HOMEWARD BOUND

**GLUCKSMAN
IRISH DIASPORA**

IN THE GLUCKSMAN IRISH DIASPORA SERIES

Edited by Kevin Kenny

Homeward Bound

Return Migration from Ireland and India
at the End of the British Empire

Niamh Dillon

NEW YORK UNIVERSITY PRESS
New York

NEW YORK UNIVERSITY PRESS
New York
www.nyupress.org

Library of Congress Cataloging-in-Publication Data
Names: Dillon, Niamh, author.
Title: Homeward bound : return migration from Ireland and India
at the end of the British Empire / Niamh Dillon.
Description: New York : New York University Press, 2023. |
Series: The Glucksman Irish diaspora series | Includes bibliographical references and index.
Identifiers: LCCN 2022003546 | ISBN 9781479817313 (hardback) |
ISBN 9781479817320 (ebook) | ISBN 9781479817337 (ebook other)
Subjects: LCSH: Great Britain—Emigration and immigration—History—20th century.
| Return migration—Great Britain—History—20th century. | Ireland—Emigration and
immigration—History—20th century. | India—Emigration and immigration—History—20th
century. | British—Ireland—History—20th century. | Protestants—Ireland—History—20th
century. |British—India—History—20th century.
Classification: LCC JV7625 .D55 2023 | DDC304.8094109045—dc23/eng/20220810
LC record available at https://lccn.loc.gov/2022003546

New York University Press books are printed on acid-free paper, and their binding materials are
chosen for strength and durability. We strive to use environmentally responsible suppliers and
materials to the greatest extent possible in publishing our books.

Manufactured in the United States of America

10 9 8 7 6 5 4 3 2 1

Also available as an ebook

To Richard Grayson and Erica Wald
for their support and constancy

And to my family:
Matthew, Gabriel and Leo,
for the above, and everything else

CONTENTS

Homeward Bound shines a light on a neglected aspect of twentieth-century Irish migration history. It compares the experience of southern Irish Protestants who left the Irish Free State after 1922 with that of the British who left India following independence in 1947. It examines how both communities experienced life as part of the British Empire and the prompts for "return" as the two countries transitioned to majority rule. By looking at these two communities living in Britain's oldest colony—Ireland—and its most important, India, *Homeward Bound* looks across national boundaries to explore both individual and collective narratives of belonging in the late British Empire. It investigates whether there was a universal sense of being part of the empire, or whether regional and historical locations precluded this. Did the sense of belonging to the empire have different meanings in the metropolitan center and the colonial periphery? These two groups have not been compared before, and the experience of southern Irish Protestants after 1922 has largely been ignored. By looking across national boundaries and focusing on the firsthand testimony of those who witnessed these events, this book offers new insights into their lives within the empire and the prompts from their large-scale migration as it receded. By using a comparative and diasporic approach, rather than a purely national one, it is possible to view Irish migration within a wider imperial framework and to include the experience of those previously forgotten by the historical record. This comparative analysis offers the possibility to read patterns of imperial rule and responses to it.

For both groups, the success of national independence movements in the first half of the twentieth century proved cataclysmic. Census records show that between 1911 and 1926 the number of non-Catholics living in what became the Irish Free State declined from approximately 313,000 to 208,000,[1] while the majority of the British population of India left after 1947. This book reveals that class, gender, and political outlook all played a part in individuals' experience of empire and its aftermath. However, by using in-depth life story recordings with twenty-two individuals from Ireland and India and comparing these with over 350 contemporaneous case files of the Irish Grants Committee—which were closed by the British government for seventy years—one can ascertain commonalities within the imperial experience as well as regional contrasts. Principally, homes in the empire were not neutral domestic spaces but rather the sites of imperial values that reinforced the difference between ruler and ruled and created imperial hierarchies as well as domestic ones. Education was actively used as a means by which to inculcate imperial values, culture, and language and create an administrative class. However, it also became a site of resistance, particularly in Ireland. Both southern Irish Protestants and the British in India felt closely part of the British imperial world, despite different geographies, so much so that on independence they often felt they had no further role or future in the new states of Ireland and India. The decision to leave was prompted by a range of factors: a reduction in their employment prospects after independence; the covert threat of violence, particularly for southern Irish Protestants; and a lack of cultural affinity on the part of both groups with the new states. Britain was chosen as the return destination because of the continuing connection with it as "home"; however, with the decision to return there was a collision of notions of "home" for both groups, as they considered different conceptualizations of home: physical, national, imagined, and imperial. However, Britain was reorienting itself to the new postwar order, but despite the apparent inclusiveness offered by the 1948 British Nationality Act, underlying narratives of racial differentiation persisted. Narratives of empire in the mid-twentieth century continued to promote Britain's role as the guardian of democratic and civilizing values, despite the increase in national independence movements. Interviews reveal the process of relocation was not always an easy transition but prompted a reevaluation of individuals' sense of belonging and demonstrate a fluid sense of consciousness that changed in relation to time and context. Both groups of migrants imagined they were part of a community of Britishness, but when the image collided with the reality, they found themselves situated within an imperial diaspora rather than a metropolitan elite.

Introduction

I think my father was definitely very Royalist and very British. . . . His father had been a sergeant in the Royal Irish Constabulary so I think that legacy of Protestant and British tied in, he never really changed. . . . He was born in 1906 and he was in service to the Bartons of Maynooth and of course society would have been British orientated for much of his life. So for him the War of Independence would have been an act of betrayal . . . he would have stoically put up with it, but he definitely was a Victorian man, not a new Irelander.
—Anne Hodkinson

I realise that packing up must have been very stressful for my father and mother because they were in their fifties and sixties, it must have been a tremendous upheaval. Compared to people in England we were living in some luxury and I acknowledge that. . . . They knew Indian independence would come and should come, but certainly before the war we had no plans to leave India.
—Paddy Reilly

These quotes are from two people born fourteen years apart on different sides of the globe. Anne Hodkinson was born into a Protestant family in Dublin during the Second World War. Her mother's family came from Antrim and had fought in the First World War; her paternal grandfather served as a sergeant in the Royal Irish Constabulary. Her parents met while working in one of the most prestigious clubs in Dublin, the Kildare Street Club. Anne grew up at the same time as the Irish Free State. The second quote is from Paddy Reilly, who was born in 1927 in Moradabad in the United Provinces (now Uttar Pradesh) in northern

India. His family on both sides originated in Ireland, but his ancestors left in the 1830s and joined the East India Company army, fighting in the Indian Uprising in 1857–58 and remaining in the subcontinent until independence and partition a century later. Following independence, he lived in South Africa and Rhodesia—until the Unilateral Declaration of Independence in 1965, when he moved to the United Kingdom. This book examines the lives of these "ordinary" people—although in many cases their lives are extraordinary—who were part of the global imperial network that composed Britain's empire. It explores two imperial communities—southern Irish Protestants and the British in India—and compares their experiences in the late British Empire, their decision to leave Ireland and India after independence in 1922 and 1947, respectively, and their "return" to Britain.

Rationale

While these events occurred more than a generation ago, the implications of Britain's empire persist and continue to affect the present. Public debates during the Brexit campaign and negotiations often centered on migration and belonging, and the British exit from the European Union will continue to affect Ireland as its borders, trade, constitutional relationships, and position of its citizens are impacted. Not since the early years of the twentieth century have both countries undergone such fundamental changes with potentially far-reaching consequences. At the same time, within Ireland, as the centenary of the founding of the state approaches, there is a fresh perspective on this period. Within Irish history, the decade 1912–22 has understandably attracted much scholarship as the Irish Free State strove to establish a new nationalist narrative.[1] However, until very recently, there was almost no research on those who had been at the forefront of society during British rule, the Protestant upper, middle, and working classes, and they subsequently became forgotten by the historical record. As Kevin Kenny has documented, research on Irish migration to the United States and Britain has focused predominantly on Irish Catholics, and as a consequence, Protestant migration has largely been overlooked,[2] as scholars of the Irish diaspora have found it difficult to research this migration due to the paucity of material.[3] Furthermore, it has often been discussed in partisan and regional terms with a focus on the eighteenth century rather than the twentieth.[4] The Irish diaspora is a significant force in shaping not only the receiving countries but also Ireland itself, as migration narratives were presented to those at home, as stories of success or illustrations of the dangers present overseas. To fully understand Irish diasporic identity, it is important to investigate the motivation of all those migrating in this key period of Irish history. *Homeward Bound* is distinctive in that highlights the experiences of those who witnessed these events, at the moment when their adventures slip from living memory to recorded history.

Context

In the period leading up to Irish independence and partition in 1922, some of the most vocally engaged were the Protestant minority who composed approximately 10 percent of the population.[5] While the majority were active in opposing Home Rule and independence, there were prominent supporters, including Douglas Hyde, W. B. Yeats, and Countess Markievicz. However, after 1922, many Protestants, in Roy Foster's words, were "keeping themselves warm in cold houses,"[6] as the new Irish Free State took a definitely nationalist and Catholic turn. Rather than political challengers, literary figures such as Seán O'Casey, Elizabeth Bowen, and Lennox Robinson critiqued the new state.[7] More recent scholarship on the decade that shaped modern Ireland, from the Dublin Lockout of 1913 to the First World War, the Easter Rising of 1916, and the events leading to the establishment of the Irish Free State in 1922, has reappraised the position of the Protestant minority over the past century.[8] In the 1990s and 2000s, these debates often centered on whether the IRA had been active in pursuing a policy of ethnic cleansing against the minority population,[9] or whether in times of war and revolution, fear and instability are commonplace, and when compared to contemporaneous events in Armenia, Poland, and Hungary, the death toll was comparatively low.[10] During the "decade of centenaries" the debate has been more nuanced and often led by Irish Protestants who have both personal experience as well as academic insight. Some continue to argue that Protestants were actively discriminated against by the state and often marginalized on an individual level.[11] However, the most significant recent work, by Ida Milne and Ian d'Alton, charts a range of experience: from integration and inclusion in a Wexford farming community to revolutionary activity and the fate of Protestant businesses.[12] *Homeward Bound* engages in these debates and, by focusing on the individual, suggests a multifaceted, nuanced experience dependent on region, class, gender, and political outlook. It also contends that over the course of the life cycle, an individual may reassess previously held views. Protestants who initially viewed the Irish Free State and Republic with trepidation in time came to accept and acknowledge it—illustrating that outlook and allegiance are not static but affected by external factors and internal motivations.

Ireland and India

These two countries represent both contrasts and similarities in their colonial relationship with Britain. They were, respectively, the first and most important colonies, and their independence from Britain marked the beginning of the end of Britain as an imperial power. English involvement in Ireland began in the twelfth century and was accelerated in the seventeenth century, and the country was formally incorporated in 1801 with the Act of Union. This brought together the four nations—Scotland, Ireland, Wales, and England, but within that union England maintained primacy. England's relationship with the Indian subcontinent began in 1600 when Elizabeth I granted the East India Company its charter to trade and the Crown took control after the failure of company rule resulted in the Uprising of 1857. India became the most important colony in the British Empire: it effectively enhanced its prestige and strength on a global stage and particularly against competing European powers. By 1921 it contained a population of 306 million,[13] provided sterling remittances to London, paid for the Indian Army, and provided employment opportunities and indentured labor throughout the empire.[14] Ireland, in contrast, was Britain's only European colony and provided strategic rather than economic benefit. Both countries bolstered Britain's military presence but simultaneously illustrated the requirement for an armed force to support British power in each country. In addition, both countries experienced partition along ethnic-religious lines, which both "preserved the imperial bond despite devolution" and created political repercussions long after independence.[15]

Although the countries were distinct in terms of their geographical position and history, there were commonalities in both personnel and policy. The East India Company was extended in the late eighteenth century under Governor-General Richard Wellesley, a prominent member of the Anglo-Irish Ascendancy and whose brother, Arthur, was successful against Tipu Sultan, before achieving fame at Waterloo.[16] In the same period, Wellesley's successor in India, Lord Cornwallis, became Viceroy of Ireland in the 1790s. In the nineteenth century, the notorious Charles Trevelyan served as a colonial administrator during the Irish Famine and later as governor of Madras. In terms of colonial policy, at the beginning of the nineteenth century, the Ordnance Survey of Ireland was established, and its director, Colonel Thomas Colby divined that this could be a blueprint for the more extensive Great Trigonometrical Survey of India.[17] In the same period and in both countries, the policy of "Anglicization" with education, often through the medium of English, inculcated British values while devaluing indigenous languages and histories. This was supported by ideas of racial superiority with the rise of "social Darwinism" in the late Victorian period.[18]

Furthermore, both countries provide fascinating insight into how Britain viewed cultural difference in the countries it engaged with and how this changed over time. As the East India Company expanded from primarily a trading enterprise in the seventeenth century into a political and military force in the eighteenth and nineteenth, the relationship with the Indian ruling class altered. Initially, senior company figures in the eighteenth century such as Governor-General Warren Hastings, the Resident at Hyderabad James Achilles Kirkpatrick, and "Hindoo" Stuart in Delhi recognized the sophistication of Mughal culture, learned the languages of the subcontinent, and often married Indian wives.[19] In the same time period in Ireland, memories of the internecine wars of the 1640s and uprisings in 1798 created a gulf between Irish Catholics and those of Presbyterian stock settled in Ireland. There would have been little appreciation by the latter of the language, religion, and culture of the former. It was only during the nineteenth century that some Protestants became involved in Home Rule and began to create cultural outputs that owed some debt to Ireland. By contrast, in India the gap between British and Indian was such that the former lived in separate areas and socialized in segregated clubs, and interracial marriage was frowned upon.

Empire

From the sixteenth century to the twentieth, Britain's empire had a significant impact on its neighbors and increasingly on the rest of the world. This global reach meant that millions of people were British subjects and looked to this small island as the center of the empire.[20] At its height, in the late nineteenth century, historian J. R. Seeley famously asserted that the empire was acquired in a "fit of absence of mind," but as it receded and was reassessed, by those in both its former colonies and its metropolitan center, it appeared it was acquired with an intrinsic belief in Britain's providential role in the world.[21] *Homeward Bound* engages with work that reassesses the impact of empire and argues that "imperialism as a cultural phenomenon had as significant an effect on the dominant as on the subordinate societies."[22] Recent work has argued that "home" and empire were inextricably linked: the formation and expansion of empire colored the way in which the British at home measured their place in the world.[23] An imperial worldview was conveyed throughout the British world by networks that linked the metropolitan center to colony, and back again, and colonial sites were part of an interconnected system that linked flows of capital, labor, and goods but also ideas. This was facilitated in the late nineteenth century by the introduction of telegraphs, railways, and news media.[24] This period was the zenith of Britain's colonial reach and led commentators at home to seek an explanation for the dominance of a small island over huge areas of the globe. As noted, while in Britain new identities were being forged in the late eighteenth and early nineteenth centuries, "different kinds of British identities were being carved out in diverse colonial settings."[25] This was then held up against the cultures of colonized people. As well as being informed by metropolitan ideologies on imperialism and race, those in the colonies were also refracting that position and refashioning it against local circumstances.[26]

The British abroad not just were brought together by a sense of common history, culture, language, and adherence to a particular form of government but were marked out in contrast to those who were visibility "other." In both Ireland and India in the early nineteenth century, surveyors mapped and codified the country, altering names and inventing new ones in an effort to reframe and make comprehensible a land they found alien.[27] The collection and assessment of evidence was used to support the superiority of British culture over those being conquered and created "the formation of a legitimatizing discourse about Britain's civilizing mission."[28] Empire colored the way in which the British viewed race and difference.[29] As migration from the empire increased in the postwar period, issues of racial difference were brought home as British subjects from the Caribbean and Indian subcontinent were often marginalized in favor of those from Ireland and the refugee camps of war-torn Europe—illustrating that ideas of race were inextricably linked to Britishness and that "formal citizenship matters less than the constructed national identity."[30] When considering the experience of southern Irish Protestants and the British in India, it is useful to reflect upon the racial construction of "whiteness." While this has been a subject of some controversy among historians of the Irish in a diasporic context, it is certainly pertinent when considering the reception of southern Irish Protestants in Britain.[31] This work argues for a transnational study of different imperial subjects in order to complement existing work on migration and diaspora within an imperial and postimperial context.

Diaspora

Homeward Bound uses the concept of an imperial diaspora as a way of thinking about southern Irish Protestants and the British in India. It argues that they saw themselves as and behaved as if they were part of a wider collective of British people representing the empire overseas and as such often shaped their behavior to conform to the colonial ideal. It suggests both were part of an imagined community of British subjects actively involved in the functioning of the empire, rather than disparate communities living in disconnected parts of the world.[32] They were linked to Britain by transnational networks that both emanated from Britain and crossed imperial borders. The link to the metropolitan center and the sense of being part of the imperial world created a diasporic consciousness.

While the concept of diaspora has ancient roots, over the course of the twentieth and twenty-first centuries both the word and the concept have become reinvigorated and expanded.[33] In *Global Diasporas* it is defined as an adherence to a sense of a shared migration history and ethnic links with those of a similar background.[34] As noted by Seeley, Colley, and others, Britain took an active role in exporting its subjects in order to establish colonies overseas[35]—in Jamestown in 1607, in Ireland during the seventeenth century, in Australia and Canada from the eighteenth century, and in India during the nineteenth century. Between 1814 and 1914 over ten million emigrated from Britain to the empire.[36] Cohen defines an imperial diaspora as a continuing connection with the homeland, a deference to and imitation of its social and political institutions, and a sense of forming part of a grand imperial design—whereby the group concerned assumes the self-image of a "chosen race" with a global mission.[37] Diasporas are marked by connections to a homeland that continues to shape them long after leaving their place of origin.[38] Kenny notes that "diaspora reveals transnational connections not only between emigrants and their homelands, but also between emigrants of common origin in globally scattered communities."[39] More recently, the concept has evolved, and "while movement, home and group solidarity arguable remain at the heart of the concept, each of these spheres of meaning has been stretched in new and thought provoking directions."[40] Other recent scholarship contends that diaspora works on three axes: difference, space, and time. The first creates a foundational claim with a boundary of separation between the diasporic and host community, spatial relationships with both homeland and new environment form the diasporic consciousness, while the sensibility of the group evolves over time and in relation to collective experience and events.[41] *Homeward Bound* argues that these two groups, based in different locales, shared a common imperial connection, but the act of independence and its aftermath crystalized their diasporic consciousness.

Diaspora is often discussed in terms of routes as well as roots,[42] and central to this work is the journey, not simply from one place to another but from one "spatial imaginary" to another—from colony to metropole. In the former, these imperial communities formed a small and influential minority essential to the maintenance of the empire; in the latter, they were absorbed unremarked into the wider population. The empire was coming home, but would they find "home" in the heart of the empire? A significant element of their sense of belonging was linked to Britain being the literal and ideological center of the world. This work is anchored by the twin notions of home and return, both of which are used imaginatively and literally.

Home links the material geography of place and national and imperial identity.[43] This link between the physical space of the home created away from the metropolitan center and the conceptualization of Britain as home in an imagined sense are important when thinking about an imperial diaspora. Scholars of both India and Ireland acknowledge this idea of Britain as home, "consciously represented and perceived as the mother-country."[44] Embedded within the British community was a reflective look to Britain as an imagined, if not literal, home.[45] As the process of decolonization took root, southern Irish Protestants and the British in India embarked on an exodus to the place that was "actively conceptualized as home."[46]

By using an imperial diasporic framework and comparing two communities in different locations, we can open up a new field of enquiry and elicit new understandings of the past. Irish migrations have long been described as diasporic, with the Famine of 1845–51 as the defining moment.[47] As noted by Young Irelander John Mitchel, "The Almighty, indeed, sent the potato blight but the English created the famine."[48] This cataclysmic event created a "rhetoric of exile" with British rule, or misrule, attributed as the cause.[49] A national framework is not sufficiently encompassing when considering colonial histories, as national histories are always shaped by transnational forces.[50] *Homeward Bound* looks at a forgotten group at a key moment in Ireland's history and suggests 1922 was their defining moment. A transnational context is important as these communities situated themselves within a wider British world rather than a purely national context.

Returnees

These two communities have been chosen because of their close affiliation with British rule in both Ireland and India. They populated the administration and the military, shared British antecedents and cultural values, and held advantageous positions vis-à-vis the majority population. They often felt culturally, ethnically, and politically separate from the majority and part of a wider British community. This sentiment came through strongly in the life story interviews—individuals reiterate that they *felt* British despite having been born and raised outside the metropole. They closely identified with Britain through its institutions—particularly the monarchy—and through the material culture of flags, anthems, and literature. This identification was compounded by the profound sense of difference many felt from the majority population. This was not just cultural and racial but also religious. Religious difference had prompted early Puritan settlers to embark on the journey to the Americas; and had created a chasm between communities in Ireland, and different ways of worship contributed to the physical and cultural justifications for conquering the East.[51] However, interviews also reveal the internal complexity and layers of belonging even within small and socially distinct groups. This dynamic became prominent as both countries fought for independence—the culmination of which caused these two groups to "return" to Britain. This work investigates their transition from colonial to postcolonial and considers whether it caused them to reconsider their outlook and sense of belonging to the wider British world. Notably, this is not a study of the majority—there has been exemplary work on Irish Catholic migrants to Britain, and on migration from the subcontinent in the postwar period.[52] This is study of those who thought, felt, looked, and determined they were British, during the imperial period and beyond.

Research Sources

Migration often adds symbolic depth to individual memories,[53] and these individuals had their lives altered by cataclysmic events that had fundamental consequences for themselves and subsequent generations. As there is a paucity of written material on southern Irish Protestants and particularly on their relocation to Britain, oral history was used to capture their experiences. This method captures historically significant events and explores the links between personal memories and their wider social context.[54] By encouraging contrasting memories and diverse viewpoints, we are reminded that history is not just a series of facts but interpreted events. Oral history records, narrates, and archives memories that might otherwise be lost forever. Recorded in sound, it is a live event, and the voice brings expression to the narrative.[55]

One of the main arguments for life story recording is that it provides access to hidden or unheard voices.[56] "Oral sources tell us not just what people did, but what they wanted to do, what they believed they were doing, and what they now think they did."[57] Recordings counterbalance written sources by encouraging reflections on relationships, perspectives, and conflicting narratives and, unlike many documentary sources, allow individuals to narrate their own stories in their own words.[58] Recordings thus illustrate how the same event or time period can be experienced differently according to a variety of factors such as age, gender, social position, or political or religious viewpoint. Moreover, there may be inconsistencies and discrepancies in written sources, and these gaps can be filled by personal recollections.[59] Oral history conveys changing perceptions and how these shift over time: the reuse of memory as socially constructed and subjective.[60] A biographical approach can uncover the complexities of the migration process and how issues of return can remain unresolved until late in life.[61]

While the British in India are primarily associated with members of the military or Indian Civil Service, who were not intended to form a community of settlement, in fact this association belies the truth in two important ways. First, "the same families served in India for generation after generation, my father's for three and my mother's for five."[62] This corresponds to those interviewed for this research. Second, while the popular image is of the district officer sporting a sola topi and bagging a tiger, in fact there were a greater number who had a more prosaic role—working as an engineer or manager on the extensive railway system, in a clerical role for the medical or forestry service, or as a managing agent for a British firm or serving in the military. Similarly, in Ireland not all were "a Protestant with a horse," to use Brendan Behan's phrase about the Anglo-Irish. There were many Protestants who had neither a Big House nor a horse but instead worked, as in India, in various capacities in the civil service, for the judiciary, or in private business. One notable difference was that land ownership was encouraged in Ireland, and therefore families often had strong regional ties, unlike in India, where families often were posted to different parts of the country. This was significant in affecting the decision to leave: for those in India, their employment and livelihood were inextricably linked, and so with the change of government they no longer had an active role. Irish Protestants were much more likely to have a farm or independent business, which meant they were more economically and regionally rooted.

This study is based on twenty-two life story interviews with individuals who grew up in Ireland and India. They range in age from their mid-seventies to their nineties and are equally divided between men and women. The group from Ireland represents a geographical mix: four are from Dublin, and the rest hail from rural locations across the country. The interviewees from India lived in a geographically diverse area across the subcontinent, but all had spent a substantial amount of time in the hill stations of the Nilgiris in the south or the Himalayas in the north, where British people concentrated and society was a microcosm of British society.[63] The interviewees from Ireland had been in a range of occupations; several were from farming families, and others had links to the military and the Royal Irish Constabulary, employment in the civil service and education, or owned private businesses. All had attended Protestant schools. The majority of those from India had been in government service: primarily in the army, although also on the railways, with only two coming from families working in the commercial sector. Therefore, in terms of social class, those interviewed from Ireland and India were, broadly speaking, middle class. None were involved at the most senior level in the administration or the military, nor were they owners of large landed estates. They all came from families who worked for their living and were broadly reflective of their respective communities. As mentioned, families in India were often presented as being more transient, but the reality was more complex. Even within the "home-born" community who often returned to Britain for education and retirement, there was a generational link, often going back centuries, while for other British Indian families, many of whom had been in India since the mid-nineteenth century, many had never left the subcontinent.

A counterbalance to the recordings are the case files of the Irish Grants Committee held at the National Archives in London. This group was first established as the Irish Distress Committee in London in May 1922 to provide support and financial assistance to the approximately twenty thousand Irish refugees who arrived in Britain fleeing from the troubled situation in Ireland.[64] Of the 4,032 individual cases submitted, I reviewed a sample of 350, just over 10 percent of the total. In order for claimants to be successful in their application, they had to demonstrate a link between their loss and loyalty to the British government. Traditionally, Protestants in Ireland had supported the Union with Britain, and the cases reflect this, with the overwhelming majority coming from Protestants (over 65 percent). While most applications cited the loss of property, there were instances of personal attacks. However, case files also document the climate of fear and uncertain prevalent at the time. This collection has generally received little scholarly attention, with few exceptions.[65] Many of the documents contained within the archive were closed for seventy years, making them inaccessible until the past twenty years. It is an important and underresearched resource for my study and provides contemporaneous accounts of those who left Ireland immediately following the formation of the Free State.

Chapters

Homeward Bound is broadly divided between the experience of both communities in Ireland and India, the prompts for their return, and their experience in Britain. The first chapter argues that home was not just a domestic space but one that often reflected the wider imperial context, with hierarchies within the home reflecting those outside. However, interviews reveal that Irish Protestants had different understandings of home: some closely identifying with it as rooted in Ireland, others allowing for multiple understandings of home that acknowledged both Irish and British loyalties. This contrasts with the British in India—many of whom had long-established links to the subcontinent but who rarely remained in one place as they relocated frequently for education and for employment. The first chapter reviews the intersection between "home" and the wider community, and the importance of the natural and built environment in shaping a sense of self and place. This work uses the language and terminology of the interviews, so Calcutta rather than Kolkata and Bombay rather than Mumbai. This is because interviewees used these place names or terms, but such terminology also indicates the strength and reach of the imperial project in (re)naming and shaping the environment.

The chapter on schooling explores the extent to which imperial values were transmitted through the education system in each country and how "reading the alphabet and reading the nation" became closely linked. In the 1830s an education policy was introduced into both countries with specific aims—to create, as Macauley suggested in his famous 1835 Minute on Education, not only Indians who were educated within an English system but "English in taste, in opinions, in morals and in intellect."[66] The curriculum was taught through the medium of English and promoted British history, culture, and language over their indigenous counterparts.[67] Class occupied different functions in British India and Ireland. In the former, division based on close metropolitan links, occupation, and social position provided a complex hierarchy that affected every aspect of an individual's life. In contrast, while Ireland had a greater proportion of the population with British origins, class distinctions were subsumed in favor of binding together coreligionists and those of the same political outlook. However, in both cases there was often significant separation between the "British" and the majority populations.

Homeward Bound argues that both groups were part of the wider British diasporic world, and the clearest manifestation of this was migrants' decision to relocate to Britain on independence in Ireland and India, which they did in significant numbers. The response of the British government, particularly to those arriving from Ireland after the establishment of the Irish Free State, also demonstrates that they were regarded as "kith and kin" as they were assisted financially through the Irish Grants Committee to the sum of one million pounds sterling.[68] This happened to a lesser extent to those arriving from India, although those directly employed in the military or civil service were redeployed.

Chapter 4 examines how Britain was repositioning itself in the postwar world. As migrants arrived from India and continued to migrate from Ireland, the country they encountered was undergoing fundamental change. The 1948 British Nationality Act appeared to break with the past in offering an inclusive, universal definition of nationality that equated British subjects with those born in the Commonwealth. However, the official narrative of inclusivity did not correspond to private government opinion, which continued to differentiate between different types of Britishness. This transitional period caused both southern Irish Protestants and the British community in India to reevaluate their own views, resulting in a range of responses, within both groups, of what it meant to be British in the postimperial world.

The final chapter explores whether "return" to Britain was a straightforward transition or a difficult adjustment. Within the lifetime of those returning from Ireland and India, there was a marked decline in Britain's status as a world power, accompanied by a reduction in the British role as a center of finance and manufacturing within the global economy.[69] The British political class moved from opposing independence to widespread acceptance within two decades and presented the process of decolonization as the logical outcome of the process of trusteeship. The firsthand accounts of those who returned reveal that both southern Irish Protestants and the British in India did in fact reconsider their sense of belonging over the course of their lifetimes, although the way in which they did so was dependent on several factors such as country of origin, class and gender, and life trajectory. Some remained imaginatively part of the British diaspora, feeling neither entirely rooted in their country of origin nor part of metropolitan Britain, but rather existing in a diasporic space.

Conclusion

As Ireland approaches the centenary of the founding of the Irish Free State, there is a need to reappraise those forgotten by the historical record as the state sought to present a new nationalist narrative.[70] Protestants left Ireland fearful of their life and livelihood, yet very little is known about this aspect of Irish migration history. This work also sits within a growing body of research on the impact of empire on the British metropole in the twentieth century, and particularly on the counterflows of empire. There remains a paucity of scholarship on those white migrants who had chosen to "remigrate" to Britain after colonial independence. *Homeward Bound* addresses this gap in the literature and in so doing contributes to debates on the impact of empire on Britain in the postcolonial period. Original oral history interviews are used in conjunction with the records of the Irish Grants Committee to compare personal reflections with official source documents in order to investigate a more nuanced sense of belonging influenced by family history, social class, political affiliation, and personal experience. A sense of belonging and affiliation is formed and created by disparate factors and can change over time. For some, their family position or relationships may be the most important element that defines them; for others, a career pathway or vocation may be central to their sense of self. These interviews allow the possibility to consider a sense of personal and national identity within a changing world. All of those interviewed for this work grew up within the British Empire, part of a global entity that controlled huge swathes of the globe, naval and trade areas, and hundreds of thousands of people. They lived through a period when that control diminished, and they returned to a country that was changing its global position. Many of those I interviewed felt a sense of pride in the achievements of that empire and regret at its demise. In the following chapters, I deconstruct their experience in the colonial period and the challenges they encountered at the end of empire.

1

Homes in the Empire

Once you stepped inside the home you were back in Cheltenham or Bath. We brought with us, in our home lives, almost
exact replicas of the sort of life that upper middle-class people
lived in England at that time. It was very homogenous in the
sense that nearly everyone in official India sprang from precisely the same education and cultural background.
—Vere Birdwood

After all he had to defend his house against some maleffected
gentlemen, and the whole business of doubt and suspicion
when the people of your country suddenly regard you as an
enemy in your own country, just because you'd only been in
the country for four generations or so.
—Peter Walton

Vere Birdwood was born into a family whose connections to India
stretched back to 1765. She came from a distinguished family: her
father was Sir George Ogilvie, and she married Colonel Birdwood of
Probyn's Horse. The family left India in 1945. Peter Walton's maternal
family had their origins in Scotland, before moving to the north of
Ireland, then migrating south to acquire land in County Carlow in
the nineteenth century. They built a large home and farmed the estate.
His parents met when his father was a British soldier stationed at the
house in the 1920s. Peter's early years were spent in Carlow; he was then
sent to preparatory school in Dublin, followed by a boarding school
in England. There were long-standing military connections, and as a
boy Peter wanted to join an Indian regiment; he later spent his career
in the British Army and served in Aden, Cyprus, and Borneo. This
chapter examines the various ways in which southern Irish Protestants
and the British in India understood and experienced home. It con-

siders the extent to which—as suggested by Birdwood—these homes were indeed replicas of life in Britain, and if this was the case, what that demonstrated about their affiliation to Britain and relationship with the host population. By questioning their experience, this chapter investigates personal and familial relationships, the role of women within the home, and the important but often uneasy relationship with servants, who were invariably members of the majority population. Importantly, as mentioned by Peter Walton, this study focuses on these two communities in the transition from imperial to national governments, so also investigates how these two groups responded as their homes became sites of discomfort. Home and empire have often been linked by imperial scholars as ways to unpick empire on a micro as well as macro level.[1] By concentrating on the experience of "home" in the domestic *and* imperial sense, it investigates whether there were similarities in imperial consciousness and asks therefore if these communities were part of an imagined community of British subjects. How did these two communities conceptualize home in the colonial context in the early part of the twentieth century? This research suggests that imperial homes were not neutral spaces but rather sites of imperial values. In India and Ireland, there were different conceptualizations of "home," with each community perceiving home differently. In India, the British were located on the subcontinent but imaginatively connected to Britain as home, whereas in Ireland there were multilayered identities—British, Irish, and imperial—that sometimes existed simultaneously. This response to the colonial situation was based on several factors: relationship to the physical environment, hierarchies and power relationships within a colonial domestic setting, and, importantly, the role of women in the imperial process. This chapter looks at home in three ways: in an imagined sense, physical sense, and personal sense.

Home in an Imagined Sense

Concepts of Home

A significant element of the imperial British diaspora was a strong attachment to the idea of Britain as "home"—as the center, both literally and ideologically, of the empire. An important component of their imperial consciousness was anchored by the interwoven ideas of

"home" and "return," both of which are used imaginatively and literally. The physical space of the home has been somewhat overlooked by
historians but has been explored by cultural geographers, who define
home in spatial terms but also as loaded with feelings.[2] The idea of
homeland—linking the material geographies of place and national
and imperial identity—is defined by Blunt and Dowling as follows:
"Homeland—whether remembered from the past, existing in the present, or yet to be created—is mapped onto national space . . . the spaces
of home, homeland and nation inscribe gendered and racialized geographies of inclusion and exclusion."[3] Recent works on the experience
of the British in India has raised questions on the relationship between
home, identity, and belonging, and this is a useful theoretical framework. Studies on the physical space of the home in British India have
discussed how the British sought to re-create an idealized space redolent
of an imagined home in Britain. In re-creating a world in the hill stations of the Himalayas in the north and the Nilgiris in the south that
evocatively re-created home, the British were able to continue their rule
of India.[4] Alison Blunt has researched the Anglo-Indian community
to ascertain how they understood ideas of home, particularly in the
period around independence. This community, created by relationships
between British East India Company servants and Indian women, had
long existed in the space between East and West. Blunt explored actual
and imagined homes as the sites of developing imperial identities.[5] In
focusing on this hybrid community, she investigated the intersections
of home and identity for Anglo-Indians and considered the ways in
which they felt both at home and not at home in India and Britain.[6]

The concept of being both "at home and not at home" has resonance
with those who grew up in India in the early part of the twentieth
century. Sue Sloan was born in Quetta in northern India in 1934, the
only child of two parents who had been born in Britain and Singapore.
Her father was originally from a farm in Kent in Britain, fought in the
First World War, and wanted a different future so joined the Indian
Army, and her mother was born into a British family in Singapore who
migrated to India. Sue Sloan's family was based in the north while her
father was fighting on the North-West Frontier. During the Second
World War, her mother joined the Women's Auxiliary Corps and Sue
was sent to boarding school, which she disliked. When reflecting on

her childhood experiences, she recalled an ambivalent feeling of both belonging in India and yet regarding Britain as home. She attributed this feeling of belonging to the fact that she was born in India and to the degree of contact she had with Indian friends, which gave her a cultural anchor to the subcontinent. Both of these factors allowed her to accept the cultural aspects of India that many British arrivals in India found shocking, such as death, disease, and poverty. Yet despite this acceptance of life in India, Sue never doubted that "home" was Britain. She explained that the sense of home was fostered through British institutions in India, particularly the club, which served as a site of British life in an Indian environment. The internal space of the club represented British culture through furnishings, objects, and imagery. British values were emphasized through the exclusive use of English as the language of communication and the "whites only" membership policy that predominated throughout the subcontinent. The link to Britain as "home" was reinforced within Sue Sloan's family as the place to which the family planned to relocate on retirement.[7] This feeling of both belonging within the physical space of India and yet being imaginatively connected to Britain was echoed in many interviews recorded for this research. John Outram was born in Malaya (Malaysia) in 1934. His father served in the Burma Rifles as aide-de-camp to the governor, and the family moved to India at the beginning of the Second World War. His mother had grown up in Argentina. John would have been sent to boarding school in England, but the outbreak of the war preventing this, so instead he went to one in Kashmir at age eight. He was aware from a very early age of the parallel lives of the British and Indians, yet at the same time his closest relationships were with his Indian servants. He returned to England aged twelve and attended Wellington College. "I was pretty focused on getting back to England. I never thought of India as my home, even though my father had been born there."[8] Yet when describing his early years, his feelings of pleasure at the landscape were evident, and when reflecting on his childhood he noted that it was hard to feel rooted in England as an adult, as he had not spent his formative years there. Both John Outram and Sue Sloan had close relatives who were born in England and were from families in which education and retirement was customarily spent in Britain. However, there were other families who had much longer standing connections to India who still felt this deep attachment to Britain. Betty Gascoyne was born in Jubbulpore in 1925. Her maternal family had been in India since 1796 and worked for the East India Company; there was German ancestry on her father's side. She lived with her two sisters in a house provided by the railway company where her father worked in the Central Provinces. She went to boarding school, St. Joseph's in Sorga, at age five. The school had a British curriculum and taught in English, with Urdu and Hindi as additional subjects. After finishing school at seventeen she joined the Fourteenth Army, where her mother was already serving as a quartermaster. Betty Gascoyne explained that within her family Britain was considered home, although her immediate family had never been to Britain and, until independence, had no immediate plans to relocate there. These interviews illustrate that within the British community in India dual meanings of home existed, allowing them to feel both "at home and not at home" in the subcontinent. This duality served to reinforce their status as members of a British diaspora who, although located in India, were always imaginatively positioned within an imperial British context.

Interviews and memoirs of Protestants living in Ireland in the early decades of the twentieth century convey ambivalent notions of home. Some strongly identified with Ireland as home, while at the same time acknowledging British antecedents and political affiliations. Yet for others this long-standing link to Britain created a barrier to identifying Ireland as home. Peter Walton's family emigrated from Scotland in the mid-seventeenth century and from the mid-nineteenth century owned an estate in rural Carlow, where Peter spent his early years. His parents met when his father was a British Army officer stationed at the family home during the civil war in the 1920s. When asked about his sense of home, he explained, "I have always regarded home as Ireland. And as I explained, three out of four of my grandparents were Irish, so I don't feel that is a bad thing or a dishonest thing. Anyway I like it."[9] In his interview, Peter Walton was able to clearly articulate that the family's origins, Protestantism, and political affiliation to Britain, demonstrated through generations of military service, provided links to Britain, yet at the same time he identified a strong attachment to Ireland. He described his grandparents as Irish, although they would have been born when Ireland was part of the United Kingdom; therefore, Peter was able to consider the possibilities of multilayered identities and understandings of home. Robert Maude was born in 1929 and grew up in North County Dublin. One grandfather was a "gentlemen's gentleman" in the Viceregal Lodge in Dublin; the other was senior in the Royal Irish Constabulary. Both parents were Protestants; his mother was from a large family, and at independence three of his maternal uncles moved to Belfast, as they felt they had no future in the new state. His father trained as an optician and had his own practice in the Quays in Dublin. Robert was one of three children and attended Dublin's Erasmus Smith secondary school, a private school that provided an education for Protestant and Jewish boys. His family had pro-British views but also felt free to practice their religion and never felt threatened or intimidated. While the family felt betrayed by the uprising in Dublin in 1916, throughout his childhood his mother impressed on Robert his Irish background and connection to Dublin, thus allowing an affiliation and connection to Britain while remaining rooted in Ireland.[10] However, not all Protestants living through the turbulent decades of the early twentieth century were able to separate home, nation, and identity. Ron Alcock was born into a large family in Dublin in the 1930s. His father was a carpenter, while his mother stayed at home and raised the family. There were strong links to Dublin, but his grandfather was a shoemaker in Wicklow. Ron attended a local Protestant National school and successfully passed his matriculation exam, at which point he left school. The area was predominantly Catholic, and from his earliest years Ron felt separate from the majority-Catholic population of his neighborhood. "When I was living in Dublin, I felt more British because people reminded me all the time, 'You don't belong here!' That may have been kid's stuff, but you were always reminded."[11] Although Ron's family had lived in Ireland for many generations and had not spent any time in Britain, their distant British ancestry and Protestantism marked them out as separate and "foreign." This caused Ron to feel alienated and resulted in a reorientation toward Britain as a site of home and belonging. These accounts suggest a multilayered understanding of home among Irish Protestants. They were able to conceptualize home as physically and imaginatively located in Ireland, while also being part of a wider British imperial community. These retrospective accounts allow interviewees to consider their understandings of home within a colonial environment. They are able to reflect upon multiple associations of home based on physical, imagined, and imperial concepts.

The Irish Grants Committee case files are contemporaneous accounts and document the experience of those who lived through the turbulent years of the founding of the Irish Free State. The purpose of the grant was to compensate those who, as a result of their loyalty to the British Crown, suffered loss or damages.[12] As such, they provide a rare contemporary insight. These rarely used accounts reveal that home moved from a site of security and prestige to a contested space for a small number of Irish Protestants living in isolated, rural areas. While direct attacks on individuals in their homes were the exception, there were various means employed that had the effect of creating a climate of unease, thus underlining the increasingly precarious environment in which these families now found themselves. One of these methods was boycott. Mrs. E. M. Troy owned a farm and butchery in rural Tipperary. Her son joined the British Army during the First World War, and from 1916 the local IRA boycotted the farm and business, prompting a sale by auction, which they then jeopardized by occupying the premises. In response, Mrs. Troy moved from the locality and bought a farm on the outskirts of Dublin.[13] The case files of the Irish Grants Committee reveal that boycott was a commonly used form of intimidation in this period. The practice usually meant avoiding the business premises of a family or individual but could also mean a ban on social interaction and had the result of alienating those who were targeted, underlining their "alien" status. George Tyner farmed 137 acres in County Cork:

> I was very vigorously boycotted, and when the R.I.C. [Royal Irish Constabulary] were coming to protect me, they were disarmed and their hands tied behind their backs. The baker refused to give me bread and the butcher meat. In order to obtain flour, I had to steal out in the night and get it from a friend.[14]

The committee files illustrate that the practice of boycott was used against those who were perceived to be an enemy of the new state and in certain cases included Protestant farms and businesses. Tyner mentions that he was suspected of giving information. Another claimant from Cork, Samuel Byford, was a "Wholesale & Retail grocer and Colonial

Produce Dealer" in Patrick Street, Cork. He was vigorously boycotted between 1921 and 1924 "by the intimidation of customers, . . . and by destroying the credit and goodwill of the business by spreading persistent rumors that it was insolvent."[15] This practice was particularly insidious, as it was covert and therefore hard to challenge, although Byford cited examples of customers who were actively dissuaded from using the store, and one who informed him that he was a "marked man."[16] In more extreme cases, such as that of George Tyner in Cork, their precarious position in the community was underlined by the inability of law enforcement to protect them. For a small number of Irish Protestants, their sense of home was threatened more directly as their property and livelihood were attacked. Although only a small minority were affected, boycotts served to create a pervasive atmosphere of threat and hostility. The Daunt family owned two farms in County Cork and "three prominent members of the IRA came to my house and asked for a subscription for their funds. When I refused he said he 'would make it hot for me and my farm.'" Daunt fled with his family to England but returned, believing the situation had calmed, however, "the IRA used to demand rooms in my house to hold court-martial and used to fire shots near my house at all hours of the night."[17] Case files reveal that Cork was particularly badly affected. During a period of the War of Independence, the British no longer had authority, so Sinn Fein courts became the effective source of justice. Cecil Stoney resided in a Georgian mansion, Oakfield Park, on an estate in Donegal, which was occupied by the IRA's anti-Treaty forces from 13 May to 10 July 1922. During this time, the family moved to Belfast, and when the "Irregulars" were subsequently driven from Oakfield Park, the house with its furnishings and appointments was in such an "indescribable state of filth and dirt" it could not be occupied by the family for some time afterward. The occupation also drove off grazing tenants who were concerned for the security of their livestock.[18] Protestant families who experienced these traumatic events had their sense of home challenged on personal and imperial levels: their property and personal safety were threatened, and the framework of security that had protected them was now in jeopardy as British authority in Ireland collapsed.

Cultural Affinity

One of the ways in which it is possible to identify an imperial diaspora is their close affiliation to the collective memory of the original
homeland while maintaining a separation from the host community.[19]
Evidence from interviews suggests a strong self-identification with Britain as either an imagined or physical home. The new states in Ireland
and India were created with a strong nationalist and cultural ethos, at
odds with the previous British administration. In Ireland, the majority of Protestants supported the continued union with Britain, but
there were high-profile Irish Protestants involved in the movement for
Home Rule for Ireland. Debates during the revolutionary period conceded a dual Irish and imperial identity. However, the inception of the
new state presented a definite cultural and nationalist shift. One of
the fundamental barriers to inclusion was the position the Catholic
Church now took in society. Its stances on censorship, contraception,
and interfaith marriage all had profound and long-lasting effects on the
population.[20] The influence of the Church on social policy was difficult
for many Protestant families to accept. One of the slogans of the revolutionary period was "Home Rule means Rome Rule," and in the Irish
Free State this seemed to be the case. Ron Alcock grew up in a large
Protestant family in a heavily Catholic area of Dublin city. He recalled,

> The Church completely dominated everybody on the street where I lived.
> And even when the Pope was celebrating his birthday, or whatever celebra-
> tion it was, they put up bunting in the street, house to house. . . . The
> Church definitely dominated the whole street and the whole of Ireland at
> the time. This is where my parents argued against it and couldn't understand
> how people could be so dominated. And it made you feel isolated.[21]

The involvement of the Church in many aspects of Irish public life
caused Protestants to feel isolated from the majority population. A further cause of separation was the Gaelic cultural ethos of the new state.
The movements that had appeared at the end of the nineteenth century, such as the Gaelic League and Gaelic Athletic Association, which
promoted the Irish language and sport, held no appeal for the majority
of Protestants. The term "Anglo-Irish" made a clear definition about

nationality, linking Protestants with Britain. Previously many within the community were clear about their nationality and allegiance but now found they were sidelined by a racial view of Gaelic superiority that cast them as the opponents in terms of both religion and heritage.

British people in India lived in a British-centric world that coexisted with the Indian one around it but accorded primacy to British values. When asked about her reasons for leaving India, one respondent confessed that she couldn't see a future for her children.

> I had left a place that was not fit for my children; I don't like saying this, but I couldn't see my children married to Indians. I couldn't see my children, for instance, their jobs, they would have had the education but they would have been given a post as a clerk in a railway station and I wanted better for my children. When the opportunity was given, well, we had to leave, it wasn't an opportunity.[22]

Migration theories often prioritize economic factors in the decision-making process. These were a factor, to some extent, as the nascent states in Ireland and India provided new employment opportunities for the "native" population. This reversal meant that positions of authority were no longer the preserve of the former imperial elite. The removal of British military forces in both these countries had a huge impact, as employment was terminated and serving personnel were relocated. Thus, former imperial administrators and military personnel who had been raised to believe in the principles of trusteeship, particularly in India, saw that their guardianship was no longer required. Both these communities had enjoyed a privileged position due to their imperial service. The nationalist ethos of these new states was something with which they rarely felt a cultural affinity. Consequently, the decision to relocate demonstrated their continued loyalty and affiliation to Britain over the lands in which they had lived, often for generations. As part of a diaspora, their notion of return to the homeland was inbuilt in their imperial consciousness.

Home in a Physical Sense

In India, British values were reinforced within the domestic sphere as families sought to re-create a familiar environment within a somewhat foreign world. As noted by contemporary historians such as E. M. Collingham, after the Indian Rebellion in 1857 the liminal space between the British and Indian communities in the subcontinent increased, with the British increasingly living in "white towns" separated from Indian areas.[23] This retrenchment was notable, particularly in the domestic space inhabited by the British. On the plains, the usual housing type was the bungalow, which was adapted from an indigenous housing form with a low, deep plan to encourage ventilation and an overhanging roof to protect it from the sun. A verandah marked the space between the private interior and semipublic exterior and was usually the place where the family would greet tradesmen and artisans. Within the bungalow, the overwhelming sense was of a British interior. Vere Birdwood's family first went to India in 1765 as writers of the East India Company and were also prominent in the service of the Crown in the nineteenth century. She was born in India, educated in Britain, and returned to India to marry Field Marshal Sir William Birdwood.

> Once you stepped inside the home you were back in Cheltenham or Bath. We brought with us, in our home lives, almost exact replicas of the sort of life that upper middle-class people lived in England at that time. It was very homogenous in the sense that nearly everyone in official India sprang from precisely the same education and cultural background. You went from bungalow to bungalow and you found the same sort of furniture, the same sort of dinner table set, the same kind of conversation. We read the same books, mostly imported by post from England, and I can't really say that we took an awful lot from India.[24]

Sue Sloan and Jill Gowdey echo the homogeneity referred to by Vere Birdwood. Unlike most of those interviewed, both of Jill's parents were from the United Kingdom and had no real connection to India. Her father had joined the South Staffordshire regiment in 1916 during the First World War. Jill was born in Lichfield, England, in 1930, and in 1934 her father was posted to India. As with many army families, they moved according to her father's postings but settled in Bangalore in the south. Jill and her two brothers had home tutors, one of whom was Anglo-Indian. Through this connection, Jill became aware of the racial inequality present in India and British attitudes to race. She later went to a boarding school. The family returned to England at the end of the Second World War. Both women recall the uniform interiors of the official British community. Sue Sloan noted that the family lived in Public Works Department houses: "They were all furnished, same curtains, same carpets throughout and we just brought our bits and pieces to make it an individual home." In order to introduce an aspect of the personal, her mother had new curtains made.[25] By re-creating an image of Britain in a colonial context, British families sought to assert their cultural separation within a foreign environment.

In contrast, Irish Protestant homes had little to distinguish them from their Catholic counterparts. Instead, it was small signifiers that indicated the religious denomination of the inhabitants. Olive Stevenson was born in Surrey near London in 1930. Both of her parents were Protestants who were born and raised in Dublin. In 1922, as they were both working in the civil service—her mother for the Bank of Ireland, her father for the Post Office—they decided their position in the new state was tenuous and moved to south London. Olive described growing up in a place where neither she nor her family had any connection. She remembered her mother's regular visits to family in Dublin. On one such trip, her mother was visiting a neighbor in the Dublin suburbs and mischievously announced, "I can smell a Protestant!"[26] Anne Hodkinson, who had Catholic relatives within her mother's family, recalled the distinction: "Oh yes, my aunts' houses had pictures of the Sacred Heart; they had little things on the doorway where you blessed yourself with holy water."[27] However, these distinctions were often subtle and rarely uniform. Some families did not visually demonstrate their difference; therefore, determining denomination would require careful and close attention. Thus, as the two denominations were not spatially separated, as in India, and often lived in close proximity, particularly in urban areas, these small signifiers of difference carried weight. Lionel Fleming, growing up in Cork at the turn of the twentieth century, noted the distinction between the two communities: "Although there was tolerance, it was quite clear that there were two worlds. The one was inhabited by a different kind of people than ours—people who on the whole were decent, respectful, and very amusing, and who would be quite all right if people didn't put ideas into their heads."[28] He noted a different kind of separation between the two communities, living in close proximity but separated by a huge cultural gulf: "The nearest of our neighbours lived a couple of hundred yards away, but as they were in a cottage that did not count—in fact, nothing counted for about three miles on any side of us because there were no Protestants until then."[29]

Another way in which the British were never fully "at home" in India was represented in their relationship with the exterior world. This was true in the defensible space of the garden, and also in the often-adversarial relationship they had with the climate and environment. In the early years of the East India Company's involvement in the subcontinent, company servants were encouraged to learn local languages, intermarry, and "acclimatise."[30] Mark Harrison's work on colonial medicine in *Climate and Constitutions* explains the changing understanding of climate and its effects in colonial India. He argues that the earlier view of British acclimatization had lost credence by the mid-nineteenth century and, rather than being a sought-after outcome, was seen as leading to racial degeneration. This encouraged the British to view the Indian climate as potentially dangerous, damaging the body but also the racial makeup of British settlers.[31] This view of the Indian environment being dangerous for the British is echoed in many of the interviews and memoirs of those living in India in the early part of the twentieth century. Consider Colonel Rivett Carnac:

> The outlook out there was entirely different to here; you had to take precautions against disease the whole time, in what you ate and what you drank, and where you walked, and where you pulled your curtains, there might be a small snake in it, or even on your bed, there were mosquitoes which carried diseases, and malaria, bed bugs in practically every bed in the rest houses in the district, and it was the land of sudden illness, especially for children.[32]

This caution had a basis in reality. Before antibiotics, vaccination, and refrigeration, India was a more dangerous place to live than Britain for Europeans.[33] This was physically represented through clothing, particularly the sola topi, a cork hat/helmet worn to guard against the sun. Many remember purchasing their topis at retailer Simon Artz in Port Said, thus marking the division from the European sphere to the eastern. It was also demonstrated through the fear of food and contamination. It was common practice to eat only at home, where food preparation could be supervised, or at the homes of other British families where similar precautions would be taken. Children were warned against eating food from the bazaar for fear of illness, and any fresh food was washed in permanganate before being consumed.[34]

Nevertheless, there were attempts to control and tame the physical environment in India. This was often illustrated in the relationship between British women and their gardens. The garden differed from the interior of the home, with its legions of servants, and was a space in which British women could attempt to create and control their environment. However, the attempts to replicate an English garden, replete with green lawns and flowering plants, were often foiled by the climatic atmosphere of the Indian plains. Lady Dring was married to an officer in the Forty-Fifth Sikhs and therefore traveled extensively with the regiment. She recalled tending to the bungalow garden and attempting to create an oasis of green with flowering plants but being overcome by the heat and constant dust present on the plains.[35] Verna Perry was born in England in 1939, but her family had long-standing connections to India. The family moved back to India when she was a baby and lived in an apartment in Bombay (Mumbai). Her father was a senior manager at asbestos cement company Turner and Newall. They were briefly sent to boarding school in England and then traveled back to Bombay. As with other families working in commerce, they mixed socially with Indians, but only those who had been educated in England. Unlike military families, they left in the 1950s and Verna and her sister went to boarding school in Kent. Verna vividly recalled her childhood in Bombay and their relationship with nature:

> My mother loved her garden. We had a huge garden; we had several wells and the gardeners would fill their cans and water the garden. We had an old gardener, who looked like a hundred years old, and he grew plants; he and my mother would cross swords because she would grow lavender and he would put his plants in, and they looked like weeds.[36]

In this garden, the borders became the disputed terrain as two con-trasting cultures competed using English lavender and Indian "weeds." The attempts to replicate the English garden within an Indian environ-ment seem to replicate the attempts by the British to tame the Indian landscape and, through determination and effort, forge a physical transformation of the landscape into one in which they could comfort-ably live. John Outram remembered the ambivalent relationship with the climate and landscape of India:

> We used to go to rocky gorges where all the stones were smoothed with flood water and we used to slide down stones and they had waterfalls. We were playing in a landscape, like you see in the Marabar Caves in Forster's *Passage to India*. They are fabulous landscapes. And the British just sported around in them. I was never taken to see a temple; never went near one, even to look at it; it was always the landscape and nature and rocks and trees.[37]

His familiarity and ease in the Indian landscape are in contrast to his experience of coming to England for the first time during the Second World War. However, John was identifying with the natural, rather than the built, landscape of India. He described the British as "playing in a landscape" and "sporting" around in them, almost using the landscape as recreation rather than perhaps having a deep sense of connection. He also referred to the fact that they never visited a temple—the physi-cal and spiritual representation of Indian life—and therefore were not engaging with a fundamental aspect of Indian life. The British were present in India, but never fully engaged with it.

   In contrast, personal and statistical evidence reveals that a large pro-portion of Irish Protestants had strong links to the land established through generations of occupancy. Writer Elizabeth Bowen describes the family connection to County Cork, originating in the mid-seventeenth century. The family home, Bowen's Court, was inhabited by the Bowen family continuously from this period to 1959. Throughout the mem-oir, Bowen frequently refers to the topography of this part of the rural southwest: "The fields undulate in a smooth flowing way," and there are "dark knolls and screens of trees." She notes the distinctiveness of this part of the country: "This is a part of Ireland with no lakes, but the sky's movement of clouds reflects itself everywhere."[38] Bowen's familiarity and appreciation of this particular location in Ireland are mirrored by her description of her father's sense of place. "His love of the country, his Ballyhoura country, was too deeply innate to be emotional—he had no contact with it through farming or sport, but all the same this was an informed love, for Henry knew about rocks and trees."[39] Bowen's comments on the landscape link the family to the land and locate them in a specific area. The description of her father's relationship to this part of County Cork uses the personal to denote the strong attachment felt by Henry Bowen. It was "his Ballyhoura country," and she uses the word "love" twice to describe his feeling for it. Lionel Fleming's family also came from rural Cork and were long established in the area. An entrepreneurial relative had bought land near Skibbereen on which he built a large house. However, the family fortune had been dispersed before Fleming's birth, and so he grew up "in small villa on the outskirts of Cork."[40] He describes the surrounding countryside:

> The world began to change into something very elemental. The vividly green fields of mid-Cork would gradually change into something barer and browner. The treeless country, the rock poking out through the soil, tiny fields out of which it seemed impossible that anyone could scratch a living. . . . My father would love it when we got out to there, it was getting back into the places of his boyhood.[41]

This close and almost emotional link to the land is reiterated throughout a recording made with Peter Walton.[42] He described the family estate of Thornville, a Georgian manor house within a farmed estate on the outskirts of Carlow, where his family had lived for over one hundred fifty years. He expressed his deep affection for the house and its environs, recalling exploring the house with its nooks full of family mementoes and enjoying the freedom to roam around the countryside. The family, not only connected by time, were literally sustained by the estate; most of the food consumed was produced on their farm.[43]

These personal memories are supported by the case files of the Irish Grants Committee. Of the 350 case files examined, the greatest numbers of applicants came from those in rural Ireland, particularly the south and west of the country. There were forty-one applications from

County Cork, fifteen from Kerry, and twenty-one from Clare. In terms of occupation, the greatest numbers of applicants were farmers, and this figure does not include large landowners. This also indicates the close links southern Irish Protestants had with the land.[44]

Roy Strong persuasively argued that the evolution of a sense of Englishness was emphasized in the nineteenth century with the landscape being an integral part of this.[45] Colin Pooley researched the impact of place on a sense of self,[46] and therefore when we look at communities living in a colonial setting away from the metropole, it is interesting to consider the extent to which the physical environment shaped the sense of identity of these British imperial communities. Irish Protestants reveal, through memoirs and interviews, their close and often emotional connection to the land and landscape. In many cases, the land sustained families and enabled their livelihoods. In contrast, the British community in India feared the Indian climate. An immediate concern was illness, but a longer-term fear was racial degeneration and the slow erosion of their British status.

Home in a Personal Sense

At Home with the "Other"—Imperial Homes and Their Servants

In Edward Said's canonical work, he asserts that Western dominance was affected through cultural hegemony of the Orient that positioned Western philosophy and political economy as superior to those practiced in the East.[47] In the domestic sphere, this thinking predicated relationships between master and servant. Said famously originated the notion of the Other to characterize relationships between Europeans and their colonized subjects, and nowhere was this relationship more charged than at home. Here, the British were still masters, but under the close and watchful eye of their Indian subjects. British historians, particularly Leonore Davidoff and Catherine Hall, have scrutinized the relationships in British metropolitan homes to find a distance between the public and private world,[48] but as E. M. Collingham has noted in the colonial context of India, the spatial dimension of the bungalow altered the dimension of hierarchy. On the one hand, the Indian areas were situated well away from the main bungalow. This was where Indian servants, and often their families, washed, slept, and prepared food for the family. However, within the bungalow itself, the spaces were laterally organized so that servants were ever present, unlike in metropolitan homes where they accessed family spaces only when summoned by a bell and were able to exit discretely through corridors and halls.[49] This meant that the private habits and intimate behaviors of the colonizer were open to scrutiny by the subjugated race. As Collingham commented, the British were influenced by the structure of Indian society, and it was accepted that certain castes performed specific tasks. It was, therefore, common for many families to have eight or nine servants.[50] Interviews also reveal that while servants were certainly not viewed as equal to their British employers, the role they played within the household, and the respect and affection in which they were regarded, varied substantially.

Wallace Burnet-Smith was born in 1922 in Calcutta (Kolkata). Both his parents were born in England and went to India for work: his father joined the Eleventh Hussars in Yorkshire after failing to qualify as an accountant, and his mother lost her mother as a girl and became a governess in India. Wallace was brought up in the British military compound of Fort William in Calcutta and was aware of the strength of the military presence and also the racial divide that existed between British and Indians. He was educated in India, then sent to Brighton College at age eight. His feelings about return were conflicted: extreme homesickness while feeling very "at home" in England. He had been encouraged to follow in his father's footsteps and joined the RAF at the outbreak of the Second World War. Interestingly, he recollects the kindness and patience with which his father treated him, but also the dismissive attitude he exhibited toward their servants. "My father, I don't think, would shake hands with any of the servants; he always addressed them as 'bearer' or 'ayah,' or 'Wallace's ayah'; we wouldn't use their first names."[51] In contrast, many others who grew up in India in the early part of the twentieth century fondly recall close relationships with their servants. John Outram, who was an only child and whose parents were rather distant, spent more time with his bearer, Chinnathumbi, than with any family member.[52] Others recall that it was their ayah they missed most when sent away to boarding school. Parents too recall the affection with which they regarded their servants, but also the respect and admiration, particularly for those who cared for their children. Vere

Birdwood lived in India as a child, and when she returned and had her own family, she hired an ayah from Madras, as they were considered the most capable. "They have this capacity to completely identify, almost from the first day they took over, with the babies and children they looked after and it seems as if they could switch on love in this extraordinary way. I've never met this anywhere else, not with nannies, not with parents even, but the Madras Ayah." She reflected on the positive impact of this on her children's development.[53]

When considering the relationship between Irish Protestants and their servants, who were predominantly Catholic, there is perhaps a more nuanced relationship. In India, even modestly paid officials could afford servants, and those with well-paying positions in the covenanted services often employed nine or ten domestic staff. However, not all Irish Protestants could afford to employ servants in their homes, and those who did often did so on a daily basis rather than having servants live within the family home. There were also divisions between domestic servants and those employed to work on farms or in family businesses. Peter Walton's family employed several members of a local family, who lived in a large cottage in the village. They were engaged in both domestic labor and farmwork. This was usually divided along gender lines, with the female members occupied within the home and men working in a manual capacity on agricultural work. While both families would have been aware of the economic and political differences between them, there also existed a geographical separation, as the employed family lived apart in their own cottage. There was also less intimate interaction: the female employees carried out washing and cleaning tasks, but did not attend to the more personal physical needs of the family.[54] This distance allowed a greater level of separation than existed in India. Sue Elmes's father's family had a farm estate in New Ross, Wexford, where they had lived for many generations. Sue mentioned that although socially limited because of the farm, they did mix, predominantly with other local Protestant families. During the civil war, the family farm was not targeted, they had good relations with their workforce. She recalled that the majority of their workers were agricultural and that domestic help was minimal. The relationship between the Elmes family and workers on the estate was long-standing and business-like rather than close and intimate, although the family was expected to provide meals and medical care for their workers.[55] The case files of the Irish Grants Committee reveal the large number of Protestant families who employed local Catholics to assist predominantly in an agricultural or business capacity.[56] There were members of the landed aristocracy who engaged a retinue of domestic servants, but personal accounts indicate that the level of domestic help and the nature of the relationship were different relative to India in several respects. Domestic help in Ireland was predominately female and occupied with washing, cleaning, and perhaps cooking, rather than bathing and dressing, so there was less physical intimacy. Importantly, servants in Ireland were usually additional help rather than the primary caretakers of children, so the mother remained central in raising children. In addition, it was rare for Protestant families to employ nine or ten domestic servants, as this was prohibitively expensive, and servants were expected to undertake several functions. The geographical separation between Irish Protestants and their servants also meant a greater degree of family privacy.

The relationship with servants also created complex hierarchies in the home, with children being considered superior to their adult servants from an early age. This underlined the perceived superiority of the British in regard to the majority Indian population. The ability of even young children to give orders with the expectation they would be carried out emphasized the power and status accorded to even junior members of the British ruling class. Colonel Rivett Carnac, whose family were among some of the earliest British settlers in India, shared,

> I think that my life in India as a small boy, of an important official, made me have a very great opinion of myself; there were many servants and many police officers and orderlies always around who treated me as if I was an adult, rather, with the same respect as they treated my father, and the result was that I was, I got a very great idea of my own importance, so much so that in later life it never crossed my mind that I could be killed or be in any danger.[57]

Consequently, relationships between British children and their Indian servants created interesting dynamics between colonizer and colonized, between young and old. Indian servants were often the primary caregivers for young children. This created bonds of affection and support, yet the colonial relationship meant that even young children were aware of their power over their servants and the Indian population. This experience corresponds to Protestants living in Ireland in the early years of the twentieth century. Although the numbers of servants were less, the distinction between master and servant was still present. Thus, even young family members were accorded higher status. This was reflected in forms of address; Peter Walton was called Master Peter by members of the staff and seated at the head of the table at mealtimes.[58] However, this relationship became more charged in the early years of the twentieth century as demands for Irish independence became more vocal. In this period, relationships within the home began to change, as those who had been in a subservient position became aware of the altering political dynamic, which then began to challenge the balance of power within the home. This had implications, particularly for Protestants who were in a minority in rural areas. Many Protestant families in these areas derived their livelihood from their farms and associated businesses, which were serviced by Catholic workers. The changing political climate meant that not only their homes but also their businesses became potential sites of discord.[59]

This hierarchy of power was also emphasized through the use of language. In India, the close contact children had with their ayahs and other domestic servants meant that they frequently spoke one, possibly two, Indian languages from infancy.[60] Household manuals often warned against the dangers of British children's familiarity with the vernacular languages, as the ability to communicate in them opened up a window into the world of the colonized. From an early age, British children became aware that English was the language of power and governance and that in order to take their place in the imperial order they must learn to speak it well and without accent. Historians writing in the nineteenth and early twentieth centuries emphasized the disadvantages posed by possessing a "chi-chi" accent—English spoken with an accent redolent of the subcontinent. British families hoped to avoid its acquisition because of the accent's close association with the Anglo-Indian community. Irene Edwards was accepted for a nursing position in the North-West Frontier province. She remembers how she had to learn to lose her "chi-chi" accent as it was considered a "terrible handicap, especially in the Mess." She also had to learn new phrasing that indicated British associations such as "how do you do" rather than "pleased to meet you," and she was never to say "cheerio or chin-chin." She had to learn a new way of speaking.[61] Those interviewed who lived in India in the early part of the century recall the steps taken to ensure a pristine accent—not playing with Anglo-Indian children, having an English-born governess, and taking elocution lessons. British values and difference were emphasized by their language being accorded primacy within the multiplicity of Indian languages. British children under-stood that theirs was the language of power, but they also understood that within the British community some ways of speaking earned more respect than others. While "chi-chi" was associated with the Anglo-Indian community, it was also seen to denote the domiciled commu-nity: those of British ancestry who were resident in India. Thus, the use of language in British India denoted not just the line between colonizer and colonized but also that between different British communities in the subcontinent.

In Ireland, the issue of language was also charged with imperial implications. The erosion of the widespread use of the Irish language in the late eighteenth and early nineteenth centuries became a cen-tral argument within the nationalist movement. This is considered in greater depth later, but how you spoke was loaded with political and cultural implications. As in India, the use of English was also nuanced and indicated an individual's class, status, and, more importantly in Ireland, religious denomination. All those interviewed for this research acknowledged the widely held view that Protestants tended to speak differently from the Catholic majority.[62] This was usually attributed to the fact that Protestants often chose private education and usually had closer links to Britain and may have spent time there. Peter Walton said that his family had an Irish accent but a "soft one" and that his aunt's accent was regionally linked to Carlow. However, when asked whether there was parity between this and how other local families spoke, he acknowledged that there was a definite difference. Elizabeth Bowen's comment indicates the accent of the Anglo-Irish gentry whose manner of speaking closely mirrored those of a similar class in England.

> I had been so often afflicted by the English remark: "Oh but you can't be Irish you haven't got a brogue." To speak with a brogue in my childhood was

to be underbred, so I used to find myself tempted into the smart retort, "Oh but you can't be English, you don't drop your h's."[63]

The role of women provides an interesting lens through which to look at both communities. In the early days of the East India Company, there were restrictions on the number of European women allowed to enter India, and thus many company servants took Indian wives or mistresses. This was initially encouraged as it was seen to provide various benefits: the women would offer access to the customs and mores of the country, provide support in learning local languages, and could potentially assist with commerce through kinship networks.[64] An additional benefit for the company was that this arrangement provided companionship for their officers without the financial contributions they would have had to offer European families. However, during the nineteenth century, changing attitudes in metropolitan Britain, prompted by the revival of evangelical Christianity and later "biological theories of racial hierarchy" that stressed differences between races (and the alleged superiority of Europeans), meant that such interracial unions, and particularly their offspring, were shunned.[65] Of particular concern was that these unions would produce children who would "dilute the racial stock, with babies ever less English."[66] As the nineteenth century passed into the twentieth, this debate was bolstered by scientific claims, notably eugenics, which argued that "good breeding" was essential to preserve the strength and virility of the imperial race. Thus, as Anna Davin has argued, by the turn of the twentieth century national and imperial considerations had altered the place of the family from the private sphere into the public, whereby an expanding and healthy population was now part of a national resource. "Child rearing was becoming a national duty, not just a moral one."[67] In the colonial context of India, Flora Annie Steel and Grace Gardiner's widely read housekeeping manual exhorted young women new to the subcontinent to direct their efforts toward the formation of the home, where each family member, and their servants, could learn their "several duties." As they explained, "Herein lies the natural outlet for most of the talent peculiar to women," which provided "a unit of civilisation."[68] While their role was seen to be in providing the new imperial generation and ensuring its survival within a well-run home, many women living in India in this period recognized how limited that role could be. Vere Birdwood was able to consider the role of women in India through several generations. Her view of her mother's generation, who were from England but married men in the civil service, was that they never entirely integrated into life in India. The evidence for this is in their limited knowledge of Indian languages: "My mother spent thirty years in India, and I doubt if she spoke more than about 30 or 40 words of Hindustani." Birdwood's assessment was that women of this generation had limited interest in the history and culture of India. She attributed this to gendered imperial roles, where the men had very specific tasks and were often given great responsibility but that Edwardian women were expected only to run a good home. Birdwood contrasted this with her own generation who visited historical sites and learned several languages. However, she commented that when she married "the army wife was not expected to do anything, or to be anything except as a decorative chattel or an appendage to her husband. Nothing else was required of her."[69]

Mary Procida acknowledged that within official circles women's roles were limited but that some women did take active roles in the empire.[70] She suggested this was often through active participation in sport, particularly hunting, in the early years of the twentieth century. As the nationalist movement of the 1920s and 1930s gathered pace, British women were more active in their support of the empire, and their mastery of the gun was an evident demonstration of this.[71]

British women were present in India in fewer numbers than men. As mentioned, their presence was actively discouraged by the East India Company. However, from 1833, when the company's charter was renewed, British women were allowed to enter the subcontinent in relatively larger numbers. In 1861, women accounted for 19,306 in a British population of 125,945 and remained a minority. In the 1901 census British women accounted for about 38 percent of the expat population.[72] Unlike men, who had a very specific function, the role of women was directly linked to the domestic sphere. However, many women who recorded their memories of life in India in this period noted that one aspect of service in the empire was the loneliness and isolation, particularly in the *mofussil,* or up-country stations, where European company was limited. Kathleen Griffiths met her husband, a member of the Indian Civil Service, when traveling to India to work as a governess.

Their first posting was to Contai in West Bengal, "where there wasn't another European for sixty miles." She considered returning to Britain as she realized she had a husband with a demanding job whose leisure hours were spent learning Sanskrit, but rather than doing so she bought a piano and "it saved my life."[73] Lady Dring echoes the loneliness that was often part of imperial service. Her husband was in the Forty-Fifth Sikhs and was often away for weeks or months at a time. "I once worked out that, in thirteen years, we'd only spent three whole years together."[74]

Another aspect of life for women in India was how strictly their sexuality was patrolled, particularly prior to marriage. As Philippa Levine noted, "Inter-racial sex was unfortunate, but inter-racial marriage was unimaginable."[75] Mollie Warner was born in Jhansi in 1913. Her father was in the Royal Hussars; her maternal grandfather also served in the army. The family lived in a military cantonment, and Mollie attended Wynberg Allen boarding school in Musoorie. She noted how protected girls were—always chaperoned and never allowed out alone. She recalled the attention given to their hairstyles and clothing when they went to dances, but also that they were always escorted as they had "to keep their dignity and respect."[76] While middle-class young women in Britain were expected to be "virtuous," in India women's sexual behavior had the added dimension of representing not just personal behavior but imperial prestige. Verna Perry was born a generation later in 1939 and lived with her sister and parents in an apartment in Bombay. The family had long-standing connections to India. Her father was a senior manager at asbestos cement company Turner and Newall. She recalled the continued levels of scrutiny on women's sexual behavior and how it was seen as a representation of British values.

> The woman was a memsahib and you had to behave whiter than white. You set the example, you were the boss and if people didn't behave they were soon told. There was one couple in Sholapur and the wife, I don't know what she did, and no-one ever told me, but she was ostracized for years because her behaviour was not British.[77]

As Levine argued, the control of sexuality, particularly female sexuality, was a fundamental aspect of colonial control and was a constant in both local and national politics. It was seen as imperative that British behavior in the colonial sphere mirrored that of the metropolitan center. "The collapse of racial difference . . . could spell not just the end of European superiority or distinctiveness but, more pressingly, the end of Empire."[78]

In Ireland, the role of women was fundamentally different to that of India. Women were an active part of the imperial process by their engagement with economic activity, such as running farms and businesses in Ireland in the early decades of the twentieth century. During the First World War, their role was imperative as many Protestant men had joined the British Army and women took over the management of family enterprises. Food production was a vital component of the war effort and needed to be consistent throughout the duration of the war. Mrs. Troy managed the family farm and butchery business in rural Tipperary while her sons were away fighting. During this period, she contended with an illegal occupation by the IRA and had to manage the sale of the original farm and purchase of a second in a different area of the country.[79] Evidence indicates it was not unusual for Protestant women to manage farms and businesses in the absence of male family members. Mrs. E. Appelby of Clonakilty in County Cork also managed the family's dairy farm during this troubled period.[80] Women were also commonly associated with the management of family businesses, such as grocery and other retail outlets. Mrs. M. K. Madden ran the family grocery business in Arva, County Cavan, when her husband was away serving in the war,[81] and Annabella Rainey ran a general drapery, millinery, and boot business in Milford, County Donegal. Although she lived on the premises with her two adult sons, the financial responsibility for the business was hers. As the family had strong Unionist connections, they were marked out when in 1921 an IRA "Flying Column" visited from Cork and "the Republican forces kept the district in fear and turmoil." Despite warnings against selling goods made in Belfast, and subsequent boycott, Annabella Rainey defied the IRA, in spite of "being put on a Black List" and "pickets placed on my door." Mrs. Rainey then took the decision to sell the property and business and move to Belfast.[82] These contemporary accounts illustrate the pivotal role women often played in family enterprises, particularly in rural areas. They took responsibility for the financial and practical management and frequently made important decisions affecting the welfare of their families. They were also doing so at a time of political upheaval when they were required to manage these decisions under pressure and often threats of violence. The fact they did so, and did so effectively, indicates the stakes and status accorded to women in Ireland in this period.

Women's involvement in the imperial process was also indicated by their participation in political life. This occurred on both sides of the political divide. Diane Urquhart charted the active role many Unionist women took in opposing Home Rule in this period and indicated that this activism occurred across social class. Aristocratic women, such as the Marchioness of Londonderry and Duchess of Abercorn, were able to argue against Home Rule as they had access to men of influence such as Edward Carson and Andrew Bonar Law. However, working women also demonstrated their opposition to constitutional reform through the signing of the Ulster Covenant and membership in the Ulster Women's Unionist Council.[83]

Emotional Responses to Home

In 2017, David Kynaston called for historians to consider the role of emotion in historical research and suggested it opened up new avenues of enquiry in ways that were difficult to access using documentary sources.[84] Traditionally neglected, emotion has been the subject of several recent studies.[85] Within oral history, there has been a recognition of the use of emotions as being socially constructed and changing to reflect the social, economic, political, and ideological contexts in which they operate.[86] There has also been acknowledgment of the difference and relationship between private and public narratives of emotion. Within certain societies, it is possible to distinguish particular emotional climates.[87] Life story recordings provide an excellent way to research emotion through the use of both language and nonverbal signals. As Alistair Thomson noted, while human experience is formally articulated through language, it is often expressed and exposed through the body.[88] And through this, one can consider how emotion was manifested in a specific cultural context and whether this altered over time. Migration stories are often charged with emotion, and it is instructive to compare how these returnees experienced this traumatic period. A further consideration is whether the expression of emotion was gendered in a colonial context. By examining the way in which individuals use emotion in their recordings, one can access a deeper interpretation than by using words as evidence. When exploring the instances of "emotion words" and emotional responses, particularly to the events surrounding ideas of home and relocation from one sphere to another, one can directly access a specific moment in the past. The contrasting responses from those in India and Ireland corroborate the more factual responses to ideas of home and belonging and underline the close link that many in Ireland felt to landscape. Home was linked to a physical space and place, as well as being part of an imperial conceptualization. Muted emotional responses from those living in India prior to independence and partition also reinforce conceptions of home as located in the metropolitan center rather than in the periphery. I also suggest that recordings with southern Irish Protestants disrupt the mainstream narrative in which the nascent Irish Free State enshrined in law religious toleration and the inclusion of its religious minority within political life. Protestants' histories after 1922 are notable by their absence, and there has been very little public discussion on how this community *felt* about living in Ireland after 1922. I suggest that some of the emotions present in interviews with Protestants are not just located within a specific event but part of wider amnesia that chose to overlook the position of the non-Catholic population in the new state. Therefore, emotion in these recordings can be read as part of a wider political discourse rather than a purely personal response. Recent studies of emotion have suggested that this is an important aspect of remembering, as it brings memories of the past vividly back to life.[89] Emotion can trigger a response in the same way sensory responses support memory. Certain emotions are a particularly poignant aid to remembering "as it gives your body every chance to re-experience the physical reactions you had at the time" and to "see yourself in that remembered scene."[90]

During the revolutionary period of Irish history in the early decades of the twentieth century, appeals to emotion, as much as those to reason, were used to influence Nationalists and Unionists. Contemporary accounts of the signing of the Ulster Covenant of 1912 document how the atmosphere "had been charged with an almost painful emotion."[91] The language used by politicians, revolutionaries, and religious leaders encouraged such conflicting emotions as fear, anxiety, hope, and optimism. Historical events were used by both sides to link current debates to the fallen dead of the past centuries: martyrs and victims of war, starvation, and oppression.[92] The uprising of 1916 began with the desperate hope of a few and ended in executions in a prison yard at dawn. The symbolism and iconography of this event colored the debates that followed, and appeals to emotion were common within public narratives in this period.

Interviews with southern Irish Protestants reveal the presence of emotion. When asked to describe the period in which the family home of Thornville in Carlow was sold, Peter Walton's answer conveys an emotional as well as factual response:

> It is still a bit sad.
>
> Within the family, was there a sense of loss?
>
> No, only me . . . I regarded it as home. I always have regarded it as home. Because I never really had a home from which I could leave my kit. I had four years at public school, and that may be, in one sense, a privilege but if you don't have a home from which to go to school and come back to, you are like a gypsy and I didn't like being a gypsy.[93]

Although calm and measured in his tone, Walton used what Jenny Harding calls "emotion words" to describe his response to the house sale,[94] and utilized the present tense to describe an event that happened many decades before, when he was a young man—it is "*still* a bit sad," the use of which suggests a continued attachment to his childhood home. He then explained why the sale of the family home had such implications for him personally in that it removed him from the one place that, throughout his childhood, rooted him to a specific location and provided an emotional base. His repeated and emphatic use of the word *home* makes clear that the loss of the family house had a significant impact on an emotional level. He went on to describe how holidays from school were divided up between a visit to his parents:

I would go from school to North Africa where my father was serving at the time, but that was one holiday a year and perhaps another holiday to Ireland which refreshed the spirit a bit and another holiday to whoever in the family would take me, which wasn't necessarily much fun. And lugging my bag with me wherever I went. That wasn't home as far as I understood it![95]

Although his use of expression and vocal tone was measured during these descriptions, Walton managed to convey a sense of dislocation and emotional discomfort. His use of understatement is, in fact, more powerful when juxtaposed against the factual reality of his existence as a young schoolboy. The listener can imagine and empathize with an existence in which one's belongings are carried from one location to another, the only relief being a visit to the family home in Carlow, where one can "refresh the spirit a bit." And it is this phrase that is the most telling. Refreshing the spirit conveys meanings linked to emotional renewal—the use of the word "spirit" can be interpreted in several ways: the more prosaic meaning linked to outlook or mood, but it also has a deeper and more spiritual connotation, suggesting the importance of Thornville as a place of comfort and restoration.

However, Thornville as a site of renewal is in contrast with the house as a place of threat. In the 1920s, there was a physical attack on the family home in which his grandfather,

had to defend his house against some maleffected gentlemen, and the whole business of doubt and suspicion when the people of your country suddenly regard you as an enemy in your own country, just because you'd only been in the country for four generations or something, that didn't make you part of it. Can you imagine what would happen now if the English turned around and said, "What are all these people doing in this country, throw the buggers out, nothing to do with us!" And it was like that. He always used to say, not in my hearing, that he would never ever trust a Catholic, which is baloney because not all Catholics thought that independence for Ireland, or certainly obtaining it by violent means, was a good thing to do.[96]

Walton's description conveys the acute sense of jeopardy and threat felt by his grandfather, who was an elderly gentleman when the incident took place. By placing this within a domestic setting, we are able to sense how unsettling this event would have been—both on a personal level but also as perhaps a harbinger of changing times. The repeated use of the possessive pronoun "your"—as in "your country" and "an enemy in your own country"—underlines the importance of their connection to the house but also perhaps to the surrounding land and environment. Perhaps understandably, his grandfather's response was to "never ever" trust a Catholic—which Walton countered. His voice pattern changed while he spoke, increasing in volume and pitch, perhaps indicating anger and frustration. There is an interesting contrast in responses: when talking about his own emotional reaction to the sale of the house he conveyed a sense of loss, but when describing the latter event, to which he was not a witness, he registered disappointment and frustration.

This is also true within Ron Alcock's interview. His use of emotional language occurred within the first recording session. During a description of the neighborhood in which he grew up, he mentioned, "We were the only Anglican family on that street. It was a bit difficult going to school sometimes because you got shouted at."[97] He returned to the subject of being bullied and verbally abused by local children several times over the course of the recording. "We were Anglican and people used to make life difficult. . . . Not our immediate neighbours . . . not being Roman Catholic we were getting some abuse."[98] As he explained,

> The kids would pelt you with stones when you were walking to church or going to school, that's what happened. . . . Oh, we are talking about seven to ten year olds and they would say . . . "Proddy waddy, on the wall, half a loaf will do you all." They kept repeating that. It didn't mean anything to us. We didn't mind. Well I say we didn't mind, but it made us a bit nervous . . . we were worried we might be jumped on. . . . But it didn't happen.[99]

Ron recorded his feelings about this particular event in his childhood. His insistence on returning to document the aggression in the neighborhood, despite my initial failure to follow up with supplementary questions, indicates the importance of this event at the time and also subsequently. Feelings of exclusion eventually led to his decision to relocate to Britain as a young man. His remarks chart the family's marginal status and that of other Protestant families during this period. However, his use of language is at odds with other communicative aspects of the interview: "It didn't mean anything to us" and "we didn't mind" conflict with his demonstrated and justified sense of jeopardy. As with Peter Walton, his use of language to describe difficult events was muted; they were "a bit nervous" and "worried" that they might be jumped on, but the recording shows the pervasive feeling of threat. While he was able to identify aspects of his childhood that created a warm and secure environment, particularly at home, and also among a close group of almost exclusively Catholic friends, it was this lurking sense of external threat, of not belonging, that resulted in his decision to leave Dublin and "return" to the place that was psychologically "home." "I always wanted to, when I got older, find a way out . . . when I was fifteen I decided I wanted to leave. And it was probably the best thing I ever did."[100]

The use of emotion by these southern Irish Protestants contrasts with interviews with the British in India. All those interviewed had their lives interrupted by the formation of new nation-states in India and Ireland. The result of this was "remigration" to Britain and the establishment of new lives. I anticipated that these stories might be troubling for individuals, particularly if they had not processed or considered this period for many decades. What was notable was the muted emotional responses both at this point in the recordings and throughout the entire interviews. This was unusual—during life story interviews it is extremely common for individuals to express emotion at some point during the recording process. During the life cycle, people experience bereavement, loss, emotional upheaval, and perhaps marriage breakdown or mental illness, and these events are commonly expressed through tears and changes in vocalization and body posture. However, this group of interviewees was unusual in that they described leaving their homes with little emotion, either in their use of language or in their expression.

Sue Sloan's reaction to being told they were leaving India was very pragmatic. "I wasn't surprised. I just thought, 'Oh well, it's come at last, I always knew this was going to happen, so here we go.' A lot of my friends were in the same boat so we didn't talk about it much."[101] When Jill Gowdey was asked about her memories of being told she was leaving, she discussed in detail the preparations and packing but did not mention how she or her family felt about leaving India.[102]

Do you remember being told you were going back to England?

Oh *yes*! Yes, yes. I had to help! I had to do a lot of the work with my mother. We had to pack up very quickly. I think we were given a month's notice and even then we were told we had to be ready by a certain date. I think we had about four weeks to pack up.[103]

The quotidian language used to describe this momentous event is remarkable. Sue Sloan's expression, "Oh well, it's come at last," suggests both passivity and resignation. Yet earlier in the recording she had described her love of India—the sound of the jackals and the myna birds, the adventure of staying on a houseboat in Kashmir, cycling around Delhi. This lack of emotion contrasts with the color and warmth evident in these earlier descriptions. Jill Gowdey's response, focused on the practical, also seems at odds with an event that would have tremendous implications for her whole family. Both Sloan and Gowdey were young women at the time, and perhaps their muted responses can be attributed to their youth and to the fact they did not have primary responsibility for their families. The same question was posed to Betty Gascoyne, a young mother in 1947:

What were your feelings about going to England?

I couldn't get away quick enough, because I was worried about June [her baby]. I was worried about whether she would survive; she had bronchitis, diarrhoea and vomiting . . . all that sort of thing.[104]

All three responses focus on the immediate and the practical rather than the emotional reaction to a major life transition. I wondered what could possibly explain this—why was there such a contrast with Irish Protestants? One possibility was that I did not press them enough to reflect on their emotional response. However, as Joanna Bornat reflected in an article on emotional responses within the interview, there are limits to the oral historian's role, and we need to be mindful to "do no harm."[105] Alternatively, they may have thought I wanted to hear about the facts of leaving, as I had indicated in my initial letter and conversations. Dana Jack and Kathryn Anderson have advocated to "listen in stereo" "to both the facts and the feelings" when conducting oral history recordings with women.[106] They point out that women's narratives can too easily be absorbed into the dominant narrative, which prioritizes male experience; therefore particular skill is required when interviewing women in order to hear both the "dominant and muted channels clearly."[107]

Another possible explanation is that these women had all experienced separation from their families at an early age. All those I interviewed from India had attended boarding school. Commonly, young children attended school for many months of the year, often in the hill stations, which were situated at a great distance from their family homes. Many talked about their difficulty in adjusting to this communal form of life and how they adopted strategies to be able to conform. There was some differentiation in expectations between boys and girls, with girls able to secure more support and comfort from school friends. In addition, girls were able to express feelings of sadness and homesickness, at least initially, without censorship. Therefore, these women had already put in place strategies to cope with dislocation: both geographical and emotional. I also suggest they had learned to cope with their emotional responses to events and how these should be managed. Sara Hoirns described this as the "entrenched emotional stoicism of British culture."[108] In her research on British families working at the Foreign and Commonwealth Office in the 1950s, she described "the culture of putting up and shutting up and hoping for the best. Of not having the space to articulate cultural or mental differences and of—probably—not crying. They were people who were unused to speaking plainly and unwilling to do so. They were unfamiliar with expressing emotions."[109] Perhaps an alternative explanation lies in the continued upholding of certain standards of behavior. As discussed earlier, the British community was expected to present a positive image of an imperial ruling class. It was this elevated standard that in part justified British rule as being more "civilized" than Indian. I wondered whether these three women had had this ideal—which Wallace Burnet-Smith described as "stiff upper lip and be British"—instilled in them to such a degree that they were not easily able to break from this, even in the private setting of their own homes.

Alternatively, perhaps it was my expectation rather than the response that was amiss. Perhaps *I* was conditioned to feel that—like many of those of both faiths in Ireland—the link to the soil of the nation, the physical landscape of place, was the intrinsic link to one's sense of self? Was it that I found it hard to accept that, in fact, an imperial consciousness was far more important, particularly to those from India? A counterexplanation is that they did not feel emotional at the thought of leaving India. If, as many interviews suggest, Britain was always the imagined homeland, perhaps it is not surprising that they received the news that they were returning to the imperial center positively.

Conclusion

Thomas Metcalf argues that imperial homes were not neutral spaces but were themselves sites of imperial power, and this is echoed in widely read housekeeping manuals such as those by Steel and Gardiner.[110] I suggest that "home" for the British in India was an ambivalent concept, as they were rooted physically in India but imaginatively located in Britain. This separation between the physical space of India and the psychological idea of Britain was reinforced through the lack of attachment many British people serving the Raj had with their homes, as they frequently moved. It was also reinforced through the contested space of the home, where ruler and ruled inhabited the same space. It was further emphasized as the British came to view the Indian environment as a hazard to be guarded against, with potential dangers, both within the home from disease and animals and in the wider environment from the climate. The limited and explicit role of women in British India highlighted their position as the bearers and guardians of the next generation of imperial subjects and therefore required a strict standard of behavior to illustrate the superiority of the imperial class.

When comparing these understandings of home to those of southern Irish Protestants, there are both commonalities and contrasting experiences. Irish Protestants had different understandings of home: some closely identifying with home as rooted in Ireland, others allowing for multiple understandings of home that acknowledged both Irish and British loyalties. Some others felt the experiences of the early decades of the twentieth century created a climate in which they could never be fully accepted. In contrast to the British in India, however, there is strong evidence of close identification with the land and landscape of rural Ireland established over generations of occupancy. Relationships with servants are more closely aligned to those in Britain in the same period, but language was certainly a signifier of difference in Ireland. One fundamental distinction between the two imperial communities was the role of women. In India, their role was limited and restricted; in Ireland, they were politically and economically active. Listening to the interviews in depth offers the opportunity to consider the other aspects of the interview: such as the use of emotion and how these compare to the words as evidence. Southern Irish Protestants used emotion when discussing home and revealed feelings of alienation in this period. This underlines the strength of feelings about home and its physical as well as psychological importance for Irish Protestants. In contrast, the British in India were much more emotionally muted. This was revealed most clearly when they spoke about relocating to Britain in the aftermath of independence, an event that would normally arouse strong feelings in those affected.

2

Reading the Nation

You are English and you should behave and sound like an
Englishman.
—Peter Walton

This chapter examines how schooling and social class informed an
imperial consciousness within British communities living in a colonial environment. It investigates the extent to which British values
were inculcated through the education system and suggests that
schooling in a colonial context aimed to clearly demarcate the imperial elite from the majority population. This, in turn, encouraged and
enforced a sense of difference and separation from the "other," which
allowed the continuation of rule by an imperial elite. In Ireland, religious observance was the principal marker of difference; in India,
racial differentiation was the way in which groups were separated. It
is worth noting that in India there were attempts by Anglo-Indians to
"pass" as Europeans, so British authorities were keen to patrol schools
in order to enforce European membership, but in Ireland the Roman
Catholic Church supported and enforced the separation of religious
groupings. This chapter examines the reasons a metropolitan education was chosen over a colonial one and whether this affected the
employment opportunities and social standing of pupils. Did attending school in Britain alter pupils' perspective on their sense of being
British? In addition, the chapter compares how social class operated
within a colonial environment. Did it forge or unify the British community? I suggest that class occupied different functions in British
India and Ireland. In the former, divisions based on close metropolitan links, occupation, and social position provided a complex
hierarchy that affected every aspect of an individual's life. In contrast,
while Ireland had a greater proportion of the population with British
origins, class distinctions were subsumed in favor of binding together

coreligionists and political allies. However, in both contexts, great care was taken to separate the "British" from the "native" population, and therefore each community was well aware of its privileged position in the face of a much greater indigenous population.

Education

In the first half of the nineteenth century there was a sea change in the way in which children were regarded in Britain. The political and economic changes in the early part of the century meant children were now seen as potential agents of change, and this was reflected in George III's announcement that every child within his dominions should be literate enough to read the Bible. Prior to this, education was seen as the responsibility of the parent, but the obvious failure of this policy meant the state now took over.[1] The elite were influenced by the reforms introduced at Rugby by Thomas Arnold, which were both educational and "character building"; these ideas would soon spread to other public schools. The state codified education for the majority when in 1870 compulsory education was introduced for young children, with the resulting establishment of Board Schools. Teachers graduating from universities and teacher training colleges pointed to the link between the health of the masses and the health of nation and the need for the former to enhance the latter in a period when social unrest, economic uncertainty, and the rise of rival powers were confronting Britain. The schooling of working-class children was now seen as equally important as that of the middle and upper classes, and they were also being prepared for their own role within the economic system.[2] As R. E. Hughes summed up in 1907, "The school is a political institution maintained by the state for the cultivation and propagation of national ideals."[3] Education in Britain in this period exposed children of all classes to the ideals of the state and the empire, with the consequence that "learning to read the alphabet and learning to read the nation, therefore, went hand-in-glove."[4] Within the colonial context, British children were educated in India or Ireland or returned "home" to Britain for their education; the repercussions of these decisions are considered next.

Schools in Britain

Why did families choose to send their children to Britain? In India, the climatic conditions of the subcontinent were deemed by contemporary commentators to adversely affect the health and development of British children. Steel and Gardiner, in their widely read household manual, outlined the necessity for mothers to supervise the feeding of children in case the servants inadvertently contaminated feeding bottles or liquids;[5] and medical practitioners advised that the child should be sent to Britain "or it will deteriorate physically and morally—physically, because it will grow up slight, weedy, and delicate, overprecocious it may be, and with general constitutional feebleness."[6] Contemporary South Asian historians have noted how the "return" of British children to the metropole was rigorously enforced despite the financial and emotional hardship that often ensued, and while the preservation of children's health was the stated reason, there were other underlying motivations. These focused on the social and cultural development of British children, which aimed to promote the image and continued influence of the British imperial presence.[7] Buettner has argued that education in Britain, particularly for boys, added value by emphasizing their white racial status and class position as members of the colonial elite, which could then be capitalized on during their return to an imperial role.[8] This was reiterated through personal accounts of those living in India in the first half of the twentieth century. Sir Percival Griffiths was a member of the Indian Civil Service from 1922 to 1937 and later a member of the Indian Legislative Assembly:

> Rightly or wrongly, we all of us believed that in those days children must come home when they were six or seven for their education. Not from any uppish feeling towards India, but we felt that children should grow up in their own country, and anyway the education system was better here than it was in India.[9]

Griffiths's comment underlines some of the prevailing views among the imperial elite that justified sending children to Britain at an early age for their education: First, they should "come home" to Britain rather than think of home as India, and as a consequence grow up "in their own country," that is, become acclimatized to the ways and mores of metropolitan Britain. Second, the education provision in England was better, although whether this was academically or culturally correct is open to question.

In Ireland, climatic considerations were not a feature in choosing a British education, but proximity to the metropole was a factor. Peter Walton attended a preparatory school in Dublin before being transferred to St. John's School in Leatherhead, Surrey. He suggested that when considering the reasons for the transfer,

> I don't think my mother was unusual in that she eventually recovered me from staying with grandparents [In Ireland] to living with her in England, because she didn't want me to develop a brogue. And I think that was because she probably felt it was unfair to my father who was completely English, although he had been to Ireland often enough, and found her, I don't think it was because the Irish are different and therefore you don't want to sound like them, it was "You are English and you should behave and sound like an Englishman."[10]

Walton's interpretation underlines several important points that affected families' decision making. First, there was the importance of not developing "a brogue," which was closely associated with the majority Catholic population. Protestant children did not look different from Catholic children and therefore could not be visually distinguished. Other markers of difference needed to be used, and one of these was accent. Walton's mother wanted him to "behave and sound like an Englishman." Becoming acquainted with English behavior and mores was much more easily achieved in an English boarding school than even in a fee-paying one in Ireland. In addition, the use of the word "recover" is symbolic in this context as it suggests that Peter would thrive in England rather than staying with his Irish grandparents.

However, removing children to the metropole entailed a significant financial and emotional sacrifice on the part of families. Vere Birdwood, whose family returned to Britain from India for boarding school education over many generations, explained that spending on children's education was prioritized because this opened up greater employment opportunities and therefore gave them financial independence as adults.[11] Birdwood was able to compare the educational experience of her father, herself, and her own children. When discussing the pain of separation, she consoled herself with the fact that for her parents' generation, separation was often for seven or eight years, whereas for herself and her children it was much less.[12] Sir Percival Griffiths and his wife decided to send their children to the Dragon School in Oxford as day pupils and they lived with Lady Griffiths as an alternative to family separation. Peter Walton's mother lived in England, while the remainder of her family stayed in Ireland.

Schooling in Britain underwent fundamental changes in the Victorian and Edwardian periods. One of the key changes was the reorientation from primarily religious teaching to more secular curricula. Bratton suggests the influence of the evangelical revival of the 1780s prompted an increase in Sunday schools teaching the Bible. As Protestantism was rooted in Bible study, the need to read in order to access this text was imperative.[13] However, from the mid-nineteenth century, school Readers moved from primarily religious content to a more overtly political one. Deference to social superiors and adherence to the social order were important pillars. Heathorn noted that within the school Reader the subtext about social roles moved from spiritual salvation "to include the far more encompassing scope of the nature of national identity, and the social roles within this imagined national community."[14] In the early twentieth century, schooling became an active tool in encouraging an imperial mindset with elementary school rooms becoming "workshops of a reformulated English nationalism." In the Edwardian period the nation was at its most imperialistic. The schools had a major role to play precisely because of their widespread influence. In this environment, working-class children forged personal and collective identities within state-sponsored, nationalist aims. Liberal educationalist Thomas Raymont noted at the time, "National ideas, are a governing factor in the direct fashioning of character, no less are they operative in the determination of curricula." For Raymont and his ilk it was important that "national culture should form the basis of instruction."[15] By examining history teaching, one can see how societies thought about and re-presented themselves. Education provided a perfect conduit for political ideas to be packaged to the young without question.[16] Organizations such as the Royal Colonial Institute influenced school curricula and actively promoted teaching about the colonies.[17] This national patriotism was reinforced by the messages present in school textbooks and other signifiers such as symbols like the Union Jack. It was their common presence and ordinariness that made them so effective in reinforcing national ideals. This was especially true of the popular publications aimed at both sexes that encouraged a sense of being part of a Greater Britain. These had two functions: to use the imperial setting as a backdrop to stories and to inculcate an imperial identity in the transitional period between childhood and adulthood.[18] As well as text and images promoting an imperial ethos, the introduction of games to the curriculum was important in promoting ideas of leadership, obedience, and team effort as well as making students physically fit.[19]

In the late nineteenth and early twentieth centuries, education in Britain was divided into establishments that catered to the sons of the affluent, which usually meant boarding schools, and day schools for the middle class. The most elite schools were the longest established, such as Eton, Harrow, Winchester, and Rugby. However, certain schools attracted pupils with empire connections. Among the most prominent were boarding schools such as Haileybury in Hertfordshire, the United Services College in Devon, and Wellington College in Berkshire. There were also day schools established by the Harpur Trust in Bedford: Bedford Modern and Grammar for boys and Bedford Secondary and Bedford Girls.

The imperial ethos of these schools could be explicit or implicit. As Edward Jones, who attended Haileybury, which merged with Imperial Service College in the 1940s, commented, "Imperial Service College, it's there in lights! You're in service: to the Empire, to the good of the nation, you're there to save souls, to win wars, to put out fires; you're there to improve the common lot. . . . That is an interesting aspect of the public school tradition."[20] For Jones, the imperial ethos was explicit, so much so that it was enshrined in the name of the school. Reflecting on his schooldays, he noted that the aim of the school was to encourage a tradition of service as much as learning specific subjects. The boys were encouraged to think of themselves as part of an imperial tradition, in which certain future careers—the military, missionary work—were considered suitable. However, his use of language was dramatic— "saving souls" and "putting out fires" suggested more than just a job.

At Haileybury, the link with the empire was illustrated through the architecture as well as the cultural ethos. The school was established in 1862 in the buildings and former grounds of East India College, which was designed by William Wilkins, architect of the National Gallery in London. The links to empire were emphasized through the use of a classical façade featuring columns and porticos and a central quadrangle. These classical references were commonly used in British public buildings in the nineteenth century when Britain aligned itself culturally to the empires of Greece and Rome, and Gibbon's *Decline and Fall of the Roman Empire* was seen as an allegory of the British Empire. Links to the empire were displayed in the interiors of the school. The dome of the chapel featured the four evangelists, painted in memory of Lieutenant N. J. A. Coghill, who died "saving the colours" at Isandlwana in South Africa,[21] and the school houses were named to commemorate Indian civil servants.

Haileybury also promoted links to the empire through cultural events such as exhibitions and competitions. The Antiquarian Society held an annual exhibition in which objects from the Science Museum were displayed and one country, "India, Egypt, the Holy Land," was "specially illustrated each time."[22] The annual essay prize was established in 1890 by two old Haileyburians who met on service in Egypt and was awarded for the best essay on a military subject. The five-pound prize was awarded on speech day. Other empire links were in the form of financial support of a hundred fifty pounds annually to St. John's College in Agra.[23] Haileybury prided itself on an imperial tradition and even up to the 1930s pupils were addressed as "Guvnor's."[24] As Edward Jones noted, Haileybury was "very militaristic with a strong connection to India."[25] Thus, the imperial tradition, which had begun with the East India College at the beginning of the nineteenth century, was continued well into the twentieth, despite Haileybury being a new school within the East India College grounds.

It was not only the major public schools that stressed imperial traditions. The schools established by the Harpur Trust in Bedford had long established links with the empire and a significant proportion of the pupils came from imperial families. The school magazine *The Eagle* kept pupils informed about the exploits of old Bedfordians, such as George Farrar, who went from the Modern School to South Africa and became notable in mining and public works. This publication also kept pupils up to date on the sixty old Bedfordians serving in the Boer War.[26] Pupils were made aware of prominent former boys such as Maj.-Gen. More-Molyneux ISC who served in the Afghan Wars of 1878–80, Capt. A. L. Tapper, RN who was aide-de-camp to Queen Victoria, and Lt. Col. F. G. Beville who was secretary to the Governor-General of the Central Provinces in India.[27] Novels such as Fred Burnaby's *A Ride to Khiva* in 1876 "fired the boys' imagination."[28] Even extracurricular leisure activities contained elements that promoted skills useful for imperial service. There were reading and debating societies, a school museum, and prizes for recitations. "Years later an old boy said he found the experience useful in keeping up the spirits of his regiment on the Indian frontier."[29]

In both minor public schools, such as those at Bedford, and more established schools, such as Haileybury, emphasis was placed on encouraging leadership skills:

> This concept of leadership must be seen against the background of the British Empire, which then seemed founded as a rock. The South African war showed that it could be challenged, and so devotion was needed to uphold and defend it: devotion too was required to administer its far-flung dominions. "For God, King and Empire," was a rallying cry till at least the end of the 1914–1918 war.[30]

Leadership skills were encouraged through the prefect system, whereby older pupils took responsibility for younger ones, or more questionably through the system of "fagging" present in boarding schools, which allowed older pupils to use younger ones as unpaid servants. Leadership and military skills were combined in the Cadet Corps, which was a feature in the majority of public schools from the Crimea War well into the twentieth century. This combined practical experience of weaponry and logistics with the experience of leading fellow pupils. The Cadet Corps taught young men to march, drill, and strip a gun. Edward Jones explained that he could "strip a Bren gun, lead a sortie, I knew how to deal with war."[31] This could be put into practice within a few short years if boys entered the military, which many from Haileybury did. Another avenue for encouraging these qualities was through sport. At boarding schools, in particular, sport was enshrined in the curriculum and many hours were devoted to the playing of it. Sport was also used to encourage physicality, team spirit, and endurance.

In 1882 the Education Code was introduced. The aim was to improve standards and widen the curriculum; history, geography, and literature were now part of the teaching syllabi. While classics still prevailed at many public schools, the introduction of these subjects encouraged children to think about themselves within a wider geographical and historical context.[32] Heathorn, examining school Readers, argued that such books detailed the ethnological origins and Britain's special place in the world. MacKenzie proposed that imperialism dominated the study of humanities from the 1890s onward as teaching moved from "the production of a large compendia of facts" to one that offered a very specific interpretation of events.[33] In school textbooks such as *Today through Yesterday* history was presented as a linear progress from the Tudor period to the present day with Britain's role as empire central to the narrative.[34]

The other aspect of schooling in Britain that was to have a formative impact on pupils from the colonies was its emphasis on class and gender difference. There were very obvious differences between the major and the minor public schools in Britain. The latter were long established, often in impressive buildings situated on extensive grounds. They were predominantly boarding schools whose tuition was significantly higher than that for the schools of the Harpur Trust in Bedford. In 1912, Bedford Grammar School charged seventy-nine and eighty-six pounds annually for boarders and between ten and sixteen pounds for day boys depending on their age.[35] Haileybury fees were significantly higher and so attracted families from the upper classes and were able to exclude others. The Bedford schools attracted boarders, but these were always a minority.

> Some of these girls were conscious of their connection with the British Raj in an Empire on which the sun never set, and behaved accordingly. Next came the town fee-paying pupils of whom many came from Anglo-Indian families who had come to Bedford for education. It was said that the richer ones went to Cheltenham, the poorer came to Bedford.[36]

At Haileybury, there were fewer distinctions between the boys themselves; instead class differences were underlined through external connections. Haileybury established links with boys' clubs in Stepney in East London. As Edward Jones recalled, "We used to go down there as young toffs and box and they would come back and have tea and we would chat. That brought home to me the class differences."[37]

It wasn't just social class that demarcated divisions between those serving in the imperial administration. Gender provided another way to underline difference. In the late nineteenth and early twentieth centuries, attitudes toward female education were undergoing revision. In 1873, the Taunton Commission advised, "We do not go into particulars as to the share which girls should have in the proposed system. It should be an integral but an inferior share."[38] In this period, Cheltenham Ladies College and North London Collegiate were the principal schools for girls seeking academic rigor. Generally, schools appealed to parents on the basis of offering an educational background that would enhance marriage prospects. Empire families often chose schools in Cheltenham or Bedford because of the imperial links: many families retired or spent furlough there, and there were a variety of residential and educational facilities in each town. The history of Cheltenham Ladies College noted, "Very often the parents were abroad, in embassies, governorships, in the Army, or the Indian Civil Service, in the mission field."[39] Cheltenham, under its formidable headmistress Dorothea Beale, was admitted as a university college for women and is mentioned in equal terms with the women's colleges at Oxbridge and London.[40] A measure of the esteem in which it was held can be judged from John Ruskin's donation to the library in 1886 of books and manuscripts, one of which was a twelfth-century illuminated manuscript of the Gospels,[41] and a first edition from the master of Balliol College's translation of Plato. However, despite this academic recognition, Cheltenham Ladies College proudly displayed a selection of "china painting, illuminations, embroidery and needlework" in the Home Arts and Industries section at its annual exhibition,[42] thus illustrating that even at an elite girls school it was necessary to have abilities in the domestic arts. This gendered distinction is also visible at the two girls' schools in Bedford. As noted in the history of the two girls' schools, "in the first place, the concept of young ladyhood survived; education must not make a girl unfeminine."[43] Therefore, girls wore gloves and pleated dresses for gym lessons. Girls' schools in Britain acknowledged the changing role of women in society but still equipped them for marriage rather than employment.

Consequently, parents who sent their children to Britain for education in order to verify their access to indisputable British status were also providing them with the values of the metropole. These included understandings of gender and class difference and expectations of the importance of their role within the imperial enterprise. While the importance of returning children to Britain for a metropolitan education has been studied, what is less known is the response of those children to this experience. Did children take on the imperial values emanating from these schools, and was the impact the same for all children coming from colonial environments?

Colonel Rivett-Carnac's family had been involved in imperial service in India for many generations, but by the time he was of school age, the family finances were limited. Therefore, rather than returning to Britain aged six or seven, as was the norm, he was thirteen on his return and placed in a class of much younger boys. This challenged the sense of superiority that had been instilled in him throughout his Indian childhood: giving orders to Indian servants and orderlies and being treated with respect as a "chota sahib"—a young master.[44] Both Charles Giles and Wallace Burnet-Smith had been educated in India in the 1920s and 1930s before going to school in England. Giles's family connection to India stretched back to the 1760s. Male family members traditionally returned to England for their education, and his father was educated at Oxford. As a young boy, he had lessons with an English governess at Government House in Bombay until he was sent briefly to Rajkumar boarding school in Raipur. The school had predominantly Indian pupils, and Giles found it difficult to form friendships with the Indian boys. He hoped to have a better experience when he moved to Horris Hill prep school in Britain. However, he found it problematic to acclimatize to the cold environment, often echoed by others returning from India to England, but Charles Giles also found that pupils commented on his sun tanned skin and foreign background. While he was accepted as British in India, in Britain boys who had grown up in the metropole questioned his Britishness.[45] His sun tanned skin and his upbringing in a foreign land all served as markers of difference and made acceptance difficult. Wallace Burnet-Smith grew up in Calcutta, the son of an army officer serving in the Hussars. He was sent to prep school and then boarding school in Brighton aged eight. "When the big parting came, I was very homesick, it made me feel at times, not suicidal, but I used to go and have a little weep, but on the whole I managed to conquer it, as my father used to say, 'stiff upper lip and be British.' He used to say, 'You have to be a man.' But I wasn't. I was a very vulnerable young child."[46] However, despite his difficulties adjusting, Burnet-Smith realized there were boys who were in a worse position. "There were quite a few boys like myself whose parents were in Africa or Malaya. I used to think, old so and so, his mother is in Africa, I don't suppose he'll see her."[47] He acknowledged that he was well cared for by a good headmaster and housemaster and was fortunate enough to live close to his aunt and cousin, who provided comfort and support. "They were just as loving to me as to John [cousin] so that was very, very good. Some of my compatriots at school used to tell me horrific stories of being bullied."[48] At school he felt "destined for the army form, for people who were going to Sandhurst, Woolwich, Cran-bourne. . . . most pupils who had a service background went into their father's regiment." Rather than choosing the army, as was his father's preference, Burnet-Smith opted for the Royal Air Force, as he didn't want to become "cannon fodder."[49] Charles Giles went to Dartmouth Naval College aged thirteen and spent his career in the Royal Navy. Both men commented on how admiration for the armed forces was instilled in them from an early age, reinforced by a belief in British military superiority. As Burnet-Smith believed, "We thought the British never lost battles."[50] Therefore, children sent to Britain from India for their education often suffered from extreme homesickness and a period of adjustment from a familial environment into a more regimented collective one. The collective over the individual was underlined by the use of family names rather than first names, sleeping in dormitories, and team activities. Away from family and familiar environs, boys in particular were encouraged to become independent and resilient and to refrain from public displays of emotion or weakness. Pupils who had been confident in their position in a colonial environment often found this undermined in a British boarding school: the absence of servants and deference underlined their reduced status. While some, like Burnet-Smith, found they were among pupils from similar backgrounds, others found their British status undermined by boys who had a secure metropolitan background, untainted by a colonial upbringing. Vere Birdwood commented on how the ethos of the British public school, influenced by Dr. Arnold's reforms at Rugby, was evident in the institutions of British India. "There's no doubt that the stiff upper lip did help young men coming out to positions of great responsibility and, in many cases, enormous loneliness, to stick it out and to make a good go of it, because they had been trained in their public schools to do just that." She opined that the training received at a British public school primed pupils to be independent and responsible in a way that was not expected for those living in metropolitan Britain.[51] The hermetically sealed world of the British boarding school created an environment in which imperial values could be presented without challenge and were, as Giles, Burnet-Smith, and Rivett-Carnac demonstrated, actively imbued, thus creating the next imperial generation.

Pupils who came from Ireland had a contrasting experience and found their link to Ireland reinforced rather than challenged by a British boarding school education. In 1907, Elizabeth Bowen came to stay in Folkestone with her mother. She initially enjoyed the "newness" of England, but once she realized her stay would be extended, "I became increasingly proud of my Irish origins and was determined to make it felt." Her cousins were more demonstrative and "resolutely paraded the Leas at Folkestone in blowing about Celtic robes of scarlet or green, with Tara brooches clamped to their shoulders."[52] Bowen felt this conspicuousness excessive but confessed that at her Folkestone day school she tried to "out-English the English" by being fashionable and correct. However, when she returned home in the evenings she sought solace in the songbooks given to her by her cousins and accompanied her mother on the piano, singing "Let Erin Remember" and "The Wearing of the Green" and particularly "Come Back to Erin."[53] Poet Cecil Day-Lewis was born in Queen's County (now Laois), the son of an Anglican rector. He came to England at the same time as Elizabeth Bowen and demonstrated his fealty to Ireland in a similar way to her cousins, "stumping along the seafront at Gorleston singing *The Harp that Once* at the top of my voice and bearing before me a huge Irish flag (the old green one with a gold harp on it, not the tricolour)."[54] It is interesting that having grown up in an environment in which links to Britain were often part of their cultural consciousness, arrival in Britain often challenged this, causing them to reconsider their sense of Irishness. What is also telling is the way in which this is demonstrated: through songs, dress, and bearing the flag, thus providing a visual challenge to representations of Englishness. Lionel Fleming grew up in rural Cork, aware of the isolation that was a condition of being part of a minority community. Like Wallace Burnet-Smith, he went to Brighton College in the early 1920s, traveling on the Fishguard boat with "my new bowler-hat in the rack above me."[55] He described a sense of excitement "which no English boy could have had." He imagined "cloisters, house matches, tea round the study fire, and dorm feasts." Even fagging was a "bearable idea, as being part of the grand old tradition."[56] He described the imagined sense he had of life in England:

> The thought of England had always been uppermost; I had heard and read so much about it that I could almost imagine I had been there already. It is a little hard to describe the mood. The nearest I can get is a comparison with the fervent Christian who regards his present life as a pale and unsatisfactory prelude to the glorious life awaiting him in the sky. Certainly England, as presented to me by my parents, and as confirmed by any books I had read, was the standard by which all things were judged.[57]

However, on arrival at school in Brighton he experienced a sense of dislocation. "My disillusionment was so sudden that even now I am uncertain about the reasons for it." He was unable to locate the reasons for this but indicated that "the growth of a feeling of 'Irishness' did contribute to it, and did tend to put me out of touch with Brighton. It did become apparent that, after all, we were not quite of the same crowd as the rest of the boys there."[58] He noted the friendly, but inwardly condescending, attitudes of his fellow pupils.[59] He responded with defiance. This culminated in a riposte to a tutor, who, when criticizing the actions during the ongoing War of Independence in the 1920s, said, "Fleming are you not ashamed of your countrymen? I said I was not, and it was a lie."[60] Therefore, in contrast to those children sent from India to be educated in Britain who had their sense of imperial community reinforced, those who came from Ireland found that they felt a closer sense of affiliation with the land of their birth. As Fleming noted, it was not easy to discern why this occurred, but perhaps it had something to do with the imagined view of England colliding with the reality. Several described the feelings summed up by Fleming: "My first admiration of England turned into a vague sourness and resentment, simply because it was so rich and powerful. It was like being introduced to a millionaire—one was not built to his scale, one disliked the discovery."[61] The close association with England had provided this small elite with a coveted and separate status while in Ireland, but close proximity to English boys at boarding school illustrated that there were discernable differences between them. The early decades of the twentieth century were a period in which there was a determined cultural revival of Irish literature and music, and interestingly it was through these forms that Irish Protestant children chose to demonstrate their difference from their English fellow students.

Education in a Colonial Context

Parents chose a metropolitan education for their children in order to access a perceived superior standard of education and, in the process, encourage an increased sense of imperial identity. The former gave them an advantage in accessing positions in the imperial administration. For those unable or unwilling to do so, education in Ireland or India was the alternative. Evidence suggests education in a colonial context had three key, but interconnected, consequences. First, and importantly, the education system had the explicit aim of separating the imperial elite from the native population, thus reinforcing separation and a sense of "otherness." Second, British values were inculcated through the curriculum, as British history, language, and technical achievements were promoted to the detriment of "native" history and language. Third, the differentiated educational system created enhanced educational opportunities for the imperial elite, which then allowed for the continuation of rule by a small British educated imperial minority.

Racial Separation

Elizabeth Buettner has argued that sending British children to schools in India had complex implications, particularly in regard to racial status. In colonial contexts, white people's hegemonic status had been preserved by complex mechanisms to create and enforce boundaries between elite and subaltern groups. "Defining who counted as white in multi-racial societies was central to this process, because racial identity historically has depended on a shifting set of subjective criteria."[62] In the latter part of British rule in India, the choice of schooling was an important component of racial status because it suggested that British children were part of the domiciled community rather than the "home-born."[63] In a society in which racial status and access to power were linked, any questioning of the former could jeopardize access to the latter. Those with strong metropolitan links viewed education in India as suspect because it underlined the possibility of mixed ancestry through long residence in India.[64]

Official discourse on education in British India reveals the level of concern over the possibility of non-Europeans "passing" as white in schools. The "Report on the Progress of Education of European Children during the Quinquennium 1912–13—1916–17" defines European as "any person of European descent, pure or mixed, who retains European habits of modes of life."[65] The following report in this series, covering the period 1917–19 and 1921–22,[66] also begins with a discussion on the meanings of the terms "European" and "Anglo-Indian" and the widespread extent of their misuse and ambiguity. The foregrounding of these definitions at the beginning of reports on education highlights the importance and sensitivity with which the authorities viewed racial definitions in British India. The Census of India of 1901 had introduced new definitions, such as Native of India and Anglo-Indian, to formalize racial status, but it was widely understood within official circles that there were Anglo-Indians who "passed" as European and Indian Christians who "passed" as Anglo-Indian.[67] Racial status was a category the authorities viewed with some suspicion and monitored closely. Official attempts to control the numbers of non-Europeans in European schools were made by introducing a rule whereby only 15 percent of those on the school rolls could be non-Europeans. There were financial penalties if the number was exceeded,[68] although how often this was enforced is difficult to ascertain. The reports also reflected a wider concern about the blurring of race and class in British India. In attempting to classify the schools according to status and pupil intake, the report acknowledged,

> Thus then the term European School as used in this report possesses a very wide connotation. Such schools educate children of pure European descent, those of mixed descent and those who belong to particular communities, they educate children who belong to various social classes—we find in them children whose parents are substantially well-off or who occupy important positions in the world of commerce and trade, we find also children of very poor agricultural population, and we find children of parents who form merely a residuum of the casual workman type.[69]

Consequently, despite attempts to classify and control the racial and social intake into European schools, the education authorities conceded that this was difficult to do in practice.

As early as the mid-nineteenth century, when the Crown took control of British India from the East India Company, there were concerted attempts by the British authorities to use the education system as a means by which to separate the British from the Indian population. As Kennedy has discussed, the increase in the British population and the need for technocrats to work in the postal and telegraph services, railways, and other infrastructure projects necessitated new educational establishments. At the same time, and perhaps with the growing number of British entering India, there was an increase in the proportion of poor whites: unemployed sailors, destitute widows, and marginal "others" who undermined the idea of British prestige in India. In response, the imperial consul Henry Lawrence founded the Lawrence Military Asylum. The first branch opened in Sanawar near Simla in 1847, and others quickly followed at Mount Abu, Ootacamund, and Murree. The objective was to provide a "morally decent" and physically bracing environment that protected children from the moral corruption of poverty, particularly in the barracks of India. The education was Christian and stressed discipline, obedience, and respectability.[70] Spurred by this initiative, Lord Canning, the first Viceroy of India, issued a government Minute on Education in 1860. The aim was to avoid a situation whereby the British "find ourselves embarrassed in all large towns and stations with a floating population of Indianized English, loosely brought up, and exhibiting most of the worst qualities of both races; whilst the Eurasian population . . . will increase more rapidly than ever."[71] Therefore, the education system provided by the British was put in place in order to prevent "embarrassment" from an expanding "loosely brought-up" population that would, by its very existence, undermine the myth of white superiority. The provision of a technical education was another way to prevent this "floating population" from sinking down the social ladder, unable to compete economically with Indians, in skilled and semiskilled occupations. Contemporary observers argued that hill stations in the Himalayas offered superior climatic conditions to the plains where European youth "educated as imperfectly as so many of them are, in the plains of India, should grow up soft, delicate, unmanly, indolent, weak both in morale and physique."[72] The archdeacon of Calcutta, J Baly, argued, "It cannot be too clearly understood, nor too strongly insisted upon, that not only good schools, but good schools in a good climate are an absolute necessity, that for the suitable education of European children in India nothing but Hill Boarding-schools will suffice."[73]

Canning's declaration offered the spur and the financial support for a range of institutions to open in the hills. Consequently, schools opened in Darjeeling, Simla, Mussoorie, Naini Tal, Ootacamund, and other hill stations in the 1850s to 1870s, offering both Catholic and Protestant single-sex education. By the turn of the twentieth century, the majority of establishments catering for Europeans were situated in the hills, some sixty institutions with 54,000 pupils in 1905.[74] Schooling in the hill stations was considered more prestigious than that of the plains: the schools were predominantly boarding schools, such as St. Joseph's College for boys and Loreto Convent, both of which were in Darjeeling, and charged higher fees. The schools in the hill stations modeled themselves on the English public schools with uniforms and prefects, English sports such as cricket, and preparation for the Cambridge exams. However, there were exceptions, such as the schools established by Claude Martin in Lucknow and Calcutta in the early nineteenth century. La

Martiniere schools were as prestigious as those in the hills, and their fees for day pupils and boarders reflected this.[75]

While contemporary observers stressed the health benefits of the hill stations, recent scholarship has argued that there were other reasons the British chose to locate schools in these environments. Kennedy suggested that the British were able to create an environment that replicated the topography and architecture of rural Britain and that the hill stations provided a demographic contrast to the plains of India in that the majority of inhabitants were British.[76] They also combined recreation and military functions, so those pupils attending school in the established hill stations of Simla, Darjeeling, and Ootacamund were able to witness firsthand the operation of the Raj.

Education in Ireland proceeded differently but soon resulted in the same separation. The British government established nationwide education provision in Ireland in 1831 with the intention "to unite in one system children of different creeds."[77] However, within a ten-year period, the hierarchy of both the Roman Catholic Church and the Nonconformist Protestant churches strenuously objected to nondenominational education.[78] Under the leadership of Archbishop Cullen, head of the Roman Catholic Church in Ireland, the synod in Thurles in 1850 stated,

> We deem it part of our duty to declare that the separate education of Catholic youth is, in every way, to be preferred to it. We have seen, with satisfaction, the British government latterly give, in England, aid towards education of Catholic children separately and accordingly to the standard of Catholic religion . . . there is no reason why the faithful Catholics of Ireland should not be treated in the same manner.[79]

The combined weight of opposition led the British government to comply with demands for separate educational facilities for children of different Christian faiths. The churches were further strengthened as they took financial control of their own schools. By the end of the nineteenth century, Parliament was spending one million sterling on Irish education, which was principally under the control of religious institutions.[80] While the policy of inclusion was challenged by both Catholic and Protestant groups, the acquiescence of the British government in this policy created a gulf between children of different faiths and an effective separation between ruler and ruled in the education system in Ireland. "It is hard to see how the religious apartheid policy that prevailed under the national system could have done anything but strengthen the barriers that separated Catholic and Protestant in nineteenth-century Ireland."[81]

Curriculum

In *Orientalism*, Edward Said discussed the association between Orient and Occident as one in which Western powers asserted a cultural as well as physical domination over the lands they occupied and presented "complex hegemony" in which Western culture, institutions, and history are depicted as more advanced than those of the Orient. This superiority became a justifying principle for the subjection of the Orient by Western powers.[82] This hegemony can be clearly seen when examining primary documents pertaining to education in British India. What is significant is the extent to which, for all grades of school, the curriculum was orientated toward instilling British history and values into pupils, irrespective of their background or ability. In reviewing examination questions for the elementary school certificate in English (the most basic level), the English composition questions asked pupils to imagine "a conversation between the ghosts of Lord Nelson and Sir Francis Drake whilst watching the English fleet fight the Germans."[83] The English literature questions required pupils to suggest the feelings Robert Burns might evoke in "the hearts of his countrymen" when he wrote the poem *Bannockburn*. A separate section of the exam offered pupils questions on the works of Shakespeare and Dickens. Perhaps more subtly, the English grammar exercises required pupils to provide the plurals of "copy, knife, mosquito, governor general" and the feminine of "fox, viceroy," thus equating the permanence and familiarity of everyday objects and animals with the longevity of the imperial system.

The history examinations expected a wide range of knowledge: from the improvements introduced by King Alfred to the attempts of the Plantagenets to conquer Scotland and Wolsey's prominence in Tudor England. More contemporary questions asked pupils to "compare the work which is now being done by the British fleet under Admiral Jellicoe with what was done over a century ago by the fleet which was commanded by Lord Nelson."[84] In case pupils were still not aware of the empire and their role in it, one of the final exam questions in the history paper asked, "What is the British Empire, how was it obtained and how is it held together? What is the position of India in this empire?"[85] Therefore, the education system in British India was explicit in introducing pupils to the details of British history from the Anglo-Saxons to the present day, with particular emphasis on the formation and purpose of the empire. All pupils were required to study English language and literature, during which time they were introduced to the topography of the British landscape through the poetry of Wordsworth and Robert Burns. They were also encouraged to place themselves in the position of protagonist during seminal battles in British history, such as Waterloo and the Spanish Armada, thus encouraging an imperial worldview of British military and naval supremacy. Pupils in the early decades of the twentieth century could not fail to have imbued a sense of the longevity and breadth of the British Empire or to have considered they were an integral part of the imperial process.

In Ireland, the education policy of the British government aimed to imbue "loyalty to the British crown," but, as Akenson notes, this aim was never fully realized.[86] Loyalty was encouraged through the presentation of British and Irish history. The former took center place within the curriculum, while Irish history between 1500 and 1800 was reduced to six pages. "It would have been very easy for a child to have finished his schooling with the impression that nothing worth noting had taken place in the world after about 50 AD."[87] Akenson also notes that Irish schoolchildren, in the period up to 1922, learned very little of the "history and culture of their own country." It was this lack of context that encouraged Irish nationalists to oppose and reject the whole system of British education, while at the same time considering the possibility of using the education policy of the new state to forefront Gaelic culture and language.[88] The other area in which there was active suppression of indigenous culture was through the decision to teach all subjects through the medium of English. In the national schools, English was the exclusive medium of instruction until 1879, when Irish was introduced as an optional subject, and it was used as a medium of instruction only from 1898.[89] As noted in the *Third Book of Lessons*, "Various languages are spoken by the nations of Europe, besides our own English. Even in some parts of Ireland a different language is spoken, viz., Irish; though all who learn to read, learn English, and prefer speaking it."[90]

While the decline in the use of Irish as the primary language was due to several factors, such as the marked drop in population after the Famine of 1845–51 and the widespread use of English internationally, the disregard with which Irish was viewed in the educational context helped to enforce the view that English was the language of commerce, industry, and power, while Irish was the language of a rural and peasant population.

Although contemporary commentators and current historians reiterated the lower status accorded to British educational institutions in India, existing and newly created recordings with those who were part of the British imperial community in the first half of the twentieth century reveal that very few of those who were pupils in that late colonial period felt this sense of reduced status. What is also revealed is the extent to which education fostered strong links between those resident in India and those in metropolitan Britain. Furthermore, interviews indicate the line between the domiciled and home-born community was rarely as clear as has sometimes been discussed. Of those interviewed, some with British-born parents were educated in India, some with Indian-born parents were educated in Britain, and there were instances of children being schooled at boarding schools in India and Britain. Mollie Warner was born in 1913 in Jhansi. Her father was from Yorkshire and joined the Royal Hussars before being posted to India. Her mother's family were from Chelsea in London, and her maternal grandfather was an apothecary before joining the army. She was sent to Wynberg Allen, a boarding school in Musoorie for the children of European descent, but recalled there were three Indian princesses in her class. She specialized in music, performing at local concerts, with the intention of becoming a music teacher. Mollie's experience questions notions of the domiciled and the home born and the class position allocated to each category. The school was not considered one of the most prestigious and had pupils of different racial backgrounds, suggesting a catchment from the domiciled community, yet Mollie's links to Britain were unequivocal through parentage and furlough spent in

Yorkshire. When asked about the educational ethos and direction of the school, Mollie asserted firmly that they studied English literature, scripture, British history and geography, and music. The only aspect of India that was introduced into the curriculum was the study of Urdu. Mollie strongly felt that the educational and cultural bias of the school was British, exemplified by teachers imported from Oxford, Cambridge, and London.[91] Similarly, John Outram had strong links with Britain through his family, who, although born in Burma, were educated at boarding school in Britain and owned newspapers in Essex. However, he went to boarding school in Kashmir until being transferred to Wellington College in Britain aged twelve. Rather than providing him with a metropolitan education that would improve his employment chances, he attributes the move to his parents' separation. At his boarding school in Kashmir, British values were reinforced through school mottos in Latin, uniforms, and food; "it was a little English oasis," including suet puddings, porridge, and meat and vegetables. He also remembered how marching in the central courtyard was a feature of school life, with boys encouraged to wave banners and flags.[92]

Even for those who were part of the domiciled community, such as Betty Gascoyne's family, the education they received in India strongly reinforced the sense that the community was part of an imperial diaspora. They were located in India, but culturally and politically aligned to Britain and to the maintenance of British rule in India. Betty attended boarding school in Sorga, Central Provinces, where subjects were taught through the medium of English with one Indian language as part of the curriculum. They learned British history and geography and studied Shakespeare and Dickens as core subjects. Visually, the importance of the empire was emphasized through objects displayed on the classroom walls, such as maps, and the Union Jack, "every school had it." During assembly, pupils sang the hymn "Jerusalem," although they were living a considerable distance from England's green and pleasant land.[93]

As a result, many children attending school in India for the entirety, or part, of their education were strongly influenced by the British curriculum and the values it conveyed. Pupils were powerfully aware of being part of the British Empire. The education system was one element that reinforced British values to the imperial diaspora in India and in doing so helped to reinforce and justify their imperial role. The physical environment in which these schools were generally located might also have played a part. As Kennedy has argued, the hill stations were an environment that nurtured the ruling class thorough a web of educational facilities, and indeed many hill stations combined multiple functions.[94] Some of the larger stations combined rest and recuperation with other functions such as the military and administration of the Raj. The largest and most established, such as Simla, was the summer capital of the Viceroy, and therefore children could visibly see the operation of the Raj and the military force that supported it.

In Ireland, the response to the British education policy was more nuanced and multilayered. Those who already felt loyalty and allegiance to the British government and supported the continuation of the Union were confirmed in their support. Lionel Fleming attended the Manor School in Fermoy, County Cork, during the years of the Anglo-Irish War. "It went without saying, of course, that the school would admit none but Protestant boys."[95] He explained how the school was entirely orientated toward Britain, in both curriculum and culture:

> It was a preparatory school whose curriculum entirely ignored the Irish secondary schools. Its pupils were not meant to go to my grandfather's school in Kilkenny, nor to St. Columba's in Dublin or Portora in Enniskillen— they were destined for Haileybury, Marlborough or Felsted, and with scholarships at that.[96]

He noted that pupils had "no contact with any part of Ireland that existed outside the school gates, either mentally or physically."[97] The school adjoined a Catholic secondary school and was located close to the town of Fermoy, but there was no contact with either, "because of the risk of infection."[98] While the school followed a British curriculum, it also promoted pursuits that fostered a sense of being part of an imperial community, particularly the Boy Scouts and marksmanship. "Every boy in the school spent hours in the cold gymnasium, firing away at targets, while Russell [their teacher] criticised and loaded the air-rifles."[99] The desired objective was to compete in a national competition with all the British preparatory schools. The scouting movement was encouraged to the extent that in place of a school uniform, the boys wore their scouting outfits emblazoned with as many badges as possible. Fleming recalled his delight when his earned his King's Scout badge with its "large gilt crown," which he wore on his left shoulder.[100]

However, the increasing rise of nationalism colored views toward the educational system, with individuals arguing that it was a tool of British imperialism. Patrick Pearse, a key figure in the Easter Rising of 1916 and also a schoolmaster, rejected the whole system of education: "It is because the English education system in Ireland has deliberately eliminated the national factor that it has so terrifically succeeded. For it has succeeded—succeeding in making slaves of us. And it has succeeded so well that we no longer realise we are slaves."[101] This guided education policy in the early years of the Irish Free State, which had consequences far beyond. From its inception its avowed aim was to provide a radically different policy from the one that preceded it. In 1921, the National Programme Conference convened to represent all major interests concerned with primary education in Ireland. The conference had a comprehensive program of reform. The result was a desire to inculcate a deep sense of Irish identity and pride, "by showing the Irish race has fulfilled a great mission in the advancement of civilization and that, on the whole, the Irish nation has amply justified its existence."[102] Thus, the political and cultural aims of the state were funneled through the educational system in order to create adherence to the state.

It was this link between education provision and cultural nationalism that would prove to be very difficult for Protestant families to accept during the early years of the Free State. As McDowell commented, "Ex Unionists were skeptical about the value of Irish and irritated by the methods employed to promote its use."[103] For families who had been brought up to support the union with Britain, this overt cultural nationalism was an affront; and many were determined to avoid it. As Peter Walton indicated, the way in which they did so was to reject the state provision of education and overwhelmingly opt for fee-paying Protestant schools: "There wasn't any question of going to day school because that would have meant going to the Board School in Carlow, and while that would have been good educationally, socially it would not have been acceptable at that time." When asked to explain, he said,

The state schools were being run as providers of learning, but also run as support to the new state of Ireland so everybody was obliged to learn Gaelic and to write it, and to learn Irish songs and the rest of it, none of which was socially acceptable to us at that time. It might be less unacceptable now, but I don't know how the schools are run now and whether that is still a requirement.[104]

As Walton's comment illustrates, Protestant families were clearly aware of the political intentions of the Irish Free State's education policy. As the Roman Catholic and Nonconformist churches resisted British control in the nineteenth century, so Protestant families actively resisted the education policy of the new state and determined to access schools that would promote an ethos with which they were more comfortable. All of those interviewed for this research attended Protestant schools, the majority of which were fee paying.[105] Those attending Protestant schools in the decades following 1922 recalled how there was a continuation of British values and outlook. Anne Hodkinson grew up in central Dublin and attended the Kildare Place Model School:

I was brought up British. I wasn't brought up Irish. I didn't know enough Irish history. When I went back to live in Ireland, my husband knew more Irish history than I did. So in the end I had to go out and buy myself a book called the *Making of Modern Ireland* and start to read. Oh yes, I knew Brian Boru and all those stories, but I didn't know; it was still very fresh in my parents' minds, about the 1920s and the Black and Tans.[106]

Anne recalls studying ancient Irish history and British history, particularly the monarchs, but little on the recent past. "It was as if the British still had a rule over the national curriculum."[107] Perhaps in an echo of the British attitude toward Irish history in the nineteenth century, the school avoided the recent past with its contested view of events and individuals. Ron Alcock, also educated in Dublin in the 1940s, recalled the absence of Irish history and how they had much greater awareness of British history.[108] Protestant schools could often reflect British values through the playing of sport. Gaelic sports such as hurling and camogie were less usually played in Protestant schools, and although there was a ban on "English sports" such as cricket, rugby, and football by the Catholic hierarchy, it was these sports that were more common at Protestant schools.[109]

The education system established by the British in 1831 under the union had the aim of bringing Irish children of different Christian faiths together in order to aid closer understanding. Within twenty years of its establishment, this policy was disrupted by each of the major Christian denominations in turn, resulting in an effective policy of religious segregation. Concessions by the British government to each of the major faith groups strengthened each financially and politically by providing a precedent for religious involvement in education policy. The establishment of the Free State in 1922 saw the new government place education center stage in shaping and creating a new Gaelic Ireland. The Irish language was now compulsory in all schools and a prerequisite for entry to the civil service and the police force. Many Protestants rejected this overt politicization of the education system by the new regime and opted instead for a private Protestant education. This, however, continued the social segregation of the previous century and encouraged a distance between the Protestant minority and the values of the new state.

Within a colonial context, some empire families sought to "return" their children to the metropole for education, as this was viewed as enhancing their educational and employment opportunities. In Britain, imperial values were inculcated through an education system that emphasized class and gender differences and where imperial service was seen as an extension of national duty. This ethos was often implicit in the architecture, emblems, and material culture of the schools, as well as explicitly in the curriculum. The military exploits of former Old Boys were proudly discussed at speech days and in school magazines and leadership skills were taught on the sports field and through the Cadet Corps.

For those children who were schooled in a colonial environment, the implications of their education were threefold. The policy of racial separation supported by the British in India from 1858 aimed to demarcate the imperial minority from those they ruled. In Ireland, as physical difference was harder to distinguish, religion was used to differentiate between groups. However, unlike India, where Anglo-Indians sought to pass as Europeans, the Roman Catholic Church actively sought to demarcate between the Catholic majority and the imperial elite. Within the colonial environment, the curriculum aimed to promote British hegemony over indigenous language, history, and culture. In the period leading up to independence in Ireland and India, children learned of British military success and to appreciate the language of Shakespeare and Wordsworth while learning little of their own culture. In the case of Ireland, this had several unexpected consequences. It created a legitimate site of resistance to British rule as the Roman Catholic and Nonconformist churches resisted nondenominational education, wrested control of aspects of the curriculum, and achieved financial control of religious schools. This had direct implications for the education policy of the Irish Free State, which also used education provision as a conduit for cultural nationalism.

Class Position and Occupation within the Imperial Elite

David Cannadine has asserted that society in the British colonial context was a mirror image (sometimes distorted) of the metropolitan one: with those at or near the top of the hierarchy wielding the power.[110] Primary source documents and interviews reveal both the commonalities and differences between colonial societies and with the metropolitan center. In order to contextualize the relationship between those who composed the imperial elite within colonial society, it is useful to consider the way in which the British state enabled and controlled entry to Ireland and India. As mentioned, the origins of British settlement in Ireland began in the twelfth century and were consolidated after the Cromwellian wars in the seventeenth century. During this period, land was removed from those who rebelled and given to loyal British subjects, with the aim of securing territory for the Protectorate and subsequently the Crown. The penal laws of the eighteenth century ensured that Catholics and Nonconformists were disbarred from the professions, political office, and land ownership. While this was challenged by Daniel O'Connell and finally repealed in 1829, research has shown that well into the twentieth century Protestant dominance continued in the professions, business, and land ownership.[111]

In India, by contrast, the East India Company was able to exert control over entry to the subcontinent until the mid-nineteenth century. Following the abolition of company rule in 1857, the Select Committee on Colonization and Settlement (SCCS) was set up the following year to consider British immigration. The conclusions of its report differed from previous policy in promoting the immigration of a small group of capitalist entrepreneurs into India. It stated that, given the large native population, it would be ill advised to encourage large-scale white settlement, particularly from lower class groups. Instead, emigration from Britain should include only "a class of superior settlers; who may, by their enterprise, capital and science, set in motion the labour, and develop the resources of India."[112] Consequently, India was not designated as a country of settlement, where British people would be encouraged to migrate in large numbers to own and work the land. There appears to be two reasons for this: first it was imperative to avoid further inflaming Indian opinion by importing a class of person who would compete with Indians in terms of labor. Also, in the aftermath of the 1857 Rebellion, the British wished to project an image of themselves as socially elevated. There was a further consideration in restricting numbers, and this was intended to protect the prestige associated with being white, which would be undermined if India became a settlement colony populated with white laborers. The SCCS was well aware of the importance of imperial prestige: "Every Englishman should go to India with a deep sense of his responsibility, not only to those whom he is about to govern or among whom he is about to reside, but to his own country."[113]

Therefore, the purpose and role of the British community in Ireland and India was fundamentally different. The Protestant population was actively encouraged to settle, to own and farm land, and to provide a loyal and stable bulwark against Catholic rebellion. The British population in India was initially controlled by the East India Company and, after 1858, by the British government. The purpose of the British community during the period of company rule was to facilitate trade and to protect the interests of the British in India, and after 1858, to administer the subcontinent and ideally represent British power and prestige in India.

Divisions within Colonial Society

As Satoshi Mizutani has argued, imperial studies have tended to focus on the colonizer/colonized dichotomy, while less attention has been paid to the internal structure of colonial society.[114] While researching Dutch colonial society in twentieth-century Java and Sumatra, Ann Stoler argues that differences within these societies have often been overlooked; but particularly in Sumatra, there are clear demarcations between operators and the corporate hierarchy in plantation society, which led to conflicts over social restrictions and labor relations.[115] Recorded evidence with those living in India in the first half of the twentieth century suggests distinctions along occupation and racial lines that had the impact of creating multiple layers within the small British community. These divisions either offered or precluded participants from employment opportunities and social advancement, determined where they lived, and impacted all areas of their lives.

One of the major distinctions was between those who were considered "home-born" and the "country-born." The latter, also known as the domiciled community, were those who were born and spent their working life in India. This group expanded as the British state imported working-class men from Britain in the late nineteenth century to work on infrastructure and communication projects that required significant technical skill. This, together with the increased numbers of subaltern soldiers enrolled to bolster British forces after the Indian Rebellion of 1857, meant that, in practice, there were a greater number of British immigrants, many of whom did not correspond with the image of a "class of superior settlers." This policy resulted in the creation of a class of Europeans who the British government now feared were about to sink "to the level of a hopeless pauperism, and to become a source of weakness to the Government, and a permanent charge upon the country."[116] The domiciled community became a political issue for the government of British India because it raised questions about racial degeneration in a colonial climate, which informed colonial policy in the nineteenth century and early twentieth.

The domiciled community was often excluded from senior administrative positions and tended to work in specific industries, particularly the railways. Their lives were often segregated residentially as well as by employment opportunities. Paddy Reilly was born in India in 1927; his Irish family had lived there since the mid-nineteenth century and inter-married with others of Irish ancestry. Initially soldiers in the armies of the East India Company, they were employed by the railway companies by the twentieth century. He reflected on social class in British India, and how the closer the link to Britain and government, the higher the social position. Paddy's family, who worked on the railways, mixed with a different stratum of Europeans:

> The very top echelons were people who came from England, lived in England, had their homes in England, but had jobs in India: in the government, in Simla. India was an administration not a settlement, unlike Africa where you had settlements. But you had the government at the top, the Viceroys, the Generals, the military chaps, then you're coming down, doctors, lawyers, but none of us aspired to that.[117]

Reilly's comment suggests awareness and acceptance of the social distinctions that existed in British India. He acknowledged that membership of the "home-born" British community allowed access to a world of employment and influence that was barred to the domiciled community. This distinction was also understood by those considered part of the elite. According to Sir Percival Griffiths,

> There were, from time to time, what we used to call domiciled Europeans who came into some of these services. They were very, very few in numbers. At one time, recruitment to the Indian Police, for example, had not been open to Europeans domiciled in India. The statutory bars were taken down later on, but there were not many of them and I think we must be honest and say there was a feeling they were not quite out of the top drawer.[118]

The racial aspect of the British community in India is important when considering how social divisions existed and were enforced in a British colonial context. Satoshi Mizutani argued that in colonial India "Britishness" was continually under assessment. "To be 'white,' in fact, was not always perceived as a permanent attribute of Europeans but was thought to require continuous care and material investment."[119] The litmus test was proximity to the metropole. Therefore, those who had been educated at Oxbridge and sent to India to work in administration were of a socially higher position than the domiciled white community in India. The concern over this group was underlined in the Calcutta Domiciled Community Enquiry Committee of 1918–19, which considered the negative impact on imperial prestige of a class of domiciled Europeans who were living in poverty among the Indian poor. The committee acknowledged the severe shortage of suitable, affordable housing for the domiciled community in Calcutta, together with restricted employment opportunities. It also accepted that education provision was limited. While it recommended various social improvements to alleviate the situation, it also suggested that the domiciled community was living in false consciousness, which allowed them to associate with the white middle classes while feeling superior to the Indian population.[120] The absence of any significant change following the report suggests the committee was more concerned to contain the spread of poverty than to permanently alter the conditions of the poorer residents domiciled in Calcutta. However, it also underlined the deep concern felt by the authorities about the prospect of the British residents in India falling into poverty and thus undermining white racial status. Discussions in the report indicate that once the domiciled community had fallen into a certain level of poverty, they were no longer part of the acknowledged British community in India but had entered into a hybrid existence, neither British nor Indian.

While the British community in India was divided along racial lines that separated those domiciled in India from the "home-born," there were also divisions based on occupation. At the top of the social hierarchy in British India were senior government and military figures. Indian civil servants were known as the "heaven-born," and as a consequence "most did become a bit aloof and conceited."[121] Sir Percival Griffiths was born in England and decided, aged thirteen, to join the Indian Civil Service (ICS). He went to India in the 1920s after having studied at grammar school and then at university on a scholarship. Entry to the ICS was via competitive entry. Griffiths recalled that the majority of the ICS had close links with Britain, having been either born or educated there. When he joined, approximately two-thirds were from the major public schools and a third, like himself, from grammar schools. His wife recalled the reaction to her engagement by a fellow passenger on board ship who exclaimed that she had done very well for herself to marry a member of the "heaven-born."[122] The ICS was the "steel frame" of British governance in India, ensuring tax collection and implementation of law and justice. The ICS was important within the social structure of British India for several reasons: their proximity to power, the large amount of responsibility with which they were entrusted, their educational background and ability, and their close association with Britain. The middle class was those in the intermediate ranks of government service. Wallace Burnet-Smith, whose father was an army officer, described how, even as a young boy, he was aware of the divisions that existed in colonial India: "We always considered ourselves as middle class. Not upper but middle. We always travelled as second class on the trains, we didn't travel first class; that was reserved for the hierarchy: senior civil servants, military officers, naval officers and people who owned factories. . . . It was important you knew your place."[123] This can, perhaps, be seen most clearly in the Warrant of Precedence. This document produced by the government press and widely distributed throughout the British community lists official rank in India from the Viceroy and senior military figures to the lowest ranks. The new hierarchy established after 1858 indicated a direct line from the Viceroy to the governor of a province, to the ICS, to the district officer. In 1921, this consisted of seventy-eight ranks.[124] The fact that this was codified in a widely distributed official document indicates the importance of class in official India. The document is illuminating by the detail of whom it includes—such as the Imperial Bacteriologist and the Superintendent, Trigonometrical Survey—but also whom it leaves out. This document records those who are involved in official functions: government officials, the military, the Church (Protestant and Catholic), the judiciary, and the administration.[125] Those involved in commercial activity, or planters, were not included. "Everywhere in British India, social rank depended on official position."[126] Those serving the imperial state in the first half of the twentieth century corroborated Cannadine's assessment.

While the Warrant of Precedence clearly stated rank and position, the commercial class were considered apart from official India. Sir Percival Griffiths suggested that the Indian civil servants were considered superior to the "box-wallahs," whom they viewed with suspicion and distrust. He claimed that this may have harkened back to the days of the East India Company when the interlopers were viewed with suspicion.[127] G. A. Carroll served in the Indian police force and also remembered the social division between the public and commercial sectors. "We looked down upon the box wallahs as we called them, of Bombay and Calcutta, as being ignorant of the real India, . . . Snobbiness is typical of all English people." John Outram, whose father was an aide-de-camp to several governors, made the assessment that the role of the British in India was in the service of the imperial enterprise and, as such, had little contact with the "capital and interest" of the business community.[128] This almost suggests that the imperial class felt their role was to govern, rather than profit, from their association with India. One of the guiding principles in India was that of trusteeship, and many interviews supported this view. Those working in an administrative capacity argued that their role was to improve the lot of the Indian population through the introduction of new technologies and education and infrastructure projects. As Elizabeth Buettner argued, the discourse of imperial sacrifice among empire families was strong, and many civil servants believed they were fulfilling their imperial duty. Therefore, the class structure of the British in India placed those who were serving the imperial state at the pinnacle, and those who were serving the interests of capital in a less senior position.

Social division in Ireland occurred along more similar lines to that in Britain, with the notable exception that Protestants of all classes felt a stronger association with their coreligionists than with those in similar occupations. Britain at the turn of the twentieth century felt the growing demands of working-class representation through the trade union movement and the nascent Labour Party, but these failed to make significant inroads in political life in Ireland. As Jack White commented, "The student of colonial societies will have no difficulty in recognising the picture. In Ireland, the contours are sometimes hard to follow because the map is three-dimensional: creed, class and political allegiance fall together in patterns always recognisable, but not always regular."[129] Arthur Aughey described this as "elected affinity," whereby the working class of each side felt more affinity with their coreligionists than with those of the same economic background.[130] He argued that when looking at the political landscape of Ireland in the early decades of the twentieth century, it is important to understand the role of religion in informing a political outlook and therefore creating bonds between coreligionists.[131] David Fitzpatrick suggested that within a sluggish economy marked by "inflexible property and marriage markets" this binding together was a way in which to advance their material position through "collective action."[132] Those interviewed for this research came from different social and economic backgrounds within the Protestant community. Several owned estates in rural Ireland that employed numbers of agricultural workers and domestic servants; others belonged to the professional and commercial class in Dublin; still others were part of the working class. Yet each attested to links within the Protestant community: forged through religious practice and a shared political outlook and allegiance and cemented through employment connections and social activities. Ron Alcock was one of eleven children. He was born in Dublin, the son of a carpenter and a housewife. One of his first jobs was for Nichols, a well-known retailer in Dublin. "I always remember when I left school, there were no jobs. And I thought the only way I am going to get a job is to go round the shops and say, 'Look, I am looking for a job.' And that's exactly what I did." He also went with his friend, Joe Murtagh, who was Catholic.

> I was fortunate. I got a job in this very famous household linen company . . . my friend who didn't get a job, was looking for weeks and weeks and I thought afterwards, I found out the company were Anglicans, whether it was because my name was Alcock, his name was something more Irish, . . . it's a funny thing once you tell people your name in Ireland . . . they know.[133]

Alcock's comment indicates how precarious the employment situation in Dublin was at the time he left school in the 1940s and that in seeking work the best method was to approach employers directly. Once a personal connection was established, employers would have a sense of the background of prospective employees. Ron noted that he was successful, while his friend, who was Roman Catholic, was not. His employers were Anglican. Ron's job involved making deliveries to the wealthy areas such as Ballsbridge and Rathgar on the south side of Dublin city, where customers were more likely to be of the same religion. His discussion of his early employment suggests that, in difficult economic times, he was more likely to find work with a Protestant employer.

Anne Hodkinson's father, Willie Lang, was employed as a young man at the wine merchant Barton and Guestier before becoming the wine waiter at the prestigious Kildare Street Club in central Dublin. His father had been a sergeant in the Royal Irish Constabulary, so Willie Lang's progression illustrated the possibility of social advancement. The Kildare Street Club was the principal gentleman's club in the nineteenth and early twentieth centuries, "a bastion of the Anglo-Irish Ascendency" and a place where the aristocracy met to discuss politics and business within an exclusive atmosphere of fine drapes, paintings, and wood paneling.[134] Anne's father later progressed to become head steward at the Church of Ireland House on St. Stephen's Green in Dublin, a position where he had close contact with the most senior members of Church hierarchy. While this could be read as an elevation within a position of service, Willie Lang's friendship with George Otto Simms, Primate of All Ireland, and the attendance of many senior bishops at his funeral suggest close contact and relationships between Protestants of different classes. Lionel Fleming's account of his early life in County Cork documents the position of the family as they moved down the social hierarchy as their economic circumstances changed. However, their family history and connections still allowed them into a world of the Protestant upper class, which would have been barred to many others. When he visited an elderly relative whose grand house had been attacked in the early 1920s in his capacity as a reporter, they greeted him as a family friend who had come to express his condolences.[135]

Consequently, class divisions in these two colonial societies were not comparable. In India, despite the small number of British within a much larger population of Indians, colonial society was riven by difference based on perceived racial differentiation, class position, occupational position, and connection to the British state. This initially seems to run against the idea of an imagined British community in an overseas location. However, by stratifying colonial society to such an extent, the outcome was that the British community fought to remain closely aligned with British interests and to be socially accepted as part of colonial society. Thus, social customs that were rather outdated in Britain in the 1920s and 1930s, such as calling cards, were still an accepted social form of interaction in India. In contrast, Irish Protestants chose to reject the strong class affiliation present in Britain in order to retain strength within their own coreligionist community. As David Fitzpatrick notes, this had the outcome of gathering working-class support for the Ascendency class, whether this was in their interest or not.[136] However, as the interviews illustrate, this ensured working-class Protestants preferential employment positions during challenging economic times.

Conclusion

Education was used in a metropolitan and colonial setting to implicitly and explicitly encourage an imperial set of values in pupils. This was through architectural language and material culture, as well as through the curriculum. In a colonial setting, educational institutions served to demarcate ruler from ruled and to provide the academic tools to the former to allow the continuation of that rule. Class position was neither a mirror of the metropole nor unified in a colonial setting. Within Ireland, despite the greater number of Protestants than the British in India, class and economic differences were put aside as Protestants unified behind their religion and cultural and political similarities. While economic differences occurred, there was a symbiotic relationship between those of different classes, which benefitted both. In British India, rigid differences existed in colonial society based on links to the metropolitan center and official position. Rather than seeking association through similarity, they sought distance through clubs and hill stations as well as through employment and residence. However, within both countries, British values were reinforced through the differentiation and separation from the "other." This difference was demarcated through access to power and wealth and their elite status. It was also reinforced through their loyalty to the British monarch based in the metropole. The following chapter examines how the British community saw their imperial role once independence was achieved in Ireland and India.

3

Endings and New Beginnings

My father was a civil servant and he had worked for the British civil service until 1920 when the change of government meant he decided he didn't want to stay any longer in Ireland. I think he was worried about the possibility of religious discrimination; he was a Protestant, and he transferred to what was then the General Post Office in England . . . well, I mean, probably there was a basis of truth in it, that when a situation had been so manifestly unjust that Protestants were favoured over Catholics, that when the change of government came the boot was going to be on the other foot and I think that was probably a fairly accurate perception on his part.
—Olive Stevenson

Following the establishment of the Irish Free State in 1922 and Indian independence in 1947, there was a dramatic reduction in the numbers of southern Irish Protestants and the British in India living in each of those countries. Between the census of 1911 and the following one in 1926, the number of non-Catholics in the Irish Free State dropped from approximately 313,000 to 208,000.[1] After Indian independence, the majority of the British community left the subcontinent. It is difficult to accurately assess numbers, but in 1921 the total European population of India was just under 157,000, including approximately 60,000 troops and just fewer than 22,000 in government service.[2] This chapter investigates the motivation for southern Irish Protestants and members of the British community in India to leave and "return" to Britain. It assesses what this decision reveals about the links these two communities felt to Britain and questions the extent to which their sense of identity and belonging was challenged or confirmed on return. It investigates how changes in employment affected the decision-making process and whether these communities felt directly threatened during the process of independence and partition. How did these remigrants make the transition from a colonial to a postcolonial environment? What were the consequences of returning to Britain in the aftermath of a world war, and to what extent did these British returnees form part of an imperial diaspora?

The chapter contends that southern Irish Protestants and the British in India left as a direct response to the transition from British governance to the incorporation of the new postcolonial states in Ireland and the subcontinent. These former elites no longer had a clearly defined role in the new era. In Ireland, a greater number owned land and businesses and therefore were less likely to leave, but the overwhelming majority did so in India. It was, in the main, a collective rather than an individual action. The British government facilitated migration by relocating service personnel and assisting with passage. In both countries, demobilization and the creation of new military and political elites meant the loss of employment. In India, violence and intimidation against the British community were rare, but in Ireland they factored into the decision-making process. Britain was chosen as the return destination because of the continuing connection with it as "home," and these communities retained a continued deference to its cultural and political institutions.[3] However, those who had previously formed a privileged elite soon became aware of their changed circumstances and altered status. This was particularly marked for the British in India. The journey on board a cramped troopship underlined their reduced status. Arrival in Britain confirmed this, and it was particularly challenging for those responsible for families, who had to find work and accommodations in postwar Britain. They found that their colonial experience was generally not valued in a country that was reorientating itself to the postwar order, and their social capital was reduced. However, for younger returnees, particularly young women, life in Britain offered hitherto unexplored possibilities. Official reception varied; southern Irish Protestants arriving in the 1920s were recognized for their loyalty and service. Supported by senior government ministers, they were assisted with grants to create a new life. In the climate following the Second World War, there was not the same level of assistance for returnees from India. At the end of empire, those who had served it realized they had entered a new postcolonial era in which they would not be lauded for their imperial service. Britain in the postwar world was orientating itself toward a new era.

As Kenny noted in a key work, although Britain was the recipient of the second largest number of Irish migrants after the United States, and after the 1920s the principal recipient, there was little sense of an ethnic identity compared with the United States. There was no equivalent of "Irish-British" as there was in the United States.[4] In fact, there was not even a separate category in the census until Mary Hickman's work in the 1990s.[5] As Donald MacRaild has accurately assessed, most of the literature on the Irish diaspora has focused on Irish Catholic migration, with particular emphasis on periods of great change such as the Famine of 1845–51.[6] As much of this work is based on sources that reflect the separateness of Irish communities within Britain, such as religion, political affiliation, and cultural association, it has tended to overlook the Protestant context to migration. "As the Ulster loyalist idea of Irishness melted into Britishness during the Home Rule crisis, Catholics gradually became the only meaningful and distinct Irish race."[7] Historians studying the revolutionary period in Ireland in the early twentieth century have identified several causal factors that prompted migration, particularly from minority communities. While scholars diverge on the extent to which the Protestant community was coerced into forced exile, Andy Bielenberg's work on this period identifies several broad factors that prompted migration, namely withdrawal of British forces and those associated with them, the redistribution of land ownership, boycott and intimidation, as well as the cold political climate now present in the new state.[8] To a large extent, those leaving stayed within an imperial environment, with twenty-four thousand going to the new state of Northern Ireland.[9] A large proportion went to Britain, where Brennan suggests there were twenty thousand in the summer of 1922.[10] The other principal destinations were Canada and South Africa.[11] These figures indicate that southern Irish Protestants stayed within the empire and therefore remained part of an imperial network. Both Enda Delaney and Mo Moulton, in their studies of the Irish in Britain in the twentieth century, have acknowledged the paucity of material on Protestant immigration, but assumed that the transition to life in Britain was a relatively easy one. In *Demography, State and Society*, Delaney argued that it required little effort for the Ascendency and the professional or middle-class Protestants to disappear without a trace into English society.[12] Mo Moulton suggested that for many Irish

Protestants "England was not a foreign country, but actively conceptualized as home, and indeed a place where many of them had spent
large amounts of time, for educational, business, or family reasons."[13]
Others have contended that Irish Protestants assimilated much more
easily than their Catholic counterparts.[14] Rhona Ward, a Protestant
civil servant who came to Britain in the late 1930s, described her daily
life in London in terms that appear to support these assumptions. She
easily found employment prior to arrival and seemed to have few difficulties in finding accommodations or making social contacts.[15] However, as research by Kenny has shown, there was in fact little space for
Irish Protestant migrants to Britain in the 1920s to carve out any kind
of hybrid identity in this period.[16] While they might be identified by
others as Irish, this was often not an identity they would have associated
with, connected as it was with Catholicism and nationalism. Southern Irish Protestants migrating in this period would have striven to
create a distance, economically, socially, but also culturally, from this
association. As Kerby Miller pointed out in *Emigrants and Exiles*, this
migration was often seen as the demonstration of the failure of British
rule, not a promotion of the power of the Union with Britain.[17] This
chapter's contention is that, within an imperial environment, southern
Irish Protestants and the British in India maintained an idea, and link,
to Britain as "home." The result of independence in Ireland and India
caused them to reconsider their position. The following section evalu-
ates the "push" factors to determine the conditions behind their relocation to Britain.

Violence

One of the most contested debates about the revolutionary period in
Ireland centers on intercommunal violence and whether it was "ethnically" motivated. Were threats of violence following decolonization a
prompt for migration? Peter Hart is one of the key proponents of this
view, arguing that Protestants in Cork, in particular, were targeted.[18]
Other scholars have assessed the death toll of civilians to be 130 in
the period between 1919 and the Truce, although they recognize that
many more were boycotted and intimidated.[19] County Cork is widely
acknowledged to be one of the most affected areas in the country,

although in David Fitzpatrick's detailed study of Cork Methodists in this period, he argues that only 230 of the 811 emigrants from Cork district left during the revolutionary years, and it was between 1911 and 1914 that 248 members left. There was an increase in members after the First World War, particularly in 1922.[20] He suggests that it is important to take account of the long tradition of migration from all faiths and that there was a decline in population in garrison towns in County Cork, such as Fermoy and Mallow, as the British Army left the country.

The records of the Irish Grants Committee are, in many ways, the most comprehensive archive of Protestant losses in this period, although the relief fund was open to all, regardless of denomination.[21] The purpose was to support those who had "on account of their support of His Majesty's Government prior to 11 July 1921 sustained hardship and loss by personal injury . . . in the area of the Irish Free State between 11 July 1921 and 12 May 1923."[22] Traditionally, Protestants in Ireland had supported the Union with Britain and the cases examined reflect this, with the overwhelming majority reviewed coming from Protestant applicants (over 65 percent). Claims were accepted up to 29 February 1928, and the final committee report was written in 1930.[23] By this date there had been 291 sittings. The total number of claims originally lodged was 3,036 and rose to 4,032. Of those, 895 were considered to be outside the scope of the terms of reference and 900 were not recommended; therefore, 2,237 cases were successful.[24] Claimants had to demonstrate a link between their loss and loyalty to the British government to be compensated.

I examined 350 of the 4,000 original case files. Although all contained claims against loss to property, it was much rarer that claimants cited personal attacks. Most of the claims were from those located in rural Ireland and were more likely to be living in isolated locations. The most common reason for a claim was the removal of farm machinery and tools, livestock, firewood, and fuel. These items were usually taken from outbuildings or farm land. It was less usual that homes were broken into, although this was not entirely uncommon. It is very difficult to firmly ascertain the motivation behind these acts. While the claim form required that claimants directly link the loss to their loyalty to the Crown, claimants seldom knew the perpetrators and therefore could only speculate on their motivation. While in some areas families could validate their suspicions by citing other Protestant families who had seemingly been targeted, elsewhere thefts were likely prompted by a lack of law enforcement in Ireland in this period. While these attacks would certainly give rise to concerns, and in some cases may have prompted the decision to leave, it is not obvious that this, in itself, would cause the significant migration that occurred in the period. This is corroborated by the case files: among the 350 cases examined, fifty-nine people left the country and twelve returned within a couple of years. However, quantitative data do not demonstrate how individuals *felt* about these events. With the benefit of hindsight it is possible to ascertain that this period of upheaval lasted for a relatively short period. However, for those who were in the midst of these events, it would not have been clear that the Irish Free State would eventually establish control. Therefore, it is instructive to compare data with personal accounts from the period. Cork, in particular, was one of the most disturbed areas of the country: it was a Sinn Fein stronghold and the site of the 1922 murder of Michael Collins. Of the cases examined, the highest number of applicants came from County Cork—forty-one. William Bateman, age thirty-five, from Timoleague, represents a typical case. He was a farmer who had sheep and cattle stolen.

> I had to leave for England at the time of the West Cork murders in 1922. My expenses while away were £20 as well as the £34 which I lost through the taking of the animals. During the trouble I was a member of Clonakilty Urban Council and always refused to acknowledge the S.F. [Sinn Fein]. I was always in a minority of one in refusing allegiance to the Irish Republic.[25]

Another, Richard Cooper, a sixty-six-year-old from Ballinrea in Cork, revealed his concerns following the war of independence and the signing of the Truce. He was an agent for the Ministry of Pensions for Cork City—a position for the benefit of soldiers, sailors, and their dependents—and therefore he was a "marked man." He describes his decision to leave Cork:

> It was impossible for me to think of returning to live in Cork after the Truce. A friend, Colonel Peacock, was shot in July 1921 at Innishannon and a near friend and neighbour, Major O'Connor was shot on the night of the Truce. . . . I therefore decided to sell my house and lands, the best price

I could get being £3000 . . . and suffered the extra expense of coming to
England and had to pay carriage on furniture brought over, viz £194.10.0.[26]

While those Protestant families actually affected by direct threats or
violence to their person were relatively small in number, the impact
on the Protestant community in this period was significant. Within a
small but interconnected community, particularly in rural areas, these
threats created a climate of fear and unease, and led Protestants to question their position in the new state. The threats also raised concerns
about the ability of the nascent Free State to uphold the rule of law
and resist more extreme Republican factions. Another case that links
attacks to the political situation at the time is that of Lord Ashtown,
whose lands in County Galway comprised 745 acres and were seized by
the First Western Division of the Irish Republican Army in April 1921.
They asserted they were assisting the Catholic population in Belfast and
other Northern towns who were being targeted "by Orange gunmen,"
and consequently "there are thousands of men women and children
homeless and starving."[27] The IRA claimed that the British government was actively enabling the Orange Order to terrorize the Catholic
population in the North: "We are also fully alive to the fact that the
British Government is supplying the necessary cash and arms to enable
the Orangemen to complete this task of exterminating all Catholics
from the North. . . . In the absence of other resources for this purpose,
the Executive Council of the IRA have decided that the Unionists and
Free Masons in the South and West of Ireland be compelled to supply
these needs."[28] Another claimant, Mrs. Henrietta L. Stopford, leased
the mansion house and residence known as Ahanesk in County Cork,
which together with outhouses, gardens, and demesne lands totaled 183
acres. Beginning in 1921, the Stopford estate was raided on numerous
occasions, with furniture and clothing stolen from the house as well as
fruit from the orchard seized. Unlike most raids, these men confronted
the owners, "used threatening language towards the staff and remained
on the premises for some time, partaking of food and using the Hall
to dance on and amuse themselves." The Stopfords were also pressed
to contribute to IRA funds, which they refused. After which, they were
boycotted.[29] It should be mentioned that class was a factor when considering attacks. Those who were part of the Anglo-Irish Ascendency,

with large estates, and who traditionally held positions of power within the administration, were much more likely than Protestants on smaller farms to have their estates targeted and to be actively linked to the British government and its policies.[30] As noted in the IRA statement to Lord Ashtown, whether accurate or not, a line was drawn linking class, religion, loyalty, and culpability.

India witnessed terrible violence as independence and partition was implemented in August 1947. Senior figures within the administration were concerned about the potential loss of British life although most of those affected were Indians. In a Top Secret and Personal Directive issued on 29 July 1947 on the Use of the British Troops after 14 August 1947, it was stated that "although British troops can NOT be employed in communal disturbances to protect Indian subjects, they may be so employed to protect British lives." This directive was issued only to the commander-in-chief in India and his three senior *British* staff officers, his counterpart in Pakistan, and the general officer commanding in chief of the Southern and Eastern Command. They were instructed to destroy the document once troops had left India.[31] Those who remember the growing demands for Indian independence recall the violence that sometimes accompanied such demonstrations. Mollie Warner remembered being called a "red-faced monkey" during such disturbances, and Wallace Burnet-Smith recalled riots in the Maidan in Calcutta.[32] Lady Sylvia Corfield evoked the civil disturbances that followed independence.

> I can remember standing above The Mall in Simla and seeing all the shops being looted, and I can remember standing on the veranda of the United Services Club which had opened its doors to women, standing there with the Bishop of Lahore and hearing the rickshaw quarters in the lower Bazaar being bombed. We felt quite helpless listening to their cries and the dull thud of the explosions.[33]

They left by an armed convoy organized by Field Marshal Auchinleck, as this was considered safer than the railway. When asked if she felt it was potentially dangerous for British people, she responded that as the army was still loyal she felt reassured. "I don't think the army would ever have turned against the Europeans or the policy and they were trying to keep order and did to a very large extent keep order."[34]

The political transition from British to Indian rule, and the resulting partition of the subcontinent on religious lines, resulted in huge
losses of life. The calamity created conflicted feelings within the British community as to their role in this transitionary period and indeed
their own imperial service. The principle of trusteeship stated that the
purpose of British rule in India was to elevate the Indian population.[35]
However, Partition seemed a visible demonstration of its failure. Those
who witnessed the bloodshed that accompanied this policy questioned
the failure to ensure a peaceful transition of power. Mollie Warner was
traveling across India with her husband from Naini Tal in the Himalayas when her train was halted on the line. The previous train had
been attacked and all those on board massacred. She recalled seeing
children being thrown into the air and lacerated by attackers. A crowd
managed to force themselves onto their carriage and hide under the
seats.[36] While not all members of the British community were witness
to such horrific attacks, they were aware of the extent of the bloodshed
and blamed British politicians, and Mountbatten in particular, for
failing to negotiate successfully for independence. This was a recur-
ring view from accounts of the period. Sue Sloan's father was serving
in the army at the time; his view was that "if Mountbatten had kept
the army in India, they could have protected the Punjabis and got to
the switchover, you know the lines you saw of people being attacked in
the trains, he could have stopped that, but he was a very vain man and
a stupid man."[37] Verna Perry's father worked for Turner and Newall,
an asbestos cement manufacturer in Bombay, and recalled the dislike
felt by many of the British community for the Mountbattens. In their
view, the poor management of this major transition from British to
Indian governance undermined British capability. Many considered
that the appointment of Mountbatten demonstrated poor judgment
within metropolitan Britain, as the Mountbattens were neither capable
nor morally suitable for the role. It also challenged their own imperial
service, as they believed their role in India was to encourage an economic and political situation whereby self-government for India could
be achieved peacefully.[38]

Therefore, although violence was a factor around the time of independence, the number of British people affected was minimal, particularly when viewed against the huge loss of life among the Indian

population. In Ireland, the number of southern Irish Protestants affected by violence and threat was higher, but there is not enough evidence to suggest this was the principal reason for the large numbers migrating in the 1920s. As John Borgonovo has argued, when contrasted with ethnic violence in other parts of Europe as dynastic empires gave way to smaller states based on racial and ethnic affiliation, the loss of life in Ireland was minimal.[39]

Employment and Livelihood

We must, then, consider other potential reasons for the exodus of southern Irish Protestants and the British in India after 1922 and 1947. Functionalist theories of migration look to economic factors to explain the decision-making process behind migration. Economic factors, such as a lack of work and opportunities offered elsewhere, are often used to explain migratory patterns.[40] To what extent, then, was the changing employment situation a factor in prompting emigration from Ireland and India? From 1858, when the Crown took control of British India from the East India Company, senior administrative, military, and technical positions were occupied by British post holders. The monarch, whose representative was the Viceroy, governed India. The position was usually occupied by a British aristocrat. The exact and precise nature of hierarchy was recorded in the Warrant of Precedence.[41] The theoretical underpinning to British rule in India was the idea of "civilising mission," or the principle of trusteeship. Utilitarian political theorists critiqued India as being governed by superstition, being ruled by despots, and failing to achieve a high degree of civilization.[42] The prescription was British rule: low taxation, codified laws, and the free market.[43] This, coupled with Macaulay's support of an education system that promoted a British curriculum taught in English, prioritized the British culture and political system over that present in India,[44] and justified the employment of British officials in senior position throughout the administration.

From 1858 to 1947, the majority of the British community in India was employed by the state. In 1921, the total British population of India was just under 157,000. There were approximately 60,000 troops and just fewer than 22,000 in government service. There were 45,000 women, the majority of whom did not work. As Judith Brown has demonstrated, employment patterns for the British community had begun to alter in the decades before independence. One of the most significant of these was the policy of "Indianisation," which took effect from the 1920s. This policy encouraged the gradual introduction of qualified Indian staff into British administrative positions in state departments. By 1929, the Indian Civil Service contained only 895 British post holders.[45] However, the most senior positions in the Indian Civil Service were still held by British personnel. Indian independence meant the role of government changed, with functions moving from British to Indian administration. The legislation enacting the revisions stipulated that His Majesty's Government had no further responsibility to the territories that formally composed British India.[46] This had a direct effect on employment as Indian post holders replaced British staff. His Majesty's Government provided compensation for those who had been employed, with members of the Indian Civil Service receiving the highest amount: eight thousand pounds on completion of sixteen years of service. Military and police and members of the Indian Political Service received similar, though slightly lower, compensation. As the document noted, "The development of the policy of His Majesty's Government for constitutional advancement in India has affected European officers and other ranks of the Royal Indian Navy, Indian Army and Indian Medical Service in a similar way to the members of the Civil Services."[47] The establishment of the Irish Free State meant that constitutionally the country remained part of the British Empire until 1948, when the Republic was unilaterally declared. Many Protestants in Ireland, particularly the class known as the Ascendency, formed an elite that provided members of the judiciary, senior administrators, and military officers. While senior figures in the British administration were replaced by their Irish equivalents, Protestant civil servants or members of the judiciary were not removed from existing posts, and therefore the transition was gradual and evolutionary rather than immediate. The Protestant Ascendency also supplied a significant number of Unionist members of Parliament. The formation of the Irish Free State created a new governing body, the Oireachtas, made up of the Dáil and the Seanad; Ireland no longer sent representatives to Parliament. While the new constitution provided representation for minority groups within

the new governing body, speeches in the Dáil during this period illustrate some of the prevailing views. On 7 January 1922, Constance
Markievicz called the southern Unionists "England's garrison, who had
battened on the country while the Irish people were dying on the road-
sides. They were capitalists of the worst kind. They were oppressors
and traders, grinding the faces of the poor."[48] William Butler Yeats, in
a speech to the Senate on the subject of divorce, accused the government of turning on the Anglo-Irish, who were "no petty people."[49] As
acknowledged by scholars of the period, Protestant members of the old
British establishment in Ireland "experienced the most intense reversals
during the nationalist revolution."[50] The change in government in Ireland ushered in cultural as well as political changes. Irish became the
language of the new state, and officeholders had to pass exams in the
language in order to obtain teaching and civil service positions.[51] Many
Protestants were ambivalent about the language and its role in the new
state and chose not to apply.[52]

Protestants had traditionally dominated business and commerce in
Ireland. While they weren't specifically targeted, they were affected by
the economic downturn, particularly in agriculture. After the civil war,
land values fell, together with a general collapse in farm prices following the inflated values of the First World War. The loss of southern
Ireland's exceptional position in the British meat market also adversely
affected farmers. For many businesses the loss in custom from wealthy
clients who had left the country was also a factor. Another significant
aspect was the Irish Land Acts that distributed large areas of land com-
pulsorily purchased on "extraordinarily easy terms" to appease the land
hunger of earlier days.[53] However, in commerce, many of the most
prestigious firms, such as the Guinness breweries, Switzers department
store, and the John Jameson distillery, remained in Protestant ownership; and Protestants continued to dominate banking and insurance up
until the 1970s.[54] As an article in the *Manchester Guardian* pointed out,
"The wealth and business of the country are still in the hands of the
non-Catholic minority."[55]

British rule, in both Ireland and India, was underpinned by a strong
military presence. Ireland was the most militarized place in the British
Empire in this period, with twenty-seven thousand soldiers and twelve
thousand armed Royal Irish Constabulary personnel stationed across

the country.[56] The change of government led to the withdrawal of the British Army and their families, which, together with Crown officials, accounted for a reduction in population of approximately thirty-four thousand.[57] This change in government placed many loyalists in a difficult position. The Irish Grants Committee noted that it was not in their remit to compensate for this constitutional change, but the disbandment of the Royal Irish Constabulary was acknowledged and provision made by Parliament under the Constabulary (Ireland) Act of 1922. A generous scale of pension was drawn up, calculated on length of service, with either ten or twelve years added.[58] Any Royal Irish Constabulary officer was also entitled to a disturbance allowance if he had to move. It is difficult to assess exact numbers, but in 1911 the Royal Irish Constabulary numbered eight thousand, and many of their number applied for assistance to the Irish Grants Committee in the 1920s.[59]

This transition from one form of government to another also had a major effect on the British in India. As with Ireland, immediate plans were put in place to evacuate British troops from the subcontinent. As early as 17 August 1947, three thousand British troops left Bombay with a formal send-off from Field Marshal Claude Auchinleck and Viscount Mountbatten.[60] However, it was agreed by the Partition Council that a proportion of British officers and other ranks should remain for a period of eight months in order to prevent a "breakdown of the whole administrative machine and the training programme." Field Marshal Auchinleck requested that military personnel should volunteer for this role rather than being coerced, in the light of "the calumny and abuse, particularly in the press, from which British officers had suffered in recent years."[61] Under the Indian Independence Act there was provision for the division of His Majesty's Indian armed forces between the two dominions of India and Pakistan.[62] There were also royal regiments stationed in India that were relocated. Therefore, independence reduced a major source of employment for British personnel. Compensation for Regular Officers of the Royal Indian Navy, the Indian Army, and the Indian Medical Service was much less than for those in the covenanted services. The highest level was £5,250, with the amount decreasing the closer an individual got to retirement age.[63] In addition, as accommodation had usually been provided as part of the conditions of employment, with the loss of position came the loss of accommodation.

Several members of Betty Gascoyne's family were serving in the army at the time of independence. Her mother was a quartermaster, her husband Fred was a sergeant, and Betty herself worked in administration in the Indian Army.[64] For those who had committed to imperial service, the change in government meant their role no longer existed. Military participation vividly demonstrated the strength of support given to British rule by southern Irish Protestants and the British in India. The demobilization of the military presence clearly showed the transition of power from imperial to national governments.

Imperial Homecomings

Returnees chose Britain for a variety of reasons: for those voyaging from Ireland it was accessible and relatively inexpensive. There were no visas or entry requirements and no language barriers. Many migrants had some prior knowledge of life in Britain, and their education and training were generally recognized. Furthermore, many Protestant families had long-established connections with Britain. The British in India had often retained family connections to Britain, and the home-born community had often spent their education or periods of furlough there. This section argues that the period of decolonization highlighted various understandings of home in a domestic, national, and imperial framework and claims that the intersection of meanings of home collided for those undertaking remigration in the postcolonial period. Interviews with those who experienced this traumatic period reveal conflicted conceptualizations of home—one rooted in a physical space and place, another existing at a national level, and a third relating to their experience as imperial migrants. The rupture caused by independence resulted in the collision of these different meanings. Verna Perry's response to the news that her family would be returning to Britain from Bombay reveals some of the complicated feelings associated with return.

> I remember feeling really happy and excited about going home . . . I remember standing on the stairs and knew we were leaving Mulund [Bombay] and going to England and I can remember thinking, "What a happy life, and I love this place," and feeling sad at leaving it and feeling apprehensive for the

future, and with a lot of difficulty getting booked on the Largs Bay [ship] and it was a big adventure.[65]

Perry's comment reveals many of the elements discussed by those "remigrating" to Britain in this period. She described her reaction to the news in terms of strong emotions: both happiness and sadness, mixed with apprehension for what this new chapter might bring. Similarly, her attachment to "home" conveys some ambivalence: she was both excited at the prospect of returning to England, which she cited as "home," while also noting her love for her physical home in Bombay. Thus "home" was a duality between her lived experience in India and her imperial attachment to Britain as the site of "home." The prospect of return elicited a range of strong, but sometimes conflicting, emotions. She indicated the difficulty finding passage on a returning ship, often a troopship, which further complicated the return journey. Perry belonged to the "home born"—she had been born in Dartford in Kent before moving with her family to India as a baby. Vere Birdwood's family had served the British imperial state for generations, and she recognized the cyclical pattern of life for those who were part of the "home-born" British community.

> I think we felt that India was the real life, because it was where we drew our pay, it was where our own home was against the home of relations. And it was where most of us spent our working lives, but we all knew—and this was like knowing that death is inevitable—we all knew that one day we would leave India. Most of us, I think did not look forward to this day. Some did, but very few.[66]

Birdwood's reflections underlined the ebb and flow of life from Britain to India that was the pattern for the "home-born" British community and in which they existed between the two worlds, with the majority of their working life spent in India, and periods spent in Britain for education and retirement. It was this regular return that allowed privileged access to metropolitan Britain and enhanced their social capital and employment opportunities. Yet she acknowledged that the embedded pattern of return to Britain was one that was endured rather than willingly accepted, so much so that "return" was closely linked to death—not just as inevitable, but as in the ending of one form of life and the morphing into another. Also revealing is her comment on the use of the word "home." She located her "own home" in India, rather than an imperial version of home—in Britain—lodging with relations. In contrast, Betty Gascoyne was part of the community who had lived and worked in India for generations. Betty's feelings of "return" to Britain were complicated by various conceptualizations of home. In her interview, she discussed how the family always referred to Britain as home, although they had never been there. Her idea of Britain as home was visually constructed by magazines imported from Britain, such as *Sketch*, *Daily Mirror*, and *Pictorial*, which she read at the Railway Institute and which formed part of the cultural idea of Britain as home. Yet when asked where home was for her, Betty responded that it was India. When she met and married her London-born husband who was a sergeant in the army, they planned to stay in India, until his regiment was reassigned and the family was relocated to Britain. This meant that Betty's sense of being part of an imagined British community in India was suddenly confronted with the actuality of "return"; thus various meanings of home—domestic, national, and imperial—collided. Members of the domiciled community retained plural views of home—a physical and national view that differed from an imperial one.

In contrast, Irish Protestants had a different relationship to their environment. Long habitation in a specific geographical area and home ownership combined to create a strong sense of home—"home" was less a metaphorical concept than a concrete reality. Evidence from recorded interviews suggests that home for Irish Protestants was rooted in Ireland. However, they also retained a strong imperial identity that linked them to Britain. Attacks on Irish Protestant homes in this period were assaults on both their physical space and their right to remain. At the same time, the end of the union with Britain threatened their imperial identity. Thus, their sense of home as a physical space was threatened at the same time as their right to remain imperial subjects.

Mo Moulton has suggested that, for southern Irish Protestants, England was not a foreign entity but rather "actively conceptualized as home." It was a place that many of them had spent time for business, education, or social reasons.[67] She identified, in the memoirs and writings of those Anglo-Irish who had relocated to Britain in the 1920s, that they were "often affected by a profound nostalgia" and were living between two worlds.[68] She suggested that home and garden provide a metaphor in these writings, with the garden serving as emblematic of British control of an Irish environment. In contrast, the Anglo-Irish home is often depicted as decaying, much like the inhabitants who are dwindling in numbers. Case files of the Irish Grants Committee reveal that the majority of applicants did not leave Ireland despite the turbulence of the period. Three hundred fifty case files were examined: of fifty-nine claimants who came to Britain, twelve returned within a couple of years.[69] This was despite the fact that they had endured the destruction of their property, in addition to boycotts and intimidation. In choosing to return, they were prioritizing their physical home over an imperial identity that linked them to Britain. The process of decolonization forced Irish Protestants to reconsider home, national identity, and imperial identity. E. J. Gwynn was a scholar and teacher at Trinity College Dublin specializing in Celtic languages. His position was, in many ways, emblematic of those who had formed the Ascendency; he was at Trinity, the long-established Anglican university in Dublin, yet specialized in Gaelic languages. Writing in 1921, he reflected upon his position: "This last year has made me feel, for the first time, that I am myself essentially English and not Irish, in spite of certain sympathies and antipathies." In considering his children's future, he said, "I do not want myself and I do not want them to feel aliens in their own country."[70] These reflections suggest that Gwynn was retaining an imperial identity while choosing to remain within a postcolonial environment; he was perhaps choosing nation over imperial connection while accepting that doing so placed him in an anomalous position sometimes between two coexisting but contrasting worlds.

The Journey

The voyage back to Britain from India raised further questions about their imperial affiliation and caused some apprehension about their future role. This experience contrasted with those traveling from Ireland, who were much nearer geographically. This section considers aspects of the journey that caused migrants to frame their position within an imperial context.

Many families in India had little or no control over the timing or organization of their journey. They recall having to wait until they were instructed to embark, which often took many weeks. This removed any sense of agency and suggested a collective rather than an individual response to Indian independence. Betty Gascoyne's husband was serving in a British regiment. She recalled that prior to being sent to England she and her family were located at the army camp at Deolali. This camp was associated with poor conditions and interminable boredom as families waited in transit. The Gascoynes stayed there for three weeks, each family sharing one room. Betty recalled that it was so overcrowded she could overhear the other families' conversations. Illness was prevalent, and she was concerned for her young daughter who had been born prematurely and had suffered with childhood illness. However, Betty was fortunate in comparison with some families, as she had her husband to assist with the children.[71]

These families' altered status was clearly illustrated during these journeys. Previously, British families in India had numerous servants to assist with household tasks and child care. Now they were traveling alone. They were also sailing in cramped and overcrowded conditions. Jill Gowdey traveled with her mother and younger brothers from the Nilgiris in the south to Bombay before embarking. She recalled her mother's astonishment when two extra passengers joined their small berth. She remembered how each person had to schedule when they got out of bed in the morning as there was limited standing room. This discomfort was compounded by embarrassment as they had to wash in the berth. When asked about bathing facilities, she said they were too anxious to take a bath in case they were torpedoed while doing so. This underlined how insecurity and danger were constant elements for many British passengers returning to Britain post independence. Jill Gowdey recalled that they traveled in a convoy that included destroyers and aircraft carriers. In the ship's hold were a group of Italian prisoners of war. All passengers had to take part in a daily boat drill in case of attack. She recalled that it was the first time she and her mother had worn trousers. They felt it would be easier to escape while wearing pants rather than dresses. The perilous nature of the journey was underlined by both the necessity of traveling in a convoy with naval vessels and the presence of mines as they passed through the Suez Canal into the Mediterranean and onto the English Channel.[72]

Interviews with these imperial migrants reveal how the perception of their experience varied according to age, gender, class, and sense of responsibility. This illustrates how the same event can be perceived differently according to an individual's personal perspective. Women traveling with children had a very different experience from teenage members of the same family or single men traveling alone. Women responsible for other family members had to endure not only the over-crowding and danger present on board ship but also in many cases the sickness of their children. Jill Gowdey's youngest brother had measles and was quarantined for some of the journey, while her mother "who was not a good traveller" experienced seasickness.[73] Betty Gascoyne had been able to spend time with her husband at Deolali, but while on board had responsibility for her young daughter and baby son while also recovering from malaria.[74] Women with children also bore the responsibility and insecurity about their future life in Britain. Mollie Warner, who was pregnant and traveling with four children, reflected, "Yes, it was an unknown future; I was coming to an unknown future with children. When we saw the skyline of India fade, I walked to a new life and a new future and that is what I did. I made a promise that my children wouldn't suffer and I don't think they did."[75]

Arriving in Britain

As discussed, the decision to relocate was often based on the idea of being part of an imagined imperial community in which Britain was the center. I suggest that life in Britain proved to be a difficult transition for many returnees, on both practical and emotional levels. Sustained by an image of Britain as the center of a great global empire, many returnees struggled with the collision of the image and the reality. Although both groups faced obstacles in finding suitable accommodations and employment, the transition was generally more difficult for the British coming from India. Their colonial existence as a minority in a great sea of Indians meant they had a social status and lifestyle that was almost impossible to replicate once they had returned to Britain.

In contrast, southern Irish Protestants, while generally having a greater economic status than many of their Catholic counterparts, did not enjoy the same lifestyle as those in India. It was rare for these families to have large retinues of servants; women were involved in household management and commonly in the running of family businesses, and Protestants could be found engaged across the economic spectrum and different social classes.

While Britain had been "home" for the great majority of the British community in India, there were many who had little or no memory of it as a physical place. One of the first shocks for those arriving in the late 1940s was the cold and desolate landscape of postwar Britain. Betty Gascoyne had an imagined view of Britain gained from studying literature and history and reading British journals and newspapers. However, the scene that greeted her at the Southampton docks in the late 1940s was one for which she was ill prepared.

> Oh I was cold, so cold, we had nothing but my clothes from India. My feet were absolutely frozen. . . . We got to Southampton and I thought to myself, it's so cold; I'm going to die in this! I looked around and it was grey, it was foggy. We weren't allowed to get off the boat because it was too foggy, it was dangerous. Thick fog. I thought, my God, this is worse than being too hot! . . . We finally got to Forest Gate, London E7 which was where his mum lived. I looked at the roads, and I looked at the houses and I thought, oh what have they done to London? And Fred [her husband] said, "I know but this is what war is." It looked awful, absolutely desolate.[76]

Betty's view of Britain was an idealized version of the imperial center woven from conversations with British soldiers, media images, and historical and literary references. The contrast with reality was one Betty found difficult to reconcile. The shock of arrival was echoed by others arriving from India in the aftermath of the Second World War. Sue Sloan also found the physical landscape of Britain a crushing disappointment on arriving in the late 1940s. "Everything was so small compared to what I was used to, and grey." She docked at Liverpool and was astonished at the small scale of the mountains they passed through on their way to London. When she saw the Thames for the first time, she couldn't believe how it paled in comparison to the mighty

Ganges.[77] Both Betty Gascoyne and Sue Sloan found it difficult to reconcile the grand imagined sense of the imperial center with the small
scale of the British landscape. In India, Britain had been presented as
a place of sophistication, the center of power, the seat of the monarchy
and government, yet the visual reality with which they were confronted
on arrival was of small mountains and lakes, lacking color and majesty.
Much of the built environment was demolished, with many urban areas
barely functioning. In India, the British community battled with the
climate; it was seen as the source of illness and degeneration, and families were encouraged to retreat to the hill stations to escape its worst
effects. Yet for Betty, the numbing cold and thick fog were more perilous than the stifling heat, and a more immediate danger.

The accounts of southern Irish Protestants arriving in the years following the establishment of the Irish Free State reveal more mixed responses. John Stewart Collis was born in 1900 into a professional family
in Dublin. He recalled the journey from Holyhead to Euston station
and the impression of strangeness and unfamiliarity with the landscape.
As the train approached Euston Station in London he had "a sinking
feeling."[78] Interviews with those who came from Ireland in this period
reveal a range of responses, from those experienced by Collis to ambivalence, relief, and even delight.

In the late 1930s, Rhona Ward traveled with her father to take up a
position in the civil service in London.

> We arrived at London at 12.15. It is very bleak looking [the station] and after
> the style of Belfast station, only bigger. Then we went in a bus to near Earl's
> Court. When we got off we had a good bit of walking and my arm ached
> with holding my things. The road to Earl's Court was very interesting. Full
> of people, buses, cars and great big shops.[79]

Rhona Ward's account suggests ambivalent feelings on arrival in
London. She found the station bleak and rather overbearing and had
some difficulty finding her lodgings in Earl's Court. Yet she was also
struck by the diversity and dynamism present in the high street in Earl's
Court. Those traveling from Ireland would not have been faced with
the difference in landscape and climate, as travelers from India were.
However, many came from small towns or rural areas and therefore

would have had to adjust to a much more urban and dynamic land-scape. Lionel Fleming detailed how, as a young man living in Cork, he always yearned to go to England. "The thought of England had always been uppermost; I had heard and read so much about it that I could almost imagine I had been there already."[80] He described arriving in the early 1920s:

> And so, after the night crossing from Cork, I had sat staring out of the train window until the dawn should reveal England . . . the evidence of wealth and power was almost overwhelming. In the brief journey across London to catch the Brighton train, it almost seemed—though of course it could not be true—that the porters and taxi-drivers were all gentry.[81]

This accords with Ron Alcock's positive experience of arriving in Britain:

> I always had a great affinity with the UK. . . . From a very early age I knew I would leave. . . . I never felt sorry for leaving, I wasn't unhappy, you know when you are leaving somewhere you have lived all your life. When I got off the train at Euston, and got on that no. 14 bus, the sun was shining glori-ously and it was fantastic![82]

Both groups, although arriving in different time periods, returned to Britain in the aftermath of a world war. Although Britain had been victorious in both cases, success had come at a price. Irish Protestants arriving in the 1920s did so against an economic backdrop that featured historically high unemployment, averaging between 10 and 12 percent in Britain.[83] Labor unrest culminated in the General Strike of 1926. The Wall Street crash of 1929 precipitated an economic collapse in the United States that reverberated throughout Europe. In Britain, unem-ployment rose to between 22 and 23 percent.[84] The social effects of this on industrialized communities were marked most visibly by the Jarrow Marches of 1936 and were documented by George Orwell in *The Road to Wigan Pier*.[85]

Families arriving from Ireland in the 1920s found that their social capital was not easily transferable, and many struggled to find work. Francis Henry Pakenham was a dental surgeon with a successful practice in Clare Street in central Dublin and a former President of the Irish branch of the British Dental Association. He estimated the value of the practice at five thousand pounds. He was "compelled to leave Ireland, my life being unbearable, my practice destroyed, my nerves shattered, and house being made uninhabitable by night firing and bomb explosions." He applied for a grant to establish a new practice in London, although his age—sixty-four years—did not make this an easy proposition.[86] Mrs. Agnes Clarke was a schoolteacher in Ruan, County Clare. She was married to a Royal Irish Constabulary officer. In July 1921, four members of the IRA visited the school and informed her "she was not fit to teach Irish children" and gave her ten days to leave the locality. She did so and went to stay with her husband in Ennistymon, County Clare, where he was stationed. Due to further harassment, the family left the country and moved to Liverpool. "My husband is unemployed and we suffer great loss and we have 6 young children."[87] In Ireland, the family had secure employment in government positions. However, the Royal Irish Constabulary was often targeted as they were seen as being closely aligned to British rule. While the Irish Grants Committee provided financial support to successful claimants, their remit was not to find the applicants work. Those in commercial occupations also found the transition to economic life in Britain difficult. The Meade family, who came from Limerick, had been employed in the lace trade, with male family members serving in the British Army. On their return from the First World War, the family were "persecuted and threatened and had to leave to come to England." They moved to Essex but were unable to find comparable employment there or in London.[88] This difficulty affected all social classes. The Ince Allens were well connected and came from a privileged background. Ernest Ince Allen arrived in England in 1922 aged sixty-two with his wife and daughter. Their hardship led to the latter having to take work as domestic servants: "Though quite unfitted for the work, I may say my wife is the youngest daughter of the late Col. Lewis William Penn, aide de camp to her late Majesty Queen Victoria." With a grant from the Irish Grants Committee, he rented three rooms in a Warwickshire vicarage and a few acres of land and started poultry farming to "keep body and soul together." When the vicar sold the property, Allen and his family had to leave. In November 1927, with an interim payment of two thousand pounds, he bought an eighty-four-acre farm, expecting to receive a further eight hundred pounds from the Irish Grants Committee, which was not forthcoming. "I am really desperate. It would have been far better to tell me in the first place that that was all that was coming . . . now I am throwing good money after bad."[89] For families like the Ince Allens, the transition to life in Britain was marked by financial penury and loss of their social position. All social classes found it difficult to find work, either in government positions or in the commercial sector. This was certainly exacerbated by the dire economic situation in Britain in the 1920s, but even so southern Irish Protestants found they were not advantaged by their loyalty or their role in the British administration in Ireland. Instead, they were forced to find work on the same terms as the rest of the population.

In contrast, in the immediate aftermath of the Second World War, Britain suffered from an acute labor shortage. This was chiefly in heavy industry: particularly in coal mining, steel production, shipbuilding, agriculture, and textiles. In January 1946, the new Labour government headed by Clement Attlee estimated the shortage of labor amounted to a deficit of between 600,000 and 1.3 million people. More specifically, the Trades Union Congress put the shortage at 585,000.[90] The civil service had been expanded during the war to allow for the new planned economy,[91] but neither of these two factors affecting employment in Britain in the mid- to late 1940s offered opportunities for those recently arrived from India. As discussed, large-scale working-class migration to India was officially discouraged in favor of those from a middle-class, educated background. While there were poor whites in India, they were considered marginal. Therefore, the majority of "returnees" from British India had been previously employed in an official capacity, and certainly would not have welcomed manual work in heavy industry. However, for middle-aged men in particular, it was challenging to find a suitable—and comparable—position in postwar Britain. Sue Sloan's father had spent his career in the army in India, and she recalled the hurdles he had in seeking work:

> He tried to get a job, had tremendous difficulty getting a job, and I, I wince when I remember this, eventually got a job as a doorman at an upmarket hotel in the West End [in London] with his uniform and everything. The

chief doorman was an ex-sergeant and really gave him hell. It really appalls me to think about it.[92]

British India was a highly stratified society in which an individual's rank and social position were carefully calibrated. Everything stemmed from employment—where one lived and socialized, the club one was a member of, even marriage prospects. Sue Sloan's father's demotion to working as a doorman caused profound discomfort within his family— used as they were to the clear and defined class distinctions in British India—and Sue did indeed wince when reliving this memory. The use of the word "appall" accurately conveyed her discomposure at their changed social position. While her father was a middle-aged man at the time, and thus may have been disadvantaged by age, Betty Gascoyne's husband Fred also struggled to locate work even though he was in his late twenties. Eventually he found a position working in a light bulb factory in London. However, the other workers, and particularly the supervisor, were hostile and accused him of taking other men's jobs. He stayed for several months and then left following a disagreement with the supervisor.[93] John Outram, whose father had a more senior position, also within the military, reflected on his father's career prospects on returning from India:

> He had spent his whole active life until fifty in India, born in India, I won't say he found it difficult, but he never occupied that level of society in England. Like a lot of people who came back from the empire. He was aide-de-camp to Governors and Mountbatten, but when he came back to England, he had his pension and a bit of property, but it was definitely not at the centre of things.[94]

John's father was financially secure, if not wealthy, unlike some younger men with families. However, as John reflects, his father's position in society and political life altered dramatically. In India, he worked in an administrative role at a very senior level and therefore was party to key discussions on the future of India within the empire. On returning to England, that role was obsolete. As a man of fifty, he struggled to find an equivalent role and instead opted for retirement, although he was not old.

While men struggled to find work, women struggled to acclimatize to a new domestic environment. Previously used to managing an array of domestic servants, but rarely involved in formal or paid work, they returned to a country in which domestic servants were scarce and many women had worked as part of the war effort. British women in India had been accorded a prestigious social position on account of their imperial status, white skin, and class. In Britain in the late 1940s, these factors no longer guaranteed status. Women who returned to Britain at this time remembered the complexities of managing a household in this new environment. Jill Gowdey recalled, "My mother understandably went to pieces quietly; she couldn't get used to the fact there was nobody to do anything for her." Unable to cope with domestic routines, and unable to find anyone to assist, Jill increasingly took on more and more domestic responsibility: "I found I was cooking and I was doing the ironing and I was doing the housework, so I was really working quite hard . . . I was my mother's maid really."[95] Sue Sloan recollected her mother's reaction to her new life in England. "My mother had a terrible time when she came back from India, a really dreadful time . . . there was rationing, and clothes rationing, she couldn't cook, she had seldom cleaned, it was an alien life completely."[96] Middle-aged British returnees of both genders found the transition to life in Britain problematic. The skills that had allowed them to manage large numbers of people, and often large geographical areas, were no longer considered assets in a society that was differently organized. The expertise that had given them status and responsibility in India was no longer valued in metropolitan Britain. The sense of responsibility and duty felt by many of those serving in British India was no longer applicable, and the skills that had been valuable in India were not easily transferable. Having worked in the empire was not necessarily a positive attribute for those seeking work in postwar Labour Britain. The country was looking forward to a new future, not back to what was increasingly seen as its imperial past.

Difficulties finding work were compounded by the scarcity of affordable and suitable accommodation. Consequently, families often had to acclimatize to reduced circumstances on arrival. James Glynn and his wife were forced to leave Ireland in the early 1920s. Mrs. Glynn recounted the tumult in Ireland and the difficult decision to leave;

however, on arriving in England the situation was not much improved: "When we got to London we were obliged to live in two small rooms (5 storeys high) in a poor locality off Camden Town and unfit for human habitation at £2 a week. During all this time I was absolutely broken down and almost distracted being in a strange country made things so much more complicated for myself and my children. This is only an outline of my physical suffering, but words fail to describe my mental strain."[97] Mrs. Glynn's description of being "absolutely broken down" and experiencing "mental strain" caused by her situation— exacerbated by being in a "strange" country—runs counter to the literature on the experience of southern Irish Protestants who felt "at home" in Britain. It suggests that, rather than a return to "home," life in Britain was unfamiliar and rather unwelcoming. The challenges of forced migration were compounded by having to acclimatize to what she perceived as being a foreign environment and resulted in suffering and strain. Mrs. B. Meade was from Limerick city. Her two sons joined the British Army and fought in World War I. After being demobilized they returned to Limerick but were persecuted, then moved to England to rejoin the army. The Meade family was ostracized for their British connections and came to England in 1922. They joined family members in Chadwell Heath, Essex. Mrs. Meade's application stated that her daughter's family had spent their savings supporting them. As the family already had four children and only a very small house, "the strain and hardship upon them have been incalculable. My son has tried to get a Council house, but has been refused as we are not Londoners."[98]

Families arriving from India post independence also had to navigate the difficult path to finding accommodation. In the major cities, particularly London, this was exacerbated by the housing shortage. Britain's housing stock was severely depleted during the war, with approximately three-quarters of a million houses destroyed or badly damaged.[99] This compounded an already acute shortage of quality housing stock, little of which had been repaired during the economic downturn of the 1930s. As reforms were put in place in the fields of national health, education, and national insurance, the issues of housing and planning were also addressed. The 1944 Town and Country Planning Act encouraged the redevelopment of bomb-damaged sites and prepared the way for the provision of the "new towns" outside London, such as Harlow and Stevenage.[100] Debates surrounding urban density and the role of modernist architecture occurred between young architects and planners, but what was accepted by both groups, and politicians, was a new plan for city development that would include high-rise housing and new road and pedestrian circulation.[101]

However, this urban planning did not address the immediate needs of those arriving in the late 1940s who struggled to find somewhere to live. Mollie Warner arrived at Tilbury Docks in January 1948 with her four children and was heavily pregnant with her fifth. Her first concern was finding accommodation, and a family friend arranged for them to stay in a boarding house in Harrow, northwest London, until they could rent a furnished house nearby. Others recall similar difficulties and how they had to resort to temporary lodgings until they could find somewhere more permanent.[102] One family arrived at Tilbury Dock on 13 July 1949. "At Tilbury our treasured belongings—photograph albums, books, homewares, bible etc were not unloaded. They must have gone missing, probably at Bombay." They initially stayed at a guest house in North London and then, as their money was running out, they applied to a Rest Centre in Chelsea, where men and women were allocated separate dormitories. After several weeks they were transferred to a flat in East London, but as they had no furniture they painted orange boxes and used them as seats and bought four bedsteads in a sale at Gamages department store. Other furniture was purchased locally on hire-purchase. A kindly neighbor offered them pieces of lino and a mangle.[103] While Betty Gascoyne was marginally more fortunate, as she was able to stay with her mother-in-law in East London, there was severe overcrowding as her relative lived in a one-bedroom flat. The difficulty faced by families in finding accommodations was in stark contrast to the situation in India, where most who worked for the imperial state as civil servants or in the military had homes provided for them. Furthermore, those homes were, in the main, spacious and comfortable, detached from other houses, with separate facilities for servants. As part of the imperial administration, the British in India had access to a superior form of housing. The stark realization for many families was that now that they were no longer part of the imperial caste, they no longer had access to those privileges.

In addition to practical difficulties associated with finding housing and employment, many of those returning to Britain also experienced emotional upheavals. Women who were interviewed often described struggling to cope, which they later acknowledged as a form of depression; several older men talked about a lack of purpose, and a number of people acknowledged struggling with their mental health. Reflecting back on their experience, those interviewed who acknowledged such difficulties did not feel at the time that they could speak out or seek help. This may have had something to do with the stigma associated with mental illness in the early twentieth century, but also seems to reflect a sense that those returning to Britain should "just be able to get on with it." This phrase, used by four interviewees, suggests an attitude of being able to endure conditions rather than accept and seek help. Interviews with those "returning" to Britain reveal complex emotional reactions, some of which they did not feel they could acknowledge at the time. Betty Gascoyne's interpretation of her reaction to "returning" to Britain is that "I just couldn't get used to it." Betty was the mother to three young children and had to cope with finding suitable lodgings, while her husband was having difficulties in adjusting to civilian life. However, retrospectively, Betty acknowledged that she found it difficult to adjust and acclimatize: "It was like walking out of a colour photograph into a black and white one."[104] Sue Sloan also mentioned the misery experienced by herself and her mother in the years following their arrival, but commented that neither was able to support the other as they were both absorbed in trying to adjust and cope. Paddy Reilly described arriving in summer and making it through his first winter in which he experienced snow. It was at this point that he began to feel enclosed and longed for open spaces. He also found the commute to work difficult and at that point "I got into a terrible depression, for five years. . . . It was absolutely dreadful. Val kept the family together."[105] Paddy had the support of his wife, but he had come from a social environment in which the family depended on the health and financial security of the male breadwinner. After a lengthy period, helped by his religious faith and family support, Paddy was able to adjust to life in England. Jill Gowdey's mother also found the transition to life in Britain problematic. Jill explained that her mother had struggled with the domestic routine on her return and gradually her health deteriorated.

Jill reflected on causal factors such as her parents' separation during the war and her mother's inability to easily adjust to life in Britain.

Olive Stevenson, whose parents came from Dublin, reflected on their experience of leaving Ireland:

> I think they were very reserved about such matters, but I do think there was probably tremendous loneliness, for my mother particularly. She came over with her stepdaughter, who was then I think about nine or something, and they lived in north London; they were extremely hard up and I would guess, very lonely. But that was tempered by the fact that not terribly long after that, my mother's sister came over from Dublin to train as a singer at the Royal College of Music. . . . And she lived with my parents for, oh, quite a number of years before she married, and I think that probably made a huge difference to their feelings, but I think there was a lot of loneliness.[106]

Olive considered her parents' experience in the light of other migrants' experience:

> I've tried to think about this in relation to the discussions we have nowadays about immigrants and so on you know, to try and think about what it's like to arrive—not as strange as people coming from the West Indies for example—but a feeling of alienation. They never made a lot of friends; it was a source of concern to me that the links—especially for my mother—seemed to be so much more with the family than with friends. I've never quite understood that.[107]

Olive was able to reflect on the position of her parents, who *felt* unable to live in Ireland, and yet were also unable to easily acclimatize to life in Britain. While they successfully found work and eventually purchased a house in the London suburbs, her mother's feelings of loneliness and alienation colored her experience of life in London and her outlook. This counters the view that southern Irish Protestants made an easy adjustment to life in Britain. Olive's parents struggled to form friendships and relationships outside the family. This lack of ease in London also had an intergenerational aspect in that it colored Olive's feelings about the environment in which she grew up. When asked about her own sense of belonging, she responded,

If people say to me, "Where d'you come from?" I have tremendous diffi-culty in answering. I mean the reality is I grew up in Purley, Surrey, a place I never felt the faintest twinge of affection for, couldn't wait to get away from the suburbs when I went to university, and really quite alienated from everything that it stood for. And a bit of me has always felt very strongly identified with the Irish thing, though it's difficult to put a finger on it.[108]

These emotional responses to the difficult transition from one envi-ronment to another could be read as a reaction to the acknowledged practical difficulties faced by migrants. Alternatively, they could be read as a more profound, but difficult to recognize, difficulty in adjusting psychologically to the new environment in which they found them-selves. As acknowledged earlier by both groups, they grew up with a sense of Britain as the center and source of all that was central to British identity. Yet when they arrived, they were confronted visually, practi-cally and perhaps also more fundamentally, with a society that neither accorded to their vision nor accepted or welcomed their contribution.

Interviews allow the possibility of understanding the same event from different perspectives, even within the same family. They also en-courage a plurality and multilayered perspective on historical events, illustrating how the collective narrative of migration can be challenged by some voices. While the majority of those interviewed, particularly older and more established members of the British community, found the transition from India to Britain a difficult one, there were oth-ers who expressed a contrary view. Young women found life in Britain opened up hitherto unexplored possibilities. There were three areas in which they could explore new opportunities: further education, work, and social and leisure time. It was rare for British women to work in India. It was also practically difficult as many families moved frequently as the husband was redeployed. However, in Britain, tertiary education provided young women with skills to enter into employment and at a time when the economy was expanding. Verna Perry, Sue Sloan, and Jill Gowdey all arrived in Britain as teenagers and opted to attend college after having finished their formal education. Sue Sloan had wanted to attend university to study history but instead chose a secretarial course and initially worked as a secretary to an osteopath, and later for Brit-ish Transport films. Verna Perry finished her education at a boarding school in Kent and then trained as a primary schoolteacher. Jill Gowdey studied household management at Battersea Polytechnic. The new education and work opportunities meant these young women had freedom of movement and an earning ability that would have been difficult to access in India. Sue Sloan recalled the pleasure with which she walked around central London during her lunch breaks: "I used to be given luncheon vouchers worth 2s and 6d and I used to get a three course meal and would try out all the restaurants around. I had a lovely time. I had never known anything like that; it was totally different for me." In London, she possessed an anonymity and freedom of movement that would not have been possible in India, and with the financial ability to choose how to spend her leisure time.[109]

Another positive aspect of life in postwar Britain was the possibility of family reunion and "putting down roots." Family life in India had been marked by frequent separations, as children were sent away to school, mothers and children sojourned in the hills during the hot weather, and parents retired to Britain at the end of their working lives. However, life in Britain offered the possibility of family members being brought together. Jill Gowdey's father was an army officer and had been away from his family for the duration of the war, but Jill recalled the delight that they could now all live together in a home in Surrey. "It was always important to put my roots down, because we never had." Her excitement was exemplified by the purchase of a chest of drawers, a piece of furniture that signified to Jill solidity and permanence after a period of constant upheaval.[110] John Outram also found life in rural Britain a welcome change from the dislocation of living in India. Although his parents had separated, he found a warm and welcoming home environment with his aunt, uncle, and cousins in Dorset, which contrasted with the rather lonely life he experienced as an only child in India. Even cold bedrooms and wartime rationing did not diminish his enthusiasm.[111] Wallace Burnet-Smith echoed their enthusiasm for return, although Wallace acknowledged this on national as well as domestic levels. Living among British people, rather than as a minority among the Indian majority, was a signal for Wallace that he was "at home."[112]

Young Irish Protestants who arrived in the decades following 1922 shared similar positive experiences. Rhona Ward arrived as a young woman in London in the 1930s. Her family prompted the decision;

therefore personal agency was not an element in her decision-making process. However, after an initial period of adjustment in which Rhona Ward familiarized herself with the city and began to form social networks, she began to appreciate the freedom offered by London. When war broke out, Rhona rejected the opportunity to return home and scorned those who did so: "I wonder why all the girls here are simply dying to get home for good? I see only a very few advantages and a whole lot of disadvantages. The chief is, I think, that I would not be able to do exactly as I like."[113] Anne Hodkinson from Dublin echoed the freedom mentioned by Ward. She noted that as a young woman in London she was able to mix with a wide social group and enjoy her leisure time without comment from her parents. On her return for a holiday, she remarked on the contrast between English parents and those in Ireland who expected to determine their children's actions well into adulthood.[114] Ron Alcock mentioned his affinity with Britain, which helped ease the transition. However, as a young man with a secondary education, whose employment options were limited in Dublin, he now found a wealth of opportunities available. He also enjoyed the anonymity of living in London. As he remarked, once you mentioned your name in Ireland, everyone made assumptions as to your background and therefore political or cultural orientation. In London, "no-one cares!. . . . When I left Dublin, I thought it was the best thing that ever happened to me, coming to England."[115]

When comparing the experience of both groups of returnees, we can see both similarities in terms of practical experience but differences in terms of emotional responses. Although both groups often shared the view of Britain as an exciting and cosmopolitan center to a great world empire, southern Irish Protestants rarely seem to have suffered the cultural and visual shock on arrival. This may be explained in part by the similarities in landscape and climate of both places, although many were coming from a rural environment and very often relocating to the capital; therefore, there would have been great contrasts in terms of infrastructure, density, and building types.[116] Neither group could expect that their loyalty or service to the British Empire in Ireland or India would result in improved access to employment, and in many cases they found that their skills were not easily transferable. In both cases, it was much easier for those who were just entering the labor market to find success as opposed to those who were older, whether they came from India or Ireland. Social position in either country did not necessarily translate to Britain. In many cases, their colonial social position was not recognized in Britain as it relied on a complex and widely understood framework of social differentiation, which could not be read in Britain in the same way.

Reception

The reaction of imperial migrants to returning to Britain has now been considered, but what was their reception within official and unofficial circles? Southern Irish Protestants had overwhelmingly supported the union with Britain. How did Britain support them in the aftermath of the upheaval of 1922? In the spring of that year, approximately twenty thousand Irish refugees arrived in Britain.[117] The response of the British government was immediate—establishing the Irish Distress Committee on 12 May 1922. The original purpose was to assist those in immediate need, and provide funds until they could either find work in Britain or return home. However, following the signing of the Treaty and civil war, it became apparent there were a significant number of displaced people. In order to establish a more permanent solution, the Irish Grants Committee (IGC) was constituted on 23 March 1923 from the Irish Distress Committee. Its terms of reference were to offer grants or loans to refugees from the Irish Free State and Northern Ireland, and it was open to those of all denominations. In the period up to July 1922, 152 Protestants, 143 Catholics, and 88 people of no professed faith applied.[118] The response of the British government illustrated the commitment it felt to those fleeing from conditions in Ireland.

> As a result of the disturbed conditions in Ireland after the Truce, there was a steady increase in the number of Irish refugees in Great Britain. Both in and out of Parliament, a widespread feeling was expressed that some measure of financial relief should be made available for such of those refugees as were stranded in this country without resources.[119]

This extract from the report written in 1930 indicates the commitment felt by the British government toward those fleeing and how this was supported publicly. However, the British government initially hoped that their outlay would be reimbursed by the government of the Irish Free State under the terms of the Anglo-Irish Treaty. The Irish Free State accepted responsibility, but with a settlement of £26,000 expected from the British government, they felt it was appropriate to reclaim the £17,651 they had expended on nationalist refugees from Northern Ireland. For several years, the three governments (British, Irish and Northern Irish) wrangled over these payments, before finally settling at the 1926 Imperial Conference.[120]

By 1924, the number of Irish refugees had drastically reduced and as the work of the (first) IGC came to a close, it considered what further action was required. It was decided that there were a significant number of people who required a more long-term settlement. Pressure was brought to bear on the British government by two organizations set up to aid the Irish loyalist refugees: the Southern Irish Loyalist Relief Association and the Irish Claims Compensation Association. Both of these organizations had influential supporters who were able to raise questions on their behalf in the House of Lords.[121] In order to avoid a formal committee, which had the potential for political tension between the government of the Irish Free State and the British government, Leo Amery supported a revised IGC, which would assess the British obligations to Irish loyalists. Lord Dunedin chaired the revised IGC. It included Lord Selbourne and Lord Northumberland. It was set up on 8 October 1926 and met for the first time ten days later. Its terms of reference were,

> to consider claims from British subjects now or formerly residing or carry-ing on business in the area of the Irish Free State who on account of their support of His Majesty's Government prior to the 11 July 1921 sustained hardship and loss by personal injuries or the malicious destruction of, or injuries to, their property in the area of the Irish Free State between the said 11 July 1921 and 12 May 1923.[122]

However, the Treasury had warned Lord Dunedin that the objective was not to fully reinstate wronged loyalists to their former position.[123] He did, though, acknowledge the special obligation of the British government toward southern Irish loyalists. Claimants had to prove that their hardship occurred before the end of the civil war. They had to formally apply, linking their loss to their loyalty to the British government. Two references were required; in most cases these came from ministers, solicitors, or doctors. In the case of damage to property a valuation needed to be supplied, and in most cases an independent authority in Ireland was contacted to verify the claims. The principle applied was that of the Sumner Scale, used for cases of victims of enemy action during the First World War: the first £250 to be paid in full, 50 percent of the next £750, and 30 percent of any remainder up to £49,000. An initial budget of £400,000 was provided, which was increased to £625,000, and finally on 22 February 1928 Prime Minister Stanley Baldwin announced that all recommendations by the committee would be paid in full.[124] Claimants were supposed to have first sought redress from the Irish Free State before applying for compensation, but the IGC accepted that those fleeing from intimidation may not have been able to do so.

Financial hardship was a factor in determining loss, but an applicant did not have to be destitute to apply. The IGC also acknowledged that "in the course of a political upheaval such as occurred in Ireland a few years ago, the whole community suffers, and it is not unreasonable that the burden of insignificant losses, and also, to some extent of losses of articles of luxury when sustained by well to-do people, should rest where it falls."[125] The last date on which claims were accepted was 29 February 1928,[126] and the final committee report was written in 1930. In total there had been 291 sittings and 4,032 claims. Of those, 895 were considered outside the scope of the terms of reference and 900 were not recommended; therefore, 2,237 cases were successful.[127] In order for claimants to be successful in their application they had to demonstrate the link between their loss and loyalty to the British government. Traditionally, Protestants in Ireland had supported the Union with Britain. Cases examined reflect this, with the majority of applicants being Protestant.

The formation of the IGC illustrated the British government's commitment to supporting their former subjects during a period of upheaval. It acknowledged their property rights and made a pledge to reimburse their financial losses. It recognized their loyalty and support throughout the period of British rule and, implicitly, their role in aiding British administration and governance in Ireland. Southern Irish Protestants received support from the wealthy and politically influential in Britain. Their plight was highlighted in both houses of Parliament and was discussed by the most senior government officials. Most notably, the support of the British government to Irish Protestants was underlined by the financial assistance given to them, which by 1930 was over one million pounds sterling. In a period of economic hardship, this spoke volumes.

The response of the British government and public organizations to those "remigrating" from the Indian subcontinent post independence was more varied. The government acknowledged their responsibility to those who had served the British state overseas, but public opinion in Britain in this period showed a lack of awareness or interest in colonial matters. Shortly before the transfer of power in India, the Prime Minister made a statement in the House of Commons in April 1947 regarding the compensation for those in government service. He provided some background to the situation and explained how the principle of dyarchy enacted in 1919 had initiated a change in employment for those serving the Crown. In order to reassure those in government service, the government had applied the "principle of assured service" guaranteeing tenure and pensions.[128] The Prime Minister said that "it was thus the intention of Parliament that officers whose careers and prospects were prejudiced by constitutional change should receive such compensation as the Secretary of State might consider just and equitable."[129] He acknowledged that the transfer of power meant the "premature termination" of their careers. Those who transferred to another Crown service on a permanent pensionable basis received a £500 resettlement grant rather than cash compensation. Those who opted to leave the service were eligible to access a scale of compensation that ranged from £2,500 for five years' service to £500 for thirty, peaking at £8,000 for sixteen years' service. Presumably those receiving £500 would shortly be in receipt of a pension. This applied to the Indian Civil Servants, military, police, and those in the Indian Political Service.[130]

However, interviews with those "returning" from India around the time of independence reflect the low level of public interest in Britain. Those who remained in a British regiment were provided with assistance in relocating, but for others who had left the services, taken early retirement, or worked for commercial enterprises, there was little help given. In a House of Commons debate on 11 December 1947, Philip Noel-Baker, Secretary of State for Commonwealth Relations, was asked what measures had been put in place to assist with employment of ex-service personnel. He responded by saying that two branches of his department dealt with policy and appointments and two sections of the London Appointment Office of the Ministry of Labour dealt with posts in business and in temporary government employment. In addition, there was an unofficial employment liaison committee in touch with the London appointment office. The Technical and Scientific Register of the Ministry of Labour also helped in specific appropriate cases.[131] The Hon. Member Col. Wheatley responded, "Is the Minister aware that after going to Tavistock Square they had been told that there is nothing doing at all, and that the only chance they have of getting a job is to find it themselves?"[132] The Secretary of State rejoined; as far as he was aware "the machinery is, I think working very well."[133] The Hon. Mr. Godfrey Nicholson replied that he had received an answer stating that "out of over 800 officers on the register at Tavistock Square, just over 200 had found work."[134]

The following year, 1948, the Colonial Office commissioned a survey to "discover the extent of public knowledge of, and interest in, the British Colonies" in order to "frame an information policy of a realistic nature." The sample consisted of 1,921 adults and concerned public knowledge, opinion, and interest in the colonies.[135] Respondents were asked to distinguish between colonies and dominions, standards of living for "native-peoples," and whether the policy of the British government was self-government for these colonies.[136] The responses varied, with professional and managerial classes being more informed than "housewives and unskilled operatives," but the survey noted that "even the best-educated Occupational Group, and those people who have traveled widely overseas, are far from being fully informed about Colonial matters."[137] Over 70 percent could not distinguish between a colony and a dominion, and only 18 percent could name more than three colonies.[138] Interestingly, it was those in the sixteen to twenty-nine age group who were most accurate. When asked about colonial independence, 46 percent responded that they were aware of the independence of India, Pakistan, and Burma.[139] The survey was framed in terms of the metropole and the periphery and the relationship between the two. Questions were asked about colonial raw materials and in what way they earned revenue for the colonial center, indicating that both the source and the respondents viewed the nature of the relationship as to benefit Britain. Many respondents also thought that the colonies paid tax directly to support Britain.[140]

While it is difficult to firmly account for the differences in responses to those remigrating following independence, it is useful to consider changing international circumstances as well as internal factors. Irish Protestants arriving in Britain in the period following independence were widely supported both within and outside Parliament as "kith and kin," as those to whom the British government had a debt of obligation. Many in the Conservative Party had actively promoted the continuation of the Union and saw the fight to retain it as part of a wider imperial struggle. Britain after the First World War was still an imperial power and had emerged from the Treaty of Versailles with a wider imperial reach, having acquired mandated territories in the Middle East. The isolationist policy of U.S. president Woodrow Wilson meant Britain's continued importance on the international stage. In contrast, Britain after the Second World War was heavily indebted to the United States in the form of Lend-Lease and politically demoted to a second-tier power. The U.S. public denouncement of imperialism and support of Indian independence gave weight to those struggling against the empire. While politicians across the spectrum, such as Atlee and Churchill, still voiced support for the empire, the tide was turning. Within Britain, public support for the Labour Party and their landslide election victory in 1945 indicated the desire for a new Britain that would be more inclusive. Britain positioned its postwar role as supporting the colonies toward self-government, and respondents to the 1948 survey supported this view.[141] Thus Indian independence could be seen in the light of a progressive policy of self-government rather than a revolutionary act. Historians have argued about the role of empire in public consciousness in the postwar world,[142] and there continues to be a debate on the extent to which it informed Britain's sense of nationhood.

Conclusion

This chapter has argued that the success of independence movements in Ireland and India led the British-affiliated communities in both countries to reconsider their position and ultimately relocate to Britain. There were concrete factors that colored the decision-making process: factors that applied to many migrants, principally fear of threat and limited opportunities for employment. However, an underlying element in prompting migration and "return" to Britain was that, within a colonial environment, these groups felt part of an imagined British imperial community overseas. Their active role in supporting the empire—and their elevated position within each country—was directly linked to their close affiliation to Britain. One of the elements of a diasporic consciousness is a separation from the host community. This separation and lack of cultural affinity was most clearly demonstrated by the independence process. Their decision to leave was fundamentally based on the desire to remain within the imperial community, and this could most effectively be achieved by return to Britain.

However, the process of return, particularly for the British in India, illustrated their altered position. Traveling on a crowded troopship, empire families were visibly made aware of the erosion of their privilege. On arrival, this was presented more forcibly as they were faced with a landscape, climate, and environment far removed from the one to which they were accustomed. These factors were not the same for southern Irish Protestants, who had a much closer geographical relationship and therefore did not have to pass through the same physical and spatial boundaries. Both groups experienced difficulties in finding suitable employment and accommodation. While this is not unusual for migrants, many of those from India and Ireland had worked for and supported Britain's interests overseas. Therefore, this harsh transition was difficult for many to bear. Some, particularly women, suffered emotional difficulties as a response. However, the experience was not uniform; rather it was tempered by social capital. Those who were young found that, in many cases, life in Britain opened up hitherto unknown possibilities. This was particularly true for young women from both countries, who had been limited by social constraints in India and

Ireland but were now able to access tertiary-level education and the possibility of paid work, and the enhanced freedom this offered.

Although both groups were arriving in the aftermath of a world war, Britain's global position had diminished considerably by the late 1940s. Southern Irish Protestants fleeing to Britain in the 1920s were acknowledged as British loyalists and treated as genuine refugees. They were supported politically and financially on the basis of their loyalty to the Britain. Those arriving from India in the late 1940s were compensated only if they had been directly employed by the British state but were expected to be self-sufficient if they had peripheral roles in trade or commerce. Only those who were directly employed in one of the covenanted services or the military were relocated if they remained in that service, but they had to find their own work if they opted to leave. Consequently, the decision to leave and return to Britain was prompted by close political and emotional links to an imagined British imperial community. However, on arriving "home," many within both groups, but particularly the British in India, became aware of the difference between those at the center and those at the periphery of the empire. The next chapter focuses on life in Britain and the process of adjustment in the new postcolonial order.

4

Brave New World?

> It is a great recognition on our part of the responsibility we
> feel for the care, the nature and the advancement of colonial
> people that we should include them in the same citizenship
> with ourselves.
> —James Chuter Ede, Labour Home Secretary, 1948

Following the Second World War, Britain was reshaping itself to
meet the challenges of the postwar era. This was occurring at the
same time returnees were arriving in Britain following Indian independence and partition in 1947 and continuing to arrive from Ireland.
In 1945, the Labour government was elected with an overwhelmingly
majority—unseating wartime Prime Minister Winston Churchill. This
government, headed by Clement Attlee and supported by key figures in
the Labour movement such as Aneurin Bevan and Herbert Morrison,
promised a "new Jerusalem." This promise was fulfilled as the government inaugurated the National Health Service in 1948, reformed the
education system in order to offer opportunity to those from all social
backgrounds, and embarked on an unprecedented building program.
The latter provided decent homes for those on lower incomes, but it
also physically transformed many British cities as these new homes and
schools and civic buildings were built in a style that echoed contemporary Scandinavian or European modernism, not traditional British
vernacular. They spoke to an inclusive democratic purpose rather than
hierarchy and elitism. It was transformational change.

This chapter asserts that in the postwar period, Britain was representing itself both to its own people and to the wider world. By examining changing legal definitions of British nationality and comparing
this with two enormously significant cultural events—the Festival of
Britain in 1951 and the coronation of Elizabeth II in 1953—we can see
some of the contrasting and ambivalent attitudes around what it meant

to be British at this time. From 1948—chosen because it was the year Ireland declared itself a republic and Britain enacted the British Nationality Act, when the *Empire Windrush* arrived from Jamaica, and just one year after Indian independence—until 1962, when the government introduced the Commonwealth Immigrants Act, Britain moved from an apparently inclusive attitude toward British citizenship to one of restriction and limitation. The 1948 Nationality Act appeared to usher in a new era in which those born in the Dominions and Commonwealth were given equal status to those born in the United Kingdom. However, following unprecedented Commonwealth migration in the 1950s,[1] restrictions were quickly put in place that limited migrants of color. I suggest this period illustrates the continuing struggles within British society and the political class over race, inclusion, and who actually counted as British—and the ongoing debates and inconsistencies over these issues. Often a seemingly tolerant official attitude masked a more restrictive view. While legal definitions of British nationality were debated in Parliament, two cultural events occurred in the early 1950s that provided contrasting visions of Britain at midcentury. The Festival of Britain in 1951 was organized as an antidote to the war and as a tribute to the British people—and as such, it promoted a modern vision of the country, democratic, inclusive, and centered on the British Isles. The coronation of Elizabeth II, by contrast, highlighted the importance of hereditary succession, of tradition, and of a symbolic monarch embodying the nation. Both took contrasting views toward Britain's global engagement— the festival was focused on the British Isles, the coronation actively included the Commonwealth of Nations. I suggest that within the two pieces of parliamentary legislation, and within the narratives of the festival and the coronation, there were enduring conflicting messages about Britain, its world role, and inclusivity and national belonging. However, for those "returning" from Ireland and India, these messages ultimately proved that they were part of a community of British subjects, despite having been born elsewhere, and illustrated how race and skin color was more important than place of birth.

The British Nationality Act 1948

The Labour government defined nationality in the 1948 British Nationality Act.[2] It provided a wide-reaching definition that included every person who was a citizen of the United Kingdom and colonies who "shall by virtue of that citizenship have the status of a British subject."[3] The Act stated that "the expression 'British subject' and the expression 'Commonwealth citizen' shall have the same meaning."[4] In addition, "every person born within the United Kingdom and the Colonies after the commencement of this Act shall be a citizen of the United Kingdom and Colonies by birth."[5] Apparently liberal in its inclusion of all British subjects, whether born in Britain, the Dominions, or the colonies, underlying this apparent generosity lay some fundamental assumptions about the nature of the colonial relationship, even at the moment when the terms were being redefined to appear more inclusive and equitable. Parliamentary debates revealed that the Act aimed to solidify the relationship between the white Dominions and Britain at a time when there were increasing demands, particularly from Canada, to control their borders and determine their own criteria for nationality.[6] It was this prompt, rather than equality between British subjects in disparate parts of the Empire-Commonwealth, that initiated the Act.

Perhaps more than the 1948 Act itself, debates in Parliament reveal the conflicts over nationality among the political class. These expose that rather than a community of equal nations, ideas of trusteeship still prevailed across the political spectrum. In Labour Home Secretary James Chuter Ede's speech he supported the Act in furthering links between the United Kingdom and the colonies and in so doing raise them to a "position of education, of training and of experience that they too shall be able to share in the grant of full self government which this House has so generously given during the last few years to other places."[7] In addition, he commented, "We believe wholeheartedly that the common citizenship of the UK and Colonies is an essential part of the development of the relationship between this Mother Country and the Colonies who are administrated in varying degrees of self government and tutelage by the Colonial Office."[8] The Lord Chancellor noted the difference between "our own people and the people for whom we are trustees."[9]

This position indicated a continued understanding of Britain as the center of the Empire-Commonwealth in both political and cultural terms despite the equality that was offered to those resident in Britain or the Dominions and colonies. This view was shared across the political spectrum. Debates during the various readings of the Bill in both Houses reveal that references to Britain as the "Mother Country" were frequent and Attorney General Sir Hartley Shawcross stated that Britain was "the metropolitan centre of the Commonwealth and the historical Motherland," and "this country is the homeland of the Commonwealth."[10] This interpretation was supported by Viscount Hitchingbrooke when he said, "We here lie at the centre and heart of a great world Empire." In the latter's speech, he emphasized the primacy of the United Kingdom over other countries and regions when he explained, "His Majesty the King resides in London and not in Ottawa or Sydney."[11] The Act also emphasized the primacy of Westminster as a governing body, as it was Parliament that was able to debate and define the terms of the Act, not the countries affected, despite the significant impact it was to have on millions of people.

Significantly, one of the most important areas of debate was over the status of British subjects in metropolitan Britain and those of the countries of the Commonwealth and Dominions. Discussions focused on the use of language to denote British subjects and Commonwealth citizens, and although in the final Act the two were claimed to be the same, the arguments indicated that many members of Parliament struggled to accept this inclusive definition. The main controversy was over whether inhabitants of the United Kingdom should have a special designation within a wider framework of British nationality. The Labour government wanted to retain the term "Citizen of the United Kingdom and Colonies," as "British subject" denoted widespread membership of the former empire.[12] Viscount Hinchingbrooke, member for Dorset, objected to changing the status of "Briton" all over the world. "This House of Commons should be the last, not the second, legislature to turn from subjecthood to citizenship." He went on to criticize the Labour government, which, he said, "touches nothing without demeaning it—the relationship and status of great imperial countries, the inspirational symbolism of nationality and subjecthood."[13] In a debate in the House of Commons on 13 July 1948, Conservative member Sir David Maxwell Fyfe objected to the use of the word "citizen" as "'citizen' essentially implies the common enjoyment of civic rights and the acceptance of civic responsibilities and is not appropriate for describing the relationship and geographical situation of this country and the Colonies." His second objection was that "citizenship of the United Kingdom and Colonies suggests assimilation of the colonies with the United Kingdom."[14]

However, Maxwell Fyfe was one of the Conservative members who supported measures outlawing discrimination based on color prejudice. On the other side of the political spectrum, Labour politician James Chuter Ede recognized attitudes on racial equality: "I know there are also some who feel that it is wrong to have a citizenship of the UK and colonies. Some people feel that it would be a bad thing to give the coloured races of the Empire the idea that, in some way or other, they are the equals of people in this country. The government do not subscribe to that view."[15] He noted that the political differences were so great, "there have been moments when I have wondered whether we had not had two Bills before us, because the views on the Measure that was apparently under consideration were so contradictory."[16] As Chuter Ede correctly assessed, there was a fair amount of political division on the Bill and it tended to fall along party lines. It was introduced by the radical Labour government of 1945 and opposed by many in the Conservative Party. The Act also emphasized difference, particularly relating to gender; female subjects could lose their British status upon marriage to a non-British national, and children of such unions were not automatically granted British status. Descent was seen to pass through the male line.[17]

Consequently, although the 1948 British Nationality Act provided a definition that was inclusive and offered all citizens the same rights and opportunities, policy makers across the political divide shared a different understanding of what it meant to be British. However, it is important to consider the context and origin of the Act. It was brought into being to retain the links between Britain and the white Dominions at a time when this was being challenged by the Dominions themselves. Furthermore, this occurred when Britain's world role was being challenged by the changing world order. The purpose of the Act was to reassure those at home and within the Empire-Commonwealth of Britain's continued relevance, not to encourage large-scale migration to British shores.

The arrival of HMT *Empire Windrush* from Jamaica in 1948, the same year as the British Nationality Act was being passed, is significant for both the optimism of the hundreds of travelers from the Caribbean on board and the anxiety caused by its arrival. The official response indicated the underlying attitudes among the governing class toward British subjects. The lack of provision and assistance given to migrants from the Caribbean was in marked contrast to "aliens" arriving in Britain in the same period who came from labor and prisoner of war camps in Europe.[18] Unlike those workers, the government made no provision to liaise with trade unions in order to facilitate the smooth transition of these British workers from the Caribbean. In fact, a working committee composed of representatives from the Colonial Office, Foreign Office, and Ministries of Labour, Agriculture, Fuel and Power, Health, and Treasury and National Assistance reported that although there was a labor deficit of 60,000 in 1948, those from the Caribbean were deemed not suited to fill those vacancies. The report stated that employment in Lancashire textile factories was not appropriate because Caribbean women would not be able to stand the climate; and employment in silk, rayon, pottery, and tin plating industries was not suitable as it was not considered acceptable that Europeans shared accommodations with Caribbean workers.[19] In the same year, a group of Labour MPs wrote to Prime Minister Attlee outlining their concerns that "an influx of coloured people domiciled here is likely to impair the harmony, strength and cohesion of our public and social life and to bring discord and unhappiness among all concerned."[20] This discriminatory treatment of British subjects from the Caribbean indicated the prevalence of racial prejudice at the very moment Members of Parliament were arguing against racial differentiation in the 1948 Act.

Personal accounts from the period support the official attitude, and many document the prevalent racism that occurred when recent migrants sought work and accommodation. Although London Transport and the National Health Service recruited staff from the Caribbean islands, new arrivals often noted that even with equivalent educational qualifications, they were placed in lower grade positions than their white counterparts. Roy Campbell from Barbados passed the test to become a bus driver but was advised to take the lower position of bus conductor, and many West Indian nurses were placed only on the state enrolled nursing course rather than the higher equivalent state registered course.[21] Teacher Beryl Gilroy's account of her search for work in 1950s London illustrated that even well-qualified candidates were often considered only for menial jobs.[22] Discrimination was most visible when Commonwealth immigrants sought accommodations. As new arrivals, the majority sought housing in the private rented sector and were subjected to rejection due to their skin color and origin. Famously, signs in boarding house windows often proclaimed, "No Blacks, No Irish, No Dogs."[23]

These signs indicate that white skin alone did not provide the necessary passport to acceptance. As in British India, some could be whiter than others. When examining narratives on Irish immigration and domicile in Britain, it can be seen that within metropolitan Britain there were conflicting discourses on what it meant to be "white." Studies on the Irish in Victorian Britain, and particularly their representation in the popular press, have argued that discriminatory attitudes often alluded to racial and ethnic differences.[24] The imagery often showed "Paddy" with ape-like features, lower down on the evolutionary scale than his evolved British counterpart. This clearly illustrated the intended meaning to a readership with limited literacy. In his ethnographical survey *The Races of Britain*, written in 1885, John Beddoe noted, "The Irish are amongst us, but not of us, and generally intermarry among themselves."[25] The issue of race to describe differences with, and between, English and Irish was fraught, but since the sixteenth century such ideas had been colored by "conquest, colonization and Anglicization."[26] During the revolutionary period in Ireland, at the beginning of the twentieth century, English and Irish characteristics were often described in binary opposites: Irish memory and English forgetfulness, Irish spirituality and English pragmatism.[27] As Radhika Mohanram observed, "The Irish are so problematic: their practice of Catholicism, the history of their colonization, their political sympathies all scandalize and problematize British whiteness, revealing the limits of its assimilative process. Are they black or are they white?"[28] Therefore, while those who were visibly different were often subject to overt discrimination, whites were not necessarily allowed unchallenged access into British life but were also subject to qualification.

The Festival of Britain 1951

While the British Nationality Act of 1948 created a legal definition of British citizenship, two events occurred that projected an image of what it meant to be British in the postwar era both to the nation and internationally. The first, the 1951 Festival of Britain, was initiated as a "Tonic for the Nation" in response to the Second World War. The second, the coronation of Elizabeth II, continued a tradition of dynastic monarchy. Although occurring only two years apart, they presented contrasting narratives: the first progressive, democratic, and centered on the British Isles; the second traditional and ceremonial and using the monarch as an embodiment of hereditary Christian rule.

The Festival of Britain in 1951 created a vision of a new Britain—one that was directed at the future rather than the past. It was "an affirmation of faith in the future."[29] The organizing committee intended to open up new ideas to the public in a way that was easily accessible.[30] As Gordon Bowyer, who designed the Sports Pavilion, noted, "It was going to show what life could be like, rather than what it was at the time; unpainted buildings and neglect and decay. It was to show people the future could be rosy."[31] The main festival site on the South Bank of the Thames was constructed on derelict land and was a modernist architectural expression of materials, technology, and engineering.[32] This was a visual break with the past.

Modern architecture in Britain before the war was a specialist interest and firmly associated with continental Europe.[33] Its exponents in Britain were often European émigrés such as Berthold Lubetkin and Serge Chermayeff from Russia and Ernö Goldfinger from Hungary.[34] Early modernist buildings were often homes for the wealthy, but the Festival of Britain would open up contemporary architecture to the masses.[35] This new architectural expression was reflected at the festival in the buildings and structures such as the Skylon, a futuristic pencil-like object anchored on tensile wires, and the Dome of Discovery, with its 365-foot span made of aluminum and triangulated lattice, making it the largest domed structure at the time.[36] The Dome of Discovery promoted the fact that "British initiative in exploration and discovery is as strong as it ever was."[37] Modern architecture was also promoted for public housing, as showcased at the Lansbury estate in Poplar, East London. This estate incorporated modernist principles with town planning, as the grounds included a children's playground, churches, schools, and shopping areas.[38] The link between the festival and modernity was also clear in the choice of artists and artwork on view. Sculptures were by well-established names such as Henry Moore and Barbara Hepworth, but also emerging talents including Eduardo Paolozzi and Lynn Chadwick.[39] As noted, "these broke with historical precedent and eschewed the usual subjects of public sculpture: kings, queens and generals."[40] Modernity was also in evidence in the newly designed furniture by Ernest Race, constructed of sculptural metal and bent plywood, and the interior of the Festival Hall with its bespoke carpet featuring sound waves.[41] In graphics too, designer Abram Games created a logo for the festival: a silhouette of Britannia that combined traditional motifs within a contemporary idiom.[42] The festival sought to represent a successful narrative of technological progress in pioneering radar, jet engines, and telecommunication through visual means.

The Festival of Britain was part of a tradition of world fairs and expositions and had a direct lineage to the Great Exhibition of 1851. In these, Britain's production and cultural influence were highlighted, as was its position as an imperial power.[43] The festival broke with this by limiting references to the Empire-Commonwealth. The three main narratives, the Land of Britain, the People of Britain, and Discovery, were much more focused on the British Isles. The festival was essentially democratic and described itself as "the autobiography of a nation," claiming "millions of the British people will be the authors of it."[44] The site, too, was democratic in its design: it was accessible in terms of cost and location; members of the public were able to access each area. The festival promoted Britain's advances in scientific endeavors, polar exploration, and new technology, thus creating a narrative of modernity and progress rather than tradition.[45] As Hugh Casson, director of architecture, reflected, "The theme was the, the achievements, past, present and future, of the British people, based on the thing they were handed, which was the, the country, and the coal and the wood, and the resources, and the people. There were two units which made England what it was, which was the actual, physical country, and, and the people."[46] At the Festival of Britain, one of the three principal themes was the Land of Britain.[47] The narrative began with the natural landscape and argued that the people had shaped the landscape "until we come to have one of the most efficiently farmed countryside's in the world."[48] Mechanization and science were shown to have increased cultivation and productivity.[49]

While many of the exhibits sought to promote Britain's leading role in the sciences and technology and prowess in the fields of art and design, the Lion and Unicorn pavilion aimed to define British national identity—"though no-one liked to admit it, the Lion and the Unicorn exhibition was less about real people and more about the promotion of an artificial national self-image."[50] However, this self-image, whether constructed or not, proved to be the most popular exhibit at the festival. The name for the pavilion was taken from the heraldic crest of the United Kingdom: "The lion was used to symbolise courage and fortitude. The unicorn, on the other hand, was used to express the eccentricity and good humour that are understood as characteristics of British social tolerance and political freedom."[51] In the aftermath of the Second World War, and in the midst of the Cold War, there would have been a strong desire to promote Britain's advocacy of tolerance and political freedom, but this made little reference to the independence movements under way in the Empire-Commonwealth. Another important part of the display was the English language, which was "linked to the historical development of romanticism, eccentricity and inventiveness. Each of these characteristics was, for the purposes of the exhibition, identified as essential to national identity."[52] As we have seen, the English language within an empire context played an important part in identifying an imperial class, and the command of the language was key to opening up both social and economic opportunities. Within Britain itself, the use of language was not neutral but conveyed a complex set of meanings linked to social class, regional background, and education.

A Queen Is Crowned 1953

In the aftermath of the Second World War, in which Britain, and its empire, had played an important role as part of the Allied Powers, it was apparent to many, both those queuing for staples that were still rationed and those in power who were navigating through the new Cold War alliances, that Britain's role in the world had fundamentally changed. Victory had come at a significant cost. While the Festival of Britain was designed to lift the nation's spirits and provide a sense of optimism for the future, all dressed up in the primary colors and contemporary patterns of the 1950s, the 1953 coronation of Elizabeth II offered a different vision. While this event was prompted by the early death of George VI, as opposed to being planned like the festival, the coronation depicted in the film *A Queen Is Crowned*, focused on a traditional view. "While the Festival looked to the future, the Coronation was an exercise in mass nostalgia, less a celebration of what could be than what was: Britain as a heritage site."[53]

Benedict Anderson has argued that the spread of print journalism allowed for the establishment of imagined national communities as events were experienced at the same time and through the same medium. By examining the festival and the coronation through the visual media of television, photographs, and film, it is possible to discern two, often contrasting, visions of Britain in the postwar world. The coronation of Elizabeth II, and particularly the official film, *A Queen Is Crowned*, linked the centuries-old tradition of coronation with the new medium of television. It glamourized constitutional monarchy within a liberal democracy and illustrated to the world the successful transition of power as well as the social contract between people and government. This was vital at a time when totalitarian governments expanded across Europe and the empire was under attack ideologically from the United States and nationalist movements.

A Queen Is Crowned illustrated the importance of hereditary succession, of tradition, of ceremony. The images of the capital center on the symbolically important Westminster Abbey, London Bridge, and the Houses of Parliament—thus linking church, state, and capital. Those featured are in uniform, either the Queen's Guardsmen or part of her armed forces—the monarchy, protected by the military. The image of the Queen herself in the gilded carriage and dressed in her coronation robes reinforced the link to history and tradition. The coronation was essentially celebrating a centuries-old tradition of dynastic monarchy where an individual embodied the nation. The role of the public in the coronation was limited to that of spectators; they were separated from the monarch, who was encased in a gilded carriage or presented on the balcony of Buckingham Palace—visible, but protected and spatially distant.[54] The film is narrated by Sir Laurence Olivier, who would have been familiar to contemporary audiences from his depiction of Henry V, released during the Second World War when Britain was poised against another European enemy. The film focused on the historical objects that formed an essential part of the ceremony: the orb and scepter, the crown and its jewels, all of which provided a direct link back to Edward the Confessor, a millennium before.[55]

Jonathan Rutherford noted that the English imagined themselves as rooted and located within the landscape of Britain in a way that was impervious to changing circumstances. "And yet for all this national myth-making there was a dissonance in the telling. We were living through the final years of the long, stubborn demise of the late Victorian imperial age."[56] In *A Queen Is Crowned*, the landscape of Britain plays an important part in defining Britain as a nation. The first six minutes of the film scanned across the British countryside showing thatched cottages and Kentish hop houses, ruined castles, and pastoral scenes. This was accompanied by Blake's "Jerusalem," but without the shots of dark satanic mills. The images are rural and picturesque, and even when the other nations of the United Kingdom are mentioned they are accompanied by images of Balmoral or Caernarfon Castle.[57] Thus, the coronation film shows a rural and traditional Britain; the built landscape is limited to rural cottages, and the industry that powered Britain's economic ascendency is totally absent.

Unlike the Festival of Britain, the representation of the Empire-Commonwealth features heavily, although the emphasis was much more on Commonwealth than on empire. The Queen's coronation oath indicated her role in governing the United Kingdom and Northern Ireland, Canada, Australia, New Zealand, South Africa, Pakistan, Ceylon, and other possessions.[58] The coronation procession featured monarchs and troops from the Commonwealth, most notably Queen Sālote of

Tonga.[59] The film devoted a long sequence to the procession of these troops, which created an impression of a large military and imperial force under the command of the commander in chief, the Queen. At the end of the coronation year, the Queen broadcast a Christmas message from Auckland, New Zealand. She realigned from an imperial position by making reference to the Commonwealth, saying that it "bears no resemblance to the Empires of the past." Instead, she defined it as "a worldwide fellowship of nations, of a type never seen before" and claimed that "the United Kingdom is an equal partner with many other proud and independent nations."[60] The Queen confirmed that "to that one conception of an equal partnership of nations and races, I shall give myself heart and soul every day of my life."[61] Newspapers often used the occasion to promote the positive view of Commonwealth and its break with the past.[62]

However, both events aimed to demonstrate to the British people and the international world that Britain continued to have an important role in the new world order. As the deputy leader, Herbert Morrison said at the opening of the Festival of Britain, "To have organised the Festival now may be madness, but it is the sort of madness that has put us on the map and is going to keep us there."[63] The message was reinforced during King George VI's address at St. Paul's Cathedral, which was broadcast internationally: "The Festival of Britain has been planned, like its great predecessor, as a visible sign of national achievement and confidence." He continued,

> Two world wars have brought us grievous loss of life and treasure: and though the nation has made splendid effort towards recovery, new burdens have fallen upon it and dark clouds still overhang the world. Yet, this is not a time for despondency; for I see this Festival as a symbol of Britain's abiding courage and vitality. . . . In this Festival, then, we look back with pride and forward with resolution.[64]

Returnees' Views of the Two Events

However, despite differences in the projected message, the public reception to both events was very positive. Approximately twenty million people watched the coronation, often on specially purchased color televisions. Neighbors often invited those without a television to watch together and share this collective experience.[65] Thousands queued at the Mall in London to watch the coronation procession. *A Queen Is Crowned* won best documentary at the Academy Awards in 1954. When it was screened in Salisbury, Rhodesia, audiences queued from dawn until five in the evening. In Britain, it was the most popular box office draw of 1953.[66] The festival had approximately eight and a half million visitors between May and September 1951. Visitors included John Outram, Jill Gowdey, and Sue Sloan, who responded positively to the message of hope and optimism and found it a welcome antidote to the rationing and austerity of the postwar years,

> It was fascinating, very interesting, . . . I went with a group of friends and we did everything. Absolutely everything. There was an exhibition about the brain, and the man who was pointing all this out was a really low grade comedian. . . . I was appalled that he was pointing all this out . . . but the Festival was an amazing thing.[67]

They echoed the excitement and optimism of the Festival of Britain. All described it as an antidote to the postwar world of damaged and decaying buildings, rations, and general gloom. In contrast, the festival was often portrayed as a sensory experience—of twinkling lights, bright colors, and music and dancing. It was described in binary opposites to the gloom of postwar London. However, few returnees mentioned the narrative as described by Hugh Casson that the festival aimed to promote a vision of Britain, "the achievements of Britain, in all facets, and effort," to show the technological and scientific achievements of Britain, thus staking a claim to its future role in the postwar world.[68] Rather they saw it as a fun day out. However, it was the coronation of Queen Elizabeth II that had much deeper resonance with returnees from Ireland and India. Many of them or their family members had served in the armed forces and therefore had pledged their allegiance to the monarch.

As Sue Sloan stated,

> I went and slept on The Mall with my friends. There were three of us. We palled up with three boys and shared our sandwiches. We slept right at

the front and watched everybody going by in their coaches, the Queen of Tonga, a large lady with bright colours . . . it was a fantastic thing to see, the King of Norway, we saw everybody! We then walked up The Mall and they appeared on the balcony at Buckingham Palace. Quite a day! My parents hired a television so they could watch it.[69]

Jill Gowdey was studying home economics in London at the time of the coronation and recalled,

I was working at Gypsy Hill training college; my boss said "they're hiring a television set for the teachers' common room and we've been invited to join them, would you like to do that or would you rather have the time off to sleep in The Mall?" I said I would like to sleep on The Mall. . . . We saw all the coaches and Queen Salote of Tonga, who is still talked about and remembered. . . . The atmosphere was so wonderful.[70]

Both were young women at the time and described the event as exciting, fun, and a break from the ordinary. Sue Sloan's memories capture the excitement of the day and the break from usual patterns of social interaction, while Jill Gowdey's comment is significant in that it shows how the coronation temporarily broke down social barriers. This was an era when social deference and class distinctions were still important parts of social life and the offer to watch the event broke down traditional hierarchies between teachers and students. What is also revealing is that Jill Gowdey was given the opportunity to reject this invitation in order to sleep on a street in central London, an activity unthinkable at any other time. By politely rejecting the offer, Gowdey was demonstrating not only the importance of being physically part of the celebration but also her active agency in the decision-making process.

However, interviews suggest that the event had a deeper resonance for those from India and Ireland. Witnessing the coronation demonstrated the importance of having a visible and physical connection to the monarch. When asked about the importance of the monarchy, the response was emphatic—Sue Sloan described her father's reaction: "He was a monarchist, from his head to his heel. He was very pro George VI and he always referred to Edward VIII as 'that failed monarch.'"[71] Wallace Burnet-Smith was brought up in a military environment in

India and later joined the Royal Air Force. His view represented the thoughts of many returnees. "Without the monarch we'd be like France with a President who you wouldn't really honour."[72] Mollie Warner, who was from a similar generation as Wallace and who volunteered as a nurse during the Second World War, declared, "Oh we loved the monarchy . . . in India too, they think the monarchy is something very wonderful for this country. Lots of people there would tell you, once the monarchy goes, England would be nothing. They keep us going."[73] Mollie's use of the word "love" is not casual but reflects the deep attachment felt toward the monarchy. This emotional response reflects a deep personal connection to the sovereign as the primary site of British institutional life. It cannot be imagined that she would use such an emotional word about another public figure. The monarch's centrality in public life creates stability, so much so that without this Britain would be "nothing." Her comments also act as a unifying device between Britain and the empire—with the monarchy binding the two together. Many returnees had chosen to join the armed forces and had seen action during the Second World War, visibly demonstrating their loyalty and allegiance to the monarch and the nation. According to Wallace Burnet-Smith,

> I had a volunteer reserve commission, but when I got my permanent commission it was a great honour to have the piece of parchment signed by my sovereign. When I look at it I think, well I have done my duty, as such, and I like to think I do it with honour and with grace.[74]

Few expressed the devotion of Burnet-Smith: "I would lay my life down for her [the Queen], no compunction. If she commanded me to do something, I would do it. Perhaps people might think that's a servile way of looking at it, but it isn't to me; it's an honour."[75] Wallace's comments, as with Mollie Warner's, underline the personal link between himself and the monarch—it is important to him that the Queen personally signed the commission. Burnet-Smith responded with the most fundamental commitment to protect and serve Elizabeth II and the whole system of government that she represents. While the oath of service requires this commitment, the fact that Burnet-Smith *felt* this close link is an indication of the personal as well as instrumental bond he felt with the Queen. Many returnees felt there was a social contract between themselves and the monarch, which was not applicable with an elected government. In a period of transition and change, it was this link that proved enduring.

So why was there such a bond? Interviews suggest that returnees felt a close link to the monarch for four principal reasons. First, the monarchy, as embodied by the young Queen Elizabeth, represented a unifying force in a country that was recovering from the effects of the Second World War and experiencing the transition to the welfare state. The fact that the Queen was politically neutral, rather than party political, made it possible for returnees to identify with her while at the same time feeling disengaged from the political parties of the time. Unlike traditional politics, which could be divisive, the monarch proffered to represent all subjects irrespective of their political persuasion. Consequently, the Queen offered constancy, which was unlike the temporality of a politically elected government. It was this permanence and unity that appealed to those returning from countries that were, themselves, in transition. Wallace Burnet-Smith's views on monarchy expressed above are contrasted to the opprobrium heaped on figures such as Mountbatten, particularly his management of the process of independence and partition in India.[76] All those interviewed expressed strong feelings about the devastating impact this had on the subcontinent. This was in contrast to the effective role of the monarchy as a binding force prior to and during the Second World War. While Churchill was admired, the abdication crisis highlighted how the monarchy managed dissent in their midst. In addition, the decision of King George VI and Queen Elizabeth to stay in London and tour areas devastated by the Luftwaffe, while participating in BBC broadcasts, strengthened morale. Many returnees commented on the reassurance provided by king and queen in the face of the bombardment of London and other British cities.

The monarch also provided a focus for loyalty and allegiance. Benedict Anderson has discussed nationalism and its ability to create loyalty to a nation-state in ways in which it would be impossible to imagine a political party eliciting. Dynastic monarchy, as represented by the House of Windsor, created a direct and clear bond between monarch and subject. This was particularly pertinent for those who had joined the armed services and engaged in action during the Second World War. As Peter

Walton pointed out, serving officers took an oath to the monarch to "be faithful and bear true allegiance to His Majesty."[77] In this public act individuals declared their loyalty and allegiance. The Queen not only represented the head of the polity but also was the commander in chief of the armed forces. In this capacity, returnees were able to demonstrate their loyalty, which was not necessarily linked to the other organs of government. Many returnees had chosen to join the armed forces and had seen action during the Second World War, visibly demonstrating their loyalty and allegiance to the monarch and the nation.

In addition, the monarchy was seen as a mystical force at the pinnacle of British society. In the Victorian and Edwardian periods, the role and symbolism of the monarchy had been extended. When Disraeli proposed that Victoria become empress as well as Queen under the Imperial Titles Act of 1876, he was acknowledging her role as head of an empire as well as the replacement for the defunct Mughal dynasty in India.[78] The British were no longer just a European nation, but part of a small and select imperial group that included the Roman Empire, the Habsburgs, the Romanovs, and the Ottomans. In Ireland and India, the monarch's representative lived in regal splendor at the heart of power in Dublin and Calcutta and later in Delhi. The coronation of Queen Elizabeth II was the visible symbol of the confirmation of dynastic rule. Many returnees were keen to participate in the ritual as spectators and went to some lengths to do so by camping out overnight on the Mall in London. The importance of witnessing the event demonstrated the significance of having a visible and physical connection to the monarch. It is notable that several of those returning collected imagery and objects, thus bringing the Queen into their domestic environment. Verna Perry explained,

> How important was the monarchy? Hugely. We'd cut out pictures of Princess Elizabeth and Princess Margaret Rose. There was awe and respect. Very, very much so. And the Union Jack. If you were on a boat, going to England from India the first port of call was Aden, and everyone would be up on deck, emotional, it was our flag. We were monarchists definitely.[79]

Perry described her response to the monarchy, and its symbols, as emotional. This corresponds with many of the other recordings. The use of emotional words, or responses, is unabashed in this context, yet when compared with emotional responses to other topics or events, particularly for those leaving India, it is startling in its contrast. Neither is it confined to gender. Overt public displays of emotion were not encouraged and were even frowned upon for men, but in this context they were considered acceptable. Perry used the word "awe" to describe her response to the monarch, and this has reverential overtones. Collecting items associated with an object of reverence has a long tradition, often associated with religious worship. Collecting images of the royal family was a popular pastime particularly among the women recorded for this research. These images—prepared for public reception and offered through popular magazines—were used in different ways by interviewees. Some women used them as style icons and copied the looks presented in the magazines; others used them as personnel mementoes linking them physically with the monarchy.

Jill Gowdey recalled that during her time in India her grandmother collected newspaper clippings about the royal family that she gave to Jill on her return. Jill continued the collection, "and now I have boxes and boxes of cuttings."[80] Elizabeth Carver recalled that there was always a picture of the reigning monarch displayed in their living room— and that both her and her sister were named after princess Elizabeth and princess Margaret.[81] Mollie Warner also collected royal memorabilia and has a large collection of mugs and photographs in her living room.[82] During our interview, the room was bedecked with red, white, and blue bunting and flags celebrating the Queen's diamond jubilee.[83] This physical connection between returnees and the monarch was important in distinguishing it from others in authority. While they acknowledged the importance of authority and the rule of law, it could not be imagined that they would collect imagery of a political figure or wait outside Parliament to view members arriving for the Prime Minister's question time.

Returnees associated the Queen with her role as monarch but also the physical embodiment of certain values that they associated with imperial service. They saw Queen Elizabeth II as the personification of national duty and sacrifice. Many felt that seeing the young Queen take up her position as sovereign following the untimely death of her father, while also maintaining a young family, personified the values in which they believed. As Sue Sloan summarized, "You had a duty to your King, your country, your family, the men you employed or looked after. Yes, duty was a very strong ethos."[84] Many who remembered the abdication of Edward VIII saw Elizabeth II as returning the monarchy to its place as a bastion of the values of duty and sacrifice over personal fulfilment. Wallace Burnet-Smith, reflecting on his service in the Royal Air Force and the commitment he made, declared, "The promise I made my sovereign, is so important, you just don't break promises."[85]

The other important aspect of the monarchy with which returnees identified was as the head of the Church of England. While religion did not seem to be a fundamental factor in either binding or creating difference among the British in India, it certainly was in Ireland. Therefore, the monarch as the head of the established church was important symbolically in representing a Protestant, Christian country. For Irish Protestants this affirmation was important in validating their experience and political choice.

While these interviews illustrate the strong and personal connection between themselves and the sovereign, there were a number who reflected upon the changing nature of the monarch as the empire became the Commonwealth. This transition had an important impact for those whose families had been integral to the maintenance of the empire.

According to Sue Sloan, "With the loss of India, and the loss of the empire, our role had changed tremendously. My father was very aware that the Americans wanted to take over, he said the Commonwealth held us together and was something we could be very proud of."[86] Peter Walton was a young army officer at the time and recalled,

When big events happened in London like the Victory parade, the Coronation in 1953 and lots of these guys [Commonwealth regiments] would be wheeled out, and marched up and down the streets and the population, who was quite narrow minded and not terribly well educated after the War, would say, look at all these people in the British Army! And it was done on purpose to spread the idea that Britain was an important part of the world and in the 1950s it still was, but in truth the Americans had taken over in defense matters.[87]

1962 Commonwealth Immigrants Act: Who Counted as British in the Postwar Order?

As discussed earlier, the 1948 British Nationality Act gave equal status to those from any part of the Empire-Commonwealth. This Act was initiated to bind the countries of the Empire-Commonwealth together, rather than encourage large-scale migration to Britain. Yet beginning in 1948, unprecedented migration to Britain occurred.[88] The Home Office estimated net immigration of 160,000 West Indians, 33,000 Indians, and 17,000 Pakistanis between 1955 and 1960. Migration from Ireland increased, peaking in 1957 at 58,000, with most settling in Britain.[89] By 1980, there were approximately 2.2 million from the former empire and Commonwealth.[90]

There had been a "foreign" presence in Britain for centuries: communities of Black sailors in the London and Liverpool docklands and around Cardiff Bay, with the Black presence in Britain in the eighteenth century numbering approximately 15,000.[91] Economic and political pressures and persecution led to increased migration from Ireland and Eastern Europe in the nineteenth century, resulting in Irish and Jewish communities in many British cities.[92] The government response was to introduce the Aliens Act of 1905, the first piece of legislation to restrict immigration,[93] which demarcated between acceptable and "undesirable" immigrants, giving the state the power to reject those deemed unacceptable.

The issue of color and immigration would persist throughout the 1950s, occasionally making front-page news as riots broke out in Notting Hill and Nottingham in the late 1950s. In 1962 the government under Conservative leadership introduced the Commonwealth Immigrants Act, redefining what it meant to be a British citizen. The Act made clear what was previously implicit—that to be British meant to be white. The first page of the Act denoted its purpose:

> To make temporary provision for controlling the immigration into the United Kingdom of Commonwealth citizens; to authorize the deportation from the United Kingdom of certain Commonwealth citizens convicted of offences and recommended by the court for deportation; to amend the qualifications required of Commonwealth citizens applying for citizenship.[94]

By comparing the clauses of the Act with the debates that occurred over the readings of the Bill in Parliament, it is possible to see how racial and ethnic difference was key to the Bill. The Commonwealth Immigrants Act of 1962 restricted entry to those individuals not born in the United Kingdom and those who did not hold a U.K. passport or citizenship of the United Kingdom and colonies. A U.K. passport was now defined as one that had been issued by the government of the United Kingdom, not one issued on behalf of the government by "any part of the Commonwealth outside the United Kingdom."[95] This gave preference to those born in the United Kingdom, in contrast to the stated equality in the 1948 Act. Those arriving had to prove they were in receipt of the correct vouchers provided by the Ministry of Labour, were following a course of full-time study, or were in a financial position to support themselves.[96] The Act gave immigration officers the right to refuse entry if such conditions were not met. The onus was on those arriving to prove their legitimacy, which could be interrogated by an official on behalf of the government. Other grounds for refusal were "suffering from a mental disorder" or rather more vaguely "undesirable for medical reasons."[97]

The 1962 Act differed fundamentally from the 1948 British Nationality Act by introducing the principle of criminality for those who entered outside the conditions of the Act. They were now committing an offense, as were those assisting them. Much of the Act was given to discussion of the various reasons for deportation.[98] It provided for the appointment of immigration and medical officers; the former were allowed to board any ship "for the purpose of exercising any of his functions under this Act."[99]

Parliamentary discussions illustrate the ongoing debates about the definition of British nationality based on racial difference. This can be seen perhaps most clearly in the discussions on whether citizens of the Republic of Ireland should be included in the 1962 Act. Under the terms of the 1948 British Nationality Act, the Irish had a unique position. They were treated as equal but accepted as different. The Irish were needed as a useful additional source of labor, so policy makers at the time eased their entry into the labor market. However, official documents reveal ambivalent attitudes toward Irish immigrants: useful to fill positions that the indigenous population rejected, but not comparable in attitudes and mores. In a survey of housing conditions, an interdepartmental committee observed that the Irish were "accustomed to living in their own country in conditions which English people would not normally tolerate."[100] Many accounts from this period attest to the difficulties faced when attempting to seek work that was anything other than menial. In contrast with the political activism of the early part of the twentieth century, in the 1950s many Irish institutions and individuals chose to remain part of a cohesive group while distancing themselves from contentious political subjects. Mary Hickman argued that by insisting on separate educational facilities, the Catholic Church created a class of good citizens who were hardworking but separate.[101] This transitional space was echoed in social clubs, which allowed the creation of a separate ethnic and cultural identity while not challenging loyalty to the state.[102] Thus, the Irish occupied an anomalous position in British public life. They were both needed as a source of relatively cheap labor that was easily accessed and could therefore adjust to changing employment requirements and preferable to migrants of color, but they were not fully accepted as part of the community of British subjects. They were white, but not white enough.

In the Commonwealth Immigrants Act, the inclusion of citizens of the Republic of Ireland seems cursory, but the debates reveal that the issue was fraught. As Mr. Chapman commented,

> I wonder whether the Home Secretary can give us the next stage of the story about the Irish. In the original Bill they were in. On Second Reading, the Home Secretary said he could not apply it to the Irish; they were out. Later in the debate the Minister of Labour said that they were in. In Committee, the Home Secretary said that they were out again. We have had this game of ins and outs, which has done no good for the ideas of British legislation during these last weeks.[103]

As Lord Balniel noted, the two main unskilled immigrant groups in this period were those from Ireland and the West Indies. During his speech, he questioned, "When we imposed restrictions and controls on the black group and allow totally unrestricted immigration by the white group, how can we possibly preach racial tolerance."[104] The debates reveal the need for continued labor to work in construction, for the

National Health Service, in factories, and on the transport system,[105] work that indigenous labor was disinclined to take on. As Sir Thomas Moore (Ayr) commented, "Without the Irish labourer our functions in this country could not be fulfilled. What about the hospitals? Where are the nurses to be found to fill the places in our hospitals—those Irish nurses who are so welcome, so cheerful and so tactful?"[106] The underlying issue was how to square the need for additional labor in industries such as construction and health care with the desire to restrict those of color. The dynamic of differentiated classes of imperial workers based on color, race, and ethnic difference persisted. The difficulty the British government had in legitimizing these different entry requirements was that the Republic of Ireland was no longer affiliated with the United Kingdom, not even as a member of the Commonwealth. As Lord Balniel commented, "We are giving preference to non-British subjects over the members of the Commonwealth."[107]

The 1948 and 1962 Acts, while seeming to present contrasting approaches to Commonwealth migration, in fact continued to illustrate differentiated understandings of what it meant to be British in the postwar world. The Commonwealth Immigrants Act subtly, but emphatically, restricted numbers from South Asia and the Caribbean Islands while allowing citizens of the Irish Republic—a country with no formal link to Britain—unrestricted entry. Within a short period, it was apparent that to effectively belong to this category meant being white. Rather than granting citizenship to those who were members of the Empire-Commonwealth, the Act restricted numbers, dividing potential immigrants into those who were suitable for entry through their skills and education. This again asserted Britain's dominant place in choosing who would be allowed entry or refused. It regarded potential applicants as suspicious unless they could prove otherwise and employed medical and immigration officers to interrogate new arrivals. Deportation was not mentioned in the 1948 Act but was considered from a variety of vantage points in the 1962 Act, anticipating that entrants might not be suitable and therefore could be legally and forcibly removed. Britain was now policing its borders, ready to refuse entry to miscreants and remove those who slipped through the net. The message was not one of welcome to those who were still members of the Commonwealth. While the tenor of these two Acts might appear to be substantially different, the restrictions present in the 1962 Act were aligned to previous colonial policy that aimed to separate groups based on perceived racial difference and allocated a specific value to each group: imperial ruling class, imperial administrative class, imperial worker. Taken as a whole, the 1962 Act seemed to conform to British ideology on race and difference, while the apparent generosity of the 1948 Nationality Act appeared at odds with it.

These two Acts clearly stated government policy toward immigration. The postwar Labour government appeared to be ushering in a new era. Alongside a commitment to rebuilding Britain along socialist lines, it seemed to also make a public commitment to its imperial subjects, many of whom had sacrificed their lives in supporting Britain during the Second World War. However, the public commitment was not reflective of the private views of politicians across the political spectrum who shared a view that members of the Commonwealth were not valued in the same way as those born in the United Kingdom. When these subjects were "no longer imperial subjects at a distance, but British citizens at home," this resulted in a reversal.[108] As a response to Commonwealth migration, the 1962 Commonwealth Immigrants Act was introduced to allow Britain to determine who should be allowed entry. This confirmed Britain's position as central in that those born in Britain had greater status than those born in the Commonwealth. Within fourteen years the apparently generous policy restricted entry and established in law Britain's ability to determine entry based on applicants' utility and racial status. Thus, postwar legislation codified previous imperial policy in creating different classes of British subjects. This policy highlighted the fact that certain subjects were more British than others. The determining factors were race and skin color.

There is a wealth of evidence highlighting how difficult it was for many migrants to find anything other than menial employment and substandard accommodation. However, what has not been explored is the reaction of those who were part of the empire and returned. The colonial system codified racial and ethnic difference, and it was this difference that was part of the justification of imperial rule. It had elevated a small group over the majority and legitimized this on the basis of ideas of trusteeship and the civilizing mission. These ideas were challenged by independence movements in both Ireland and India, causing many who had been integral to the working of the empire to leave and return to Britain. Yet shortly after their arrival, there was an influx of migrants from India and Pakistan, in addition to Commonwealth migration and renewed migration from Ireland. How did returnees respond to this counterflow of empire now that the empire was coming "home"?

British policy and public reaction to immigration supported the view that some subjects were more British than others. This view confirmed for returnees that they were considered part of the community of British subjects. Thus, British immigration policy continued and confirmed British colonial policy in differentiation based on skin color and perceptions of whiteness—separating and valuing differently the ruling class from those over whom they ruled. This suggests a continuation of imperial thinking that, although originating with policy makers in Westminster, had resonance with southern Irish Protestants and the British in India. Interviews with returnees reveal how clearly they understood the implications of different communities of Britishness in this period.

Returnees understood racial and social distinctions in ways that were more subtle and complex than in the metropolitan center. While class differences were clearly demarcated and understood by those in British society, in a colonial context there were varying degrees of difference, based on economic status, racial and social distinctions, and loyalty and affiliation. Return migrants arriving in the immediate postwar period were doing so against increased migration from the Caribbean and South Asia. This prompted national debates about who could, and should, be allowed entry into Britain and again revealed distinctions based on race and proximity to the metropole. Within these discussions, returnees reflected upon how they interpreted British identity and inclusion and revealed complex and multilayered understandings of both.

Asking returnees to discuss racial difference was often a thorny and contentious subject. They were often aware that the values and social mores with which they had grown up were now questioned and challenged, not just by those who were negatively affected but by mainstream society. They were concerned about appearing "racialist" and were wary of discussing a subject that could place them in a compromised position. This was compounded by the fact that they were being asked to discuss, and perhaps reevaluate, the way in which they thought about their family life and values on which it was based. Returnees differed in their responses, revealing complex and multilayered interpretations. Some were reflective and acknowledged the existence of changing value systems, others demonstrated ambivalent responses, while a small number continued to adhere to the values and social mores of their childhood. Whatever their level of reflexivity about these changes, their views on different layers of Britishness seemed to reflect some of the wider debates on nationality. Jill Gowdey grew up in India, Anne Hodkinson in Ireland. When asked about their reaction to postwar migration, they gave similar responses. Hodkinson said,

England had been to war twice. Everything that the English held dear was thrown up into the air and came down with a massive bump. And not only that, you had a people who were used to being an empire, and then suddenly having to change their thinking because of all these people coming in, who now regarded themselves as British. I say if you go out and take sugar and coffee and tea virtually for free, from the riches of another nation, and use them for yours, and all you give them in return is citizenship, there will come a day when they want to use that citizenship.[109]

Gowdey shared,

I thought it was sad that so many people couldn't accept other races in our country because when you think about it the British went all over the place and always assumed that they were better than anyone else. . . . There were people [in Britain] who thought they were better than anybody else and why should somebody from another country come in. And they assumed they were less than the dust, but they were human beings and had as much right as we did to be here. And I still feel that.[110]

Both women, despite their different origins, shared similar views of those arriving from the Commonwealth in the two decades following the Second World War. They saw the direct link between those arriving and the role of the British Empire in taking raw materials, and labor, from the colonies. They both stressed that Commonwealth migration was a direct result of British imperial policy and that these migrants should be treated as part of an imperial family. However, both acknowledged perceived differences between those arriving and "indigenous" British people. Jill's comment of "other races in our country" and Anne's remark regarding "people coming in, who now regarded themselves as British" acknowledged a racial differentiation between British citizens based on racial difference. However, both Jill and Anne accepted the responsibility Britain had toward those arriving from the Commonwealth and that Britain should honor its commitment to give them citizenship. The views of these two women echo the parliamentary debates on the British Nationality Act of 1948, as members of Parliament struggled with definitions of British nationality. Jill and Anne's comments are evidence of the fact that despite having grown up in societies in which ethnic and racial difference was an accepted part of the social fabric, both considered the consequences of this policy and chose to reject the values on which it was based. They recognized that the empire was able to take advantage of less developed countries and in the process, introduced ideas of racial superiority. Anne's comment that "everything that the English held dear was thrown up into the air" not only is reflective of the certainties of the political class but also was true for the families in which she and Jill had grown up. Both identified how difficult it was for their parents to accept the new order and particularly the change in their social position as a consequence of this transformation. Both women had experienced the upheavals of the Second World War and its aftermath and were witness to the changes that followed. However, as adults, both had actively decided to consider the implications of imperial policy and reevaluate the past.

Other returnees acknowledged and accepted Commonwealth migrants into British life but were perhaps ambivalent about their status. When reflecting on those from the subcontinent living in Britain, Wallace Burnet-Smith commented,

> I have got to know so many Indian people myself. We have quite a few in our establishment here, who come to do care work. I always like to talk to them. And I try to talk a bit of Hindustani. I have a lot of time for the Indians. If I see any on the buses I ask, "Where in India do you come from?" And if they come from Pakistan I say, "Which part, East or West, or Bangladesh?" . . . I tell them I was born in Calcutta. But I always mention that

I was born in Calcutta, but my father was part of the British Raj, so they know. Some of them know, but with the younger generation I don't think it counts for much.[111]

Wallace's remark reveals some of the conflict between the values of his childhood in India and the world of the Brighton sheltered housing in which he now resides. For the son of a British Army officer living in Fort William in Calcutta, the difference between the small number of British inhabitants and the mass of Indians in the city was visibly and forcibly illustrated. They lived in a fortified compound, with cannons pointed across the Maidan, where there was "a clear line of fire." His father, to whom Wallace was close and who was killed by a German bomb in the Second World War, enforced racial difference both within the home and on a national level. Wallace could see during his childhood that Indians wanted independence. "They wanted the British out, quite rightly so."[112] Wallace returned to Britain, joined the Air Force, and fought in the Second World War. He acknowledged that the war caused dramatic changes in British life that were for the better. When Indians arrived in Britain, Wallace attempted to initiate contact with them and spoke to them in their language. He had "a lot of time for the Indians" and tried to establish commonalities by asking where in the subcontinent they were from and informing them that he too was born in India. However, he could not move away from the differences that were established in his early life, and it was important to him that Indians knew he was a product of the British Raj. Those of his generation understood the implications of this, but for the younger generation this had less relevance. Wallace was caught between reaching out while at the same time establishing distance. For him contact with Indians had come full circle. As a child, a retinue of Indian servants cared for the family; as Wallace and his wife moved into a care home, they were also supported and cared for by Indians. However, the relationship is now subtly different, as the staff are under the control of the home's management rather than employed directly by Wallace. However, his comment reveals the complexity of the transformation of this relationship—while wanting to reach out to Indians resident and working in Brighton, Wallace could not entirely escape the legacy of his colonial childhood.

Peter Walton reflected on the ambivalence felt toward Commonwealth migrants within British society in the 1950s:

> Everybody got used to the idea of black conductors on buses in London
> after the war. By the time I was working in London in the 1950s, it was
> normal but then there weren't that number of them, and they were mostly
> first generation from the West Indies. Indians, we were as a nation ambiva-
> lent about, on the one hand, they were of colour, but on the other, many of
> them were highly educated and, in fact, better educated than many English
> people.[113]

His use of the expression "got used to" suggests both a gradual and grudging acceptance toward the new Caribbean arrivals among the British population. The implication is that West Indian bus conductors were accepted because their numbers were marginal and they were first generation. However, evidence from the period suggests West Indians in public-facing roles were often subjected to hostility and verbal abuse. Also, these arrivals had come in larger numbers only since the late 1940s, so the use of time to indicate acceptance among the host population was perhaps imagined rather than literal. Furthermore, the use of the word "normal" suggests that their arrival was not "normal" or usual, that it interrupted the demographics of the places to which they arrived. The differentiated understanding of migrant groups based on perceived class differences is also illuminating as it seems to run contrary to the evidence. Many arriving West Indians in the 1950s had higher skill levels than those from the subcontinent, who tended to come from rural areas. However, this comment indicates a view not commonly held at the time—but that was often the case—that many migrants were indeed more educated than was commonly perceived, and often more so than the average British person. As noted during the war, their knowledge of Britain was far greater than the average Briton's knowledge of the empire.

Interviews with Jill Gowdey, Anne Hodkinson, and Wallace Burnet-Smith reveal a level of reflexivity in thinking about the impact of Commonwealth migration on British society. However, other returnees thought about migration in a different way and rather than acknowledge it as the result of British imperial policy, had difficulty in accepting that those arriving in the postwar period were genuinely part of a British "family." One interviewee said,

> People from Commonwealth countries, Asians, West Indians, I just wonder how many of those support sporting events that England is involved in. You never see them shouting for England. When the cricketers come over, they shout for the country they came from! The reason I am saying that is when I came here, I always shouted for England. I have always supported England. . . . I am afraid immigrants from Asia and the West Indies; they don't always have that view. They are not fully integrated.[114]

Rather than question the right to live and work in Britain, which had already been enshrined in the 1948 British Nationality Act, this quote raises questions about the loyalty of Commonwealth migrants. The narrator used a sporting event—an example of a public space where people come together for leisure—to illustrate that their loyalty is superficial and their true allegiance is to "the country they came from." The interviewee does not accept that they can retain emotional links to their ancestral homeland while feeling loyal to Britain. In order to demonstrate their loyalty, they must do so publicly, offering a visible demonstration in order to fully partake in British citizenship. However, by requiring these arrivals to demonstrate their commitment to Britain, the interviewee suggests a more stringent test than one required for those from the Dominions, or indeed British-born natives. They compare this perceived disloyalty with their own visible loyalty: "I have always shouted for England. I have always supported England."[115] The interviewee used the issue of loyalty, rather than race, to question the integration of Commonwealth citizens into British life.

The attitudes revealed in recordings with imperial returnees indicate ambivalent responses to increased migration from the Commonwealth and former empire in the postwar period. Some indicated they understood the background to this migration and also Britain's obligation to those from its former colonies. Several people accepted these migrants as part of the wider imperial family, while at the same time differentiating between different strands of "Britishness." Others doubted whether these migrants could really be as loyal to Britain and therefore could not easily integrate into life in Britain. This ambivalence suggests both

a continuation of differentiated streams of British subjects and a soften-
ing of this attitude, which accommodated their right to be part of the
British metropolitan community.

Commonwealth migration reinforced returnees' sense of Britishness.
Faced with the "otherness" of these migrants, their position within the
heart of the metropolitan British community was strengthened. As migration from the Commonwealth increased and became more visible in
British towns and cities, and debates within the media centered on conflict, such as the riots in Notting Hill and Nottingham in the late 1950s,
returnees could see the differentiated attitudes toward those arrivals
from the Commonwealth and themselves. It was against this backdrop
that some returnees sought a further distancing of themselves from
British subjects of color. As they all shared the same legal right to live
and work in Britain, and as the term "British subject" and the expression "Commonwealth citizen" had the same meaning,[116] some returnees sought a different classification of belonging. As noted in the quote
above, Britain was becoming replaced by England as the new political
entity with which some returnees identified. In identifying with England, another interviewee described, "I was English rather than British,
because there were an awful lot of Indians who were British. So I made
myself distinct from them by being English and that was a conscious
decision, which was probably of no credit to me but nevertheless that is
how it was."[117] This rejection of "British" in this context is in order to
differentiate from the wider definition offered to the Commonwealth
as part of the 1948 Act. As noted, British in this context was not limited to a particular racial definition but had a wider inclusiveness that
encompassed people of diverse racial backgrounds. This narrator perhaps used the example of Indians because they had been born in India,
part of a small imperial ruling class. The prospect of now being legally
equivalent to Indians arriving in Britain was difficult to accept. As acknowledged, this was "of no credit to me," but it was something they
nevertheless felt. In considering Commonwealth migration, this person
made distinctions between different groups of migrants based on their
geographical origin and allocated distinct behavior types to each. When
discussing those coming from the Caribbean, the interviewee differentiated between those migrants and Indians expelled from Uganda by Idi
Amin: "I identified with the Ismailis, . . . why I don't know. . . . We

welcomed the Ismailis because they fitted into our lifestyle; they spoke extremely good English and had the same mores."[118] The interviewee distinguished between groups based on perceived similarities of behavior and the ability to fit into "our lifestyle," despite the Ismailis being of a different religion.

Why were there disparate views among returnees? What were the factors that influenced their outlook? When considering these responses to Commonwealth migrants—and interestingly no one mentioned the large numbers of Irish migrants who also came to Britain in the 1950s and 1960s—it is important to note that country of origin did not directly affect views toward increased migration. Both Jill Gowdey and Anne Hodkinson, from India and Ireland, respectively, accepted that migration was a consequence of British policy and therefore those arriving should be treated as equal citizens, partially as recompense for their earlier mistreatment. Wallace Burnet-Smith wanted to reach out to Indian workers in Brighton but was constrained by some of the embedded values of his childhood toward those of different racial background. But other interviewees from India and Ireland were opposed to thinking in equal terms of Commonwealth migrants and sought either further proof of their loyalty or wanted a more exclusive definition of Britishness. Therefore, country of origin was not necessarily a factor in determining outlook. Age did not seem to be a factor either. Wallace Burnet-Smith and Mollie Warner were the oldest interviewees, both well into their nineties when the recordings took place. While both had different experiences, as they were well into adulthood before independence in 1947, there did not seem to be a generational difference when considering the role of the British in India or how they thought about race and identity subsequently. In contrast, political affiliation did prove to be a marker of difference. Those who were most keen to stress different strands of British subjecthood were committed Conservatives: "I am a royalist and a Conservative, but more a royalist than a Conservative."[119]

Those who were most reflective about the role of the empire and the creation of racial and ethnic difference were women who had actively participated in religious life and in the process had actively considered the formation of their own attitudes and behavior. Anne Hodkinson was raised in the Church of Ireland but became a Quaker and, like many who choose a new religious path, actively participated in the Society of Friends. She appreciated Quaker values of social responsibility and activism and also the practice of questioning one's own values and behavior. Jill Gowdey married a Church of England vicar and also took an active role in supporting her husband's pastoral work. Although based in Britain, the Gowdeys served in several different parishes, so Jill had contact with people from many different backgrounds and environments. Both women's involvement in religious life caused them to reflect on the implications of social divisions and, perhaps as a consequence, question the values of the society in which they grew up.

Conclusion

The British Nationality Act of 1948 appeared to break with the past in offering an inclusive, universal definition of British nationality that equated British subjects with those born in the Commonwealth. Although the 1948 Act offered an apparently inclusive definition of British nationality, underlying this there remained long-held views on differentiated communities of British subjects. However, the official narratives of racial inclusivity did not correspond to private government opinion, which continued to differentiate between different types of Britishness, and within fourteen years the Commonwealth Immigrants Act had restricted entry: prioritizing those born in Britain and favoring white immigrants over those of color. The 1948 Act could have undermined returnees' status as part of an imperial elite. The discussion focusing on what Britishness meant in the postwar period caused returnees to reevaluate their own views and position. Within this framework, some accepted these migrants as part of a process that saw the empire expand across the globe and, during its retraction, bring home those who had been part of the imperial process. Others rejected these migrants as not being fully British and sought to redefine themselves as English, thus once again separating imperial classes. As British nationality was legally debated and defined in Parliament, two events in the early 1950s projected an image of the country onto the global stage. The Festival of Britain and the coronation of Elizabeth II showed that Britain was still a significant political and cultural force, while offering contrasting narratives. The festival presented a vision of the future that was modern and democratic and placed its faith in emerging technologies. It was centered on the British Isles and made little reference to the Empire-Commonwealth. The coronation confirmed a position of continuity and stability through the centuries-old tradition of dynastic Christian monarchy. The coronation oath committed the Queen to governing and protecting the British Isles, Dominions, colonies, and other possessions. While many of those returning visited and enjoyed the festival and the vision of modernity and prosperity it presented, it was the coronation that offered them a signal of continuity and reassurance. They felt the new Queen embodied the values of duty and sacrifice that were integral to the running of the empire. It was the monarch, rather than the government, whom they professed loyalty to.

5

Twilight of Empire

I had come home. I had been programmed to come home. I
hadn't been programmed to mourn the loss of Empire. Not at
all. Perhaps I should have been. I forgot all my Hindustani in
six months. I never thought of India again. It vanished. Extraordinary really.
—John Outram

I never planned to leave India, neither did Dad. It was our
home. History overtook us.
—Paddy Reilly

This chapter explores whether "return" to Britain for southern Irish
Protestants and the British in India was the straightforward transition
suggested by John Outram or the difficult adjustment faced by Paddy
Reilly. It considers how these remigrants adapted to life in Britain over
the longer term and the extent to which the changing social context of
life in postwar, postcolonial Britain caused them to reframe their sense
of identity and belonging. Within the lifetime of those returning from
Ireland and India, the role, size, and significance of the British Empire
changed fundamentally. There was a marked decline in Britain's status
as a world power, accompanied by a reduction in its role as a center of
finance and manufacturing within the global economy.[1] The British
political class moved from opposing independence within the empire
to widespread acceptance within two decades. Winston Churchill, in an
often-quoted speech at the Mansion House in 1942, stated that he had
not become Prime Minister in order to oversee the dismemberment of
the British Empire.[2] While Churchill's adherence to empire may seem
emblematic of his aristocratic background and conservative political
allegiance as well as his service as First Lord of the Admiralty and Secretary of State for the Colonies, his radical successor, Clement Attlee,

also supported continued links with the Empire-Commonwealth.[3] In a policy document issued by the Foreign Office in the late 1940s, Britain was noted as having "world responsibilities inherited from four hundred years as an imperial power" that required a foreign policy that maintained Britain's international standing while maintaining living standards at home.[4] However, events in the mid-1950s at the Suez Canal underlined the fractures in political life toward the empire. Public opinion was split: thousands of demonstrators tried to force their way into Downing Street. Edward Heath, chief whip at the time, noted, "This was not a demonstration organized by a few left-wing extremists. It was supported by thousands of people who genuinely believed that what was happening was politically, militarily and morally wrong."[5] The invasion highlighted Britain's relative military weakness and marked its decline in the region. As has been well documented, the lack of support from the United States highlighted the new balance of power in global politics. Historians in the decades following the Second World War tended to downplay the impact of the empire on Britain, comparing the lack of public resistance to decolonization to the upheavals in France during the war in Algeria from 1954 to 1962.[6] More recently, researchers, particularly those featured in the Studies in Imperialism series initiated by John MacKenzie, have countered by contending that this transition was felt in Britain, but the reaction was more subtle than in other countries extricating themselves from their imperial commitments. Many of those returning to Britain had taken an active role in the empire, as had their parents. Their relocation was prompted by the transition from British rule to national governments in Ireland and India. Did a return to metropolitan Britain provide a different lens through which to view the empire? How did they view their role in this period of transition, and did those returning to Britain in the aftermath of independence question their role in the imperial process?

Retreat from Empire

On first reading, their accounts support the view that decolonization in the 1950s and 1960s was met with resignation by the British public. Several of those who returned from Ireland and India were in the armed forces: Wallace Burnet-Smith in the Royal Air Force and Charles

Giles in the Royal Navy. Several others were directly part of the process of decolonization: Ron Alcock did National Service during the emergency in Kenya and in Suez; Peter Walton served in the army in Aden, Cyprus, Malaya, and Borneo. Ron Alcock recalled,

> I was called up, National Service . . . it was during the Kenya Mau Mau crisis. I was detailed to go, I didn't volunteer, you don't volunteer for anything in the army if you can help it, I was detailed to go and learn how to drop supplies over the jungle, and that lasted three weeks and then the Suez crisis in October of that year broke out. That caused an amazing kerfuffle.[7]

In explaining the events, Alcock noted that the British invasion was halted by "the American refusal to block the invasion." When asked about his response to the crisis at Suez, he replied, "I was in the Army, and there was an emergency and that was it. You had to do what you were told. Nobody questioned anything. That was army life. But I never thought I would actually go."[8] Alcock's response suggests a passive rather than an active response to the crisis, in contrast to the resistance noted by Edward Heath. Rather than give a personal response, he answered in the plural—"You had to do" and "Nobody questioned anything." By using a collective voice rather than a personal one, he suggested this was a widespread view but also distanced himself from the decision making. He explained that unquestioning obedience was a feature of army life, and therefore the uniform response was to acquiesce. However, these young men were conscripted and had not actively chosen to join the army. When asked about the more general public response to the crisis, he surmised, "People were too busy trying to get the country back on its feet and building on those bombsites that were everywhere. No-one came up and said, 'Oh, it's a shame, India's gone independent, we've lost half an empire.' That never happened."[9] This accords with Wallace Burnet-Smith's response when initially asked about decolonization: "It was a bit of an upheaval in my life; I was recently married, we were raising a family, I rather neglected any thought of what India was doing."[10]

Ron Alcock and Wallace Burnet-Smith's responses suggest that both individuals and the nation as a whole were preoccupied with the quotidian aspects of life in 1950s Britain. The shortage of housing and the difficulties of raising a family during a period when rationing had only just finished were more pressing than political events in distant lands. However, when pressed, returnees revealed complex underlying reactions to the dismantling of empire. When asked again about the empire, at the very end of his interview, Wallace reflected,

> I always think of my father, and what he would have thought of it? He was part of that big empire. There was sadness to it. They were all new countries, they got their independence, some did it with dignity, some did it with ulterior motives, but it made me feel that, what good we had done, because the colonial service was a good service, in the main, very honest, very little bribery, but that all came back with a vengeance with some, most, of the countries that got their independence. It was a pity. But we couldn't have carried on really, in practice.

It is important to note that Wallace's first thoughts were with his father, who spent his life in the service of the empire. Rather than considering imperial retrenchment as an objective fact, he immediately considered decolonization in the personal sense. His concern was whether the ending of the empire nullified his father's imperial service. The principle of trusteeship, as Wallace and others saw it, was to improve the situation in a colonial context, and he referenced bribery as an example of practices that were quashed during the Raj and were now resurrected. His concern was whether the framework the British built will now crumble and the "good we had done" will now disintegrate. He also noted the various motivations for national independence, "some . . . with dignity, some . . . with ulterior motives," which seems to indicate that not all were deserving or ready for independence. When he lamented the end of the empire, "it was a pity" and "there was sadness to it," it is difficult to know whether he was considering whether decolonization was a pity for Britain or for those countries that no longer operated within a framework of British values. However, he clearly expressed regret for the ending of empire and for the endeavor to which many devoted their lives.

Peter Walton came from a family in which military service was common among male family members. He sought to join the British Army and did so in a logistics role. This saw him deployed to regions transitioning from the empire to national governments. He served in Cyprus in the late 1950s, then Aden, Malaysia, and Borneo. His role was to ensure supplies rather than to take part in active fighting. His views on the process of decolonization contrasted with Wallace's in that he considered this from a position of geopolitics:

> I don't think anything to do with empire was an issue, and then it became one recognisably, and dramatically, when you are involved in the political decision to get out of it, and I was on the ground all too often. So I went from Cyprus, where the emergency got the better of the politicians . . . and then I went from there . . . to Aden in 1962–3. Not long after that Mr. Wilson decided he couldn't afford to keep the place, so before the army had the chance to sort itself out, he said, "We are leaving" which immediately gave the terrorists the chance to kill everyone who was not on their side.[11]

Walton's remarks suggest that, before joining the army, he had not necessarily engaged with the idea of Britain's imperial role, although generations of family members had participated in the British and Indian armies. His interpretation was that politicians, intent on furthering their own political interests, took decisions relating to independence rather than being concerned with long-term stability. He assumed the army had an impartial tactical role. When questioned about the withdrawal of British forces, he accorded his view with the principle of trusteeship in that the British were there to aid the transition to self-government within an appropriate time frame. In addition, he assumed the decision of politicians to withdraw prematurely caused the deaths of significant numbers of local inhabitants.

The three men had returned to Britain as a result of imperial withdrawal in Ireland and India. As they became both witness and protagonist to a continuation of this process of decolonization, their comments initially suggested a passive response to decision making. They did not voice outright support, nor were they active in disclaiming this process. However, they voiced measured dissent to the way in which decolonization was managed by the political class in the 1950s and 1960s. Peter Walton was the most overt in stating that the actions of politicians directly caused the deaths of individuals, as they hastily withdrew from former colonies. He cited two examples in which poor decision making led to a hurried exit and resulted in future instability.

The process of decolonization had a different effect on returnees than on those who had always lived in Britain. In the main, they had been active agents in the imperial process. Therefore, they were inextricably linked to the values and exercise of British imperial power. However, both groups had already experienced the outcome of independence movements. The overwhelming majority of Protestants had opposed Home Rule in Ireland, and yet an Irish nationalist government governed those who lived in what became the Irish Free State. In India, British rule was based on the principle of "trusteeship" and therefore eventual self-government for the Indian people, but as Paddy Reilly said, "we thought we'd be in India for a thousand years."[12] Therefore, independence had been foisted upon them. They were the victims of imperial retrenchment, and yet unlike those nationalists in Ireland and India who could celebrate this new historical era, those who were members of the imperial administration had no such reason to celebrate. While not overtly critical, their comments suggest a distance from the political class in light of the process of decolonization.

It is interesting to compare returnees' responses with narratives of imperial retrenchment presented in the British media in the 1950s. Contemporary primary sources on two sites of decolonization within Africa in the 1950s illustrate different aspects of imperial narratives occurring at the time. The Mau Mau Uprising (1952–1960) in Kenya and Colonel Nasser's nationalization of the Suez Canal in Egypt in 1956 were both attempts to remove British power in Africa and replace it with national governments in each country. However, the ways in which they were portrayed in the British media were substantially different. Discussions of the Suez crisis tended to focus on its impact within Britain and also the effect on Britain's standing in global politics. Consequently, national newspapers discussed the power struggles within the ruling Conservative Party, which ended with Prime Minister Anthony Eden's resignation.[13] The British public was made aware of the consequences of the crisis, the "heavy costs to bear" of the drain upon gold and dollar reserves.[14] Reactions from European and American politicians were also regularly featured. In a speech to the Roman Catholic conference, West German chancellor Konrad Adenauer commented that "the Suez crisis had revealed the passing of Europe's former influence, and there was a danger its moral influence would also be dissipated."[15] Newspapers across the political spectrum revealed the extent of internal dissent over Suez in a way that is not apparent in reporting of the events in Kenya.[16] The discussions of the attacks by the Mau Mau Kenyan rebels/fighters in British newspapers often focused on the domestic: articles detail individuals, often on isolated farms, a lone farmer attacked in his bedroom by a "beast" with a twelve-gauge shotgun, a female farmer whose dogs were poisoned by her staff and who had to lock herself in her bedroom with a gun,[17] a young boy literally cut in half.[18] Novelist Graham Greene wrote a study of the situation in Kenya for the *Sunday Times*, in which he began an account detailing the "bestial obscenity" of the oaths taken by rebels.[19] However, he also noted the negative influence of the British: missionaries offering "rites apt to vary with every individual missionary" and "agricultural policy varied with every agricultural officer."[20] However, the commonality is the role of Soviet influence in promoting dissent and funding for rebels in Kenya and Colonel Nasser in Egypt.

These narratives offer insights into the various ways in which imperial retrenchment was represented to the British public. The resistance to British rule in Kenya was portrayed as being advanced by "savages" whose barbaric methods targeted vulnerable individuals. The methods used, and described in detail, suggested to British readers that self-government was not appropriate in these circumstances. In contrast, the reports of the Suez crisis position Colonel Nasser as a usurper who had unconstitutionally seized an international waterway and who must be challenged by a consortium of democratic governments. Both newspaper reports of the crises depict Britain's role as mediator, trying to find a reasonable solution to "native" aggression and lawlessness. In these accounts, the illegality of Nasser and the Mau Mau was highlighted and contrasted with British efforts to negotiate through the United Nations over Egypt and to navigate between competing interests in Kenya. The failure of Britain to do so was blamed on American prevarication, communist support, and the unreasonable nature of the protagonists themselves. Thus, Britain was cast as the moderate, law-enforcing body faced with unreasonable "natives" supported by international forces using these sites as places to play out Cold War battles. There was no real suggestion in newspaper accounts that these events were the legacy of British imperialism in Africa.

Of the two, Colonel Nasser's action at the canal in Suez had the greatest impact for returnees, particularly those from India. Suez was an important staging post on the transcontinental journey from Britain to India. Wallace Burnet-Smith remembered stopping "at Aden, that was a British territory and then we went up the Red Sea. Going up the Suez Canal was interesting, we could see ships pass, and had to have a pilot to navigate the canal. . . . The water barges were brought alongside at Suez to replenish our supplies."[21] The technology that enabled the construction of the canal illustrated European prowess as well as providing easier access to India. For many returnees, Suez was a liminal space between East and West. As they passed through the canal, they were about to enter the European sphere and leave behind the East. Nasser's nationalization of the canal was a clear sign of the erosion of British power and the ebbing of empire.

Decolonization took place against a backdrop of political disapproval of European empires. In 1960, the United Nations passed a resolution on the extermination of colonization and the United States supported self-determination for national minorities. While this was occurring, a different sort of empire was emerging in Eastern Europe, and U.S. policy formally asserted its right to oppose communist regimes across the globe, even if they had been democratically elected. Britain's withdrawal from its empire was positioned domestically as the conclusion of the doctrine of trusteeship, as these new countries would continue to receive British support in the Commonwealth. However, for returnees who had experienced the British withdrawal from India and Ireland, this policy of decolonization was seen as politically expedient rather than furthering self-government within individual territories.

Shifting Imperial Identities—Is Britishness a Singular Noun but a Plural Experience?

Imperial elites often existed as part of an imagined collective, and individual comportment was seen as not just a reflection of personal action but a representation of colonial mores. Personal accounts demonstrate how, within an imperial setting, personal behavior was monitored and restricted.[22] Thus marriage, particularly to "undesirables," was managed and women's sexuality was closely controlled. In India, women were chaperoned until the 1920s and 1930s, long after this was common practice in metropolitan Britain. Public displays of intemperance and fighting were punished, although aggression toward the colonized was a regular feature of everyday life.[23] Therefore, returnees' cultural identities reflected shared historical and cultural frames of reference. After independence and relocation to Britain, these returnees were no longer part of a collective imperial elite. How did they reframe belonging in the postcolonial world? As Stuart Hall has suggested, when considering colonial identity it is instructive to think of it as something fluid rather than fixed, as something that is continually in process.[24] Cultural identity, in this sense, is a matter of "becoming" as well as "being."[25] He suggested, "Identities are the names we give to the different ways we are positioned by, and position ourselves within, the narratives of the past."[26]

This fluid, shifting sense of belonging has resonance with both those born in Ireland and those born in India, although these interviews suggest their association with postwar Britain was often reframed differently within each group. Those from India, once removed from an imperial setting, reconsidered belonging in a different way, which moved from a national/imperial framework to a more personal one. Those from Ireland often moved from a framework that referenced British and imperial connections to one that acknowledged their Irish antecedents.

Robert Maude grew up in a middle-class family in County Dublin. While noting loyalty to Britain, demonstrated by singing "God Save the King" during the Second World War at his parish church, he was also encouraged to think of himself as Irish by his family. He grew up in the Church of Ireland, but also with his grandmother's stories of the banshee and ghosts. His decision to come to England was prompted less by a feeling of being unable to remain in Ireland and more specifically by the need to study an advanced degree in mycology at Nottingham University. He did not feel this was a difficult transition; he suffered little or no discrimination and attributed this to the background of colleagues at Wellesbourne Research Unit, who were interested in science rather than politics. His decision, much later in life, to join and then run an Irish-language study group from his home suggests a different sense of association with Ireland later in life. He did not read this shift as problematic because, for much of his life, his identity was linked with his work as a biologist rather than essentially rooted in a national sense of identity.[27]

This shifting, fluctuating sense also has resonance with Peter Walton. During his lengthy recording, when asked about his sense of identity as a young adult, he responded by stating,

> I was very proud of being British. What I knew about life was far more about England and this country than Ireland, even though I had spent so much time in Ireland. Ireland was home and that was sufficient. It wasn't a country in the sense I needed to owe allegiance to it as a geographical entity. And it didn't occur to me that it was a different country. Of course, I knew it was a different country but it didn't seem any particular importance.[28]

However, later in his recording, when discussing the latter part of his life, he reflected,

> [I'm British], I think the idea that I am more Irish than English only began to hit me rather later in life. . . . I did the family trees and then I got all the papers out and got stuck into it all and then it struck me that the bulk of the background on both sides of my family is Irish. My father's father was a Church of England—High Church actually—priest, but he died during the War, and I suppose it was about then, by the time I had logged endless people who lived in Ireland or worked in Ireland or, indeed, were Irish soldiers in someone's else's army. . . . I thought this is slightly more romantic and slightly more interesting, and I began to think what am I? By birth, I am three quarters Irish.[29]

Peter's two quotes suggest a fluid movement over time. In his early years, although raised in Ireland until being sent to boarding school in England and associating Ireland with "home," he connected to "being British." This was an active positioning away from his early childhood connections and home to his adult life that saw him take an active role in the British Army. However, as an older man, while reviewing his family tree, he reconnected with his family antecedents in Ireland. This, again, was an active positioning based on a greater understanding of his family history, but also because he felt this tradition was "slightly more romantic and slighting more interesting." What is also significant is that he moved between being British, English, and Irish as though they were elements of a whole, rather than contrasting or conflicting notions of national allegiance. For Peter, they were all elements of his own identity.

When she was a young woman growing up in Dublin, Anne Hodkinson's family was closely linked to the Church of Ireland. Her father was steward at Church of Ireland house in central Dublin, and the clergy were frequent visitors. Anne acknowledged the continued links with Britain throughout her childhood. These were reinforced through the education she received.[30] "When you're a kid, you accept what's there. You only really stop to think about things as you get older. You start challenging things."[31] When asked about her identity as an older woman, she responded, "As far as I am concerned I am Irish, end of story."[32] She also told a revealing anecdote about buying some winter gloves that happened to have the Union Jack emblem on them, but how she was uncomfortable wearing such a symbol.

Robert Maude, Peter Walton, and Anne Hodkinson all actively repositioned their sense of belonging and connection over the course of their lifetime. Their interviews show that an individual's identity is a combination of self and the society in which the person lives. However, for others, this fluctuating association was more problematic. Rhona Ward came to London from Ireland in the 1930s. As a young woman, she kept a diary of her experiences and decades later was interviewed about her life. When asked about her identity as an older woman, she responded,

> I would never have thought of myself as being Irish, not really. I would have thought of myself as having Scottish connections. . . . I thought I was nearer to the Scottish than the southern Irish. I always regarded the southern Irish as foreigners; well I thought I was British. I thought I was English. I considered myself English. I was British, I wasn't Irish. Not really.[33]

Within the same sentence, Rhona Ward moved between her Scottish heritage, a rejection of the southern Irish as being foreign, and a conceptualization of simultaneous English and British identity. Yet, unlike Peter Walton, Robert Maude and Anne Hodkinson, this response was not part of an active imagining but was a response to being asked directly. Unlike the others, Rhona rejected a connection to Ireland, but by using the phrase "not really" twice she suggested an uncertain, rather than emphatic, rejection. Her diary details her enjoyment of Irish music and events and evokes a cultural rather than a political link to her country of birth. As with Peter Walton, she used "English" and "British" as though they were interchangeable, although having been born in Ireland would suggest she was not English by birth.

However, this sense of fluidity was not present among all interviewees from Ireland. Ron Alcock's decision to "return" to Britain confirmed his British connection. As a young Protestant in a large family in Dublin, he felt culturally and politically distant from his neighbors and contemporaries. The family commemorated Remembrance Sunday, and in contrast to their neighbors, they "never wore shamrocks on St. Patrick's day," although he did march in the parade in O'Connell Street with the Boy's Brigade. Ron felt that being Anglican meant "your origins weren't really Irish" and "we all knew we weren't always part of Irish culture because, sometimes, if you got into an argument with some of your friends . . . they'd throw that up at you."[34] From an early age he decided to move to London, and on arrival he felt that he had "come home."[35] Within a short time, he lost his accent, and after having completed his National Service, he felt completely part of British life. This distance from his Irish birthplace was consolidated during the Troubles, when Ron felt an affinity with his coreligionists in the six counties. When asked about his view of home as a retired businessman, he responded, "Either I say I'm from London, or if I am in Dublin, I say Chelmsford [in England], but mostly I say London where I spent my teenage years . . . but I never say I'm from anywhere other than London. People wouldn't understand if I said I was from Dublin, but it doesn't come up, I don't have many Irish friends."[36] Southern Irish Protestants who returned to Britain in the two decades following the establishment of the Irish Free State in 1922 often developed a fluid sense of connection as they entered into their later years. Interviews reveal that although connected to Britain through their ancestry and Protestant faith, when they considered their sense of belonging after having lived in Britain for decades, there were many instances of reconnecting with their origins in Ireland.

The British in India also reconsidered their affiliation when moving from a colonial to a postcolonial environment in Britain. However, the links were less to national origins and more personal in definition. John Outram returned to Britain during the Second World War. The country he arrived in was under attack, but despite the danger John enjoyed reconnecting with family members in rural Dorset. However, when he was introduced into country society, a world of "hunt balls and chairs with chewed cushions," he found little interest in it. He reflected that his father "never got me bolted on here." Instead, John found a passionate interest in architecture, which he began studying in the 1950s. It was a period when there were great opportunities for young architects, as the state was rebuilding Britain in a modernist idiom. In housing, health care, and education, ideas of the welfare state were being refashioned through the built environment. This was a world in which access to decent housing and education was seen as the birthright of all, rather than of those who could pay for them. This offered an entirely new way of thinking about society and, for those with the relevant skills, the possibility of creating a mark on the urban landscape. John commented, "I was very happy doing my architecture. I was very happy inventing entirely synthetic worlds."[37] Thus, for John ideas of identity were less connected with the nation and more rooted in creative expression and social ideals. Throughout his professional career, he continued to consider urban space and combined architectural practice with teaching. At the end of his working life, he compiled an anthology of architectural theory outlining his views of the city.[38]

Betty Gascoyne and Paddy Reilly had been part of the resident community in India. Several generations of their family had been born in the subcontinent; therefore, unlike those belonging to the "home-born" with closer ties to Britain, their connection to Britain was imagined rather than rooted in lived experience. Both experienced a migratory pathway, as explored later, but when questioned about their life in Britain in their later years, it was less connected to nation and much more connected to personal relationships. When asked about home and belonging after having settled in Peterborough once her husband had retired from the Army, Betty said, "My home is with my family. Wherever my family is, I am."[39] This had resonance with Paddy Reilly, who also linked his sense of home and belonging to his family. He had grown up within a large extended family in India:

> The two fundamental things in our family, probably because it knitted us together because we were a big Irish crowd, the O Days, O Brien's, the O Reilly's, and various other Irish names that had come from Ireland, I think the religion and the isolation of being at the bottom of the heap of a fairly large European population and a big Hindu and Muslim population. This united us, the religion and the family. It had a tremendous influence.[40]

It was the strong familial link that helped create a unifying cohesiveness when they lived in India, and it was the bond with immediate and extended family that helped Paddy through the transition to life in Britain. As he also mentioned, religion was also a factor in creating a sense of unity that was separate from a national sense of identity. "In our bedroom, there was a little shelf with pictures of Our Lady, and a crucifix and a little situation where you sat and prayed, and the same thing applies over here." As discussed, Paddy found it difficult to adjust to life in Britain. His wife was a great support, as was his faith. "I went to mass every day, and that is what kept me going."[41]

However, not everyone was able to consider or interested in considering a conceptualization of "Britishness." Jill Gowdey trained as a home economist, but much of her life was spent raising her three children and supporting her husband in his work as a vicar. Jill's life was directly rooted in caring for her family and, through her husband, their parish community. When asked what it meant to be British, she responded, "I never really thought about it; obviously I loved my country, but I never thought about actually being British as anything special. I took it for granted, I suppose."[42]

Repositioning

Alessandro Portelli has advocated for the use of oral history on the basis that "sources tell us not just what people did, but what they wanted to do, what they believed they were doing, and what they now think they did."[43] Much of the oral evidence so generously shared by interviewees centered on the details of their lives in both a colonial and postcolonial environment, and how they thought about those events. However, by looking at the interview in its entirety, it is possible to see underlying narratives that reveal more subtle indicators than words alone. Other forms of expression, underlying and conflicting accounts, and even the tenor of the voice allow the possibility to view how individuals composed their stories over the course of a life retold: how and what is remembered and presented within a narrative form.

The initial prompt for this research was to investigate the experience of southern Irish Protestants in the period around the formation of the Irish Free State. Although many Protestants had been vocal in the period leading up to 1922, their voices were notable by their absence in the years following its foundation. These interviews reveal the complex and contrasting viewpoints of Protestants in this period. The narratives that emerge demonstrate the contrast between the official narrative of inclusion in the nascent Irish Free State and the subtle, and sometimes overt, manifestations of exclusion. Anne Hodkinson, who lived in central Dublin and had predominantly Catholic friends, gave an example of being approached by a young priest who enquired of her attendance at mass and confession on the assumption that she must be Catholic—and was shocked to learn that she was not. Robert Maude, when asked directly whether his family had suffered intimidation or threats during the revolutionary period, responded,

> I don't think they would have, I've never felt there were any reprisals as far as my family were concerned and I don't see why there would have been, apart from the fact they fought in the First World War. When I lived in Swords [north County Dublin], some of the local people were ex-IRA and that never impinged on meeting them socially, as neighbours, it was never a problem.[44]

However, when asked about his family's feeling about the Easter Rising in 1916, he declared,

> I think, well from my mother, she would have thought it was a betrayal. Irish people were laying down their lives [in the Great War] and this happened. But whether it happened then, it would have happened some time,

maybe later on. What they were hoping for was a more harmonious Ireland. Ireland suddenly became very Catholic with the introduction of people like Cardinal McQuaid and so on, and the Irish government was heavily influenced by Maynooth but they would have felt, it is a Catholic country and you have to look after the majority population. But my mother probably felt a sense of betrayal that they went out and fought and they'd been let down.[45]

Robert Maude also described how during the Second World War the family felt at odds with the nation's foreign policy of neutrality. This was manifested in the defiance of the congregation at their Church of Ireland parish church, singing "God Save the King" during the service, which would not have been advisable in any other public gathering.[46]

Much later in time, when violence broke out in the late 1960s in Derry and Belfast, and later across Northern Ireland, several respondents, who wanted to remain anonymous, noted "Brits Out" graffiti being daubed in public spaces in their hometown of Sligo and on Benbulben's Head. "We weren't Brits, but some people might have perceived us in that way." Another member of the Church of Ireland from the same area, who also wanted to remain anonymous, recalled instances of Protestants at national schools in rural Ireland being referred to as "pagans" by the teachers. These examples contradict the mainstream narrative of inclusion and are revealing, as Protestant history was all but neglected in the decades following independence. These recorded accounts illustrate an underlying, and widespread, narrative of exclusion, which often created an uncomfortable hybrid position for Protestants in the early decades of the new state.

When we look at the underlying narratives present in recordings with the British in India, spontaneous comments throughout the interviews highlight a level of discomfort with aspects of racial differentiation present within that society. One way in which the interviews reveal ambivalent responses to imperial rule is through the unprompted discussion of Anglo-Indians. The Anglo-Indian community originated in the seventeenth and eighteenth centuries when East India Company servants were encouraged to marry Indian women in order to become familiar with Indian languages and customs. This was a period when few British women were living in India. However, from the early nineteenth century, this practice became frowned upon and deemed socially unacceptable. Despite the fact the community was a direct result of the British presence in the subcontinent and loyally served the administration in specific and prescribed employment, all those interviewed spontaneously mentioned how Anglo-Indians were routinely and systematically discriminated against and how they were restricted from mixing with Anglo-Indian children. Verna Perry said,

> We weren't allowed to play with Anglo-Indian children. The reason, when we questioned it, was because we might get a chi-chi accent—like Welsh sing-song. Actually, it was lonely. We were only allowed to play with the Indian officials: we were only allowed to play with the Collector, the District Superintendent, we were allowed to play with their children, but they had all been to Dulwich College, but not anyone who was Anglo-Indian at all.[47]

Wallace Burnet-Smith described how it was frowned upon for a British man to marry an Indian woman. Children of such unions were regarded as "painted by the tar-brush" and were "despised both by the Indians and the Europeans."[48] Jill Gowdey recalled that her home tutor was Anglo-Indian and how she was aware of the prejudice toward Anglo-Indians from both English and Indians and how unfair this seemed to her as a child.[49]

> She was Anglo-Indian. They are a bit beyond the pale.
> In what way?
> You are neither fish, flesh nor good red herring. They are looked down upon by the English and they are looked down upon by the Indians.
> Why?
> Because originally, they were Indian women who consorted with the army men. Then, they were looked down on by both, because you don't marry out of your colour or creed or anything. I don't know when this started but even my father was very chary about it. She [the tutor] had a daughter and she was allowed to play with me but I wasn't allowed to go to her house because she was Anglo-Indian. It always struck me as very unfair. I can remember very early on thinking, "Well there is no difference at all if you have a different colour skin," but in those days it did matter.[50]

Although interviewees rarely outwardly denounced this prejudice, as Jill Gowdey did, careful reading of the interviews indicates that there was discomfort caused by this racial demarcation. All those interviewed brought up this subject unprompted and often gave examples of Anglo-Indians being excluded from social clubs or promotion as a result of their heritage. When discussing the social context and background to the Anglo-Indian community, the most commonly expressed view was that this was another layer of demarcation within a society riven by differentiation. However, when interviewees moved from discussing the public realm into the more personal, the consequences of this socially constructed division based on racial and social differentiation showed the negative implications for both Anglo-Indians and the British.

During her interview, Verna Perry revealed that her parents' attitudes toward Anglo-Indian children meant she had an isolated childhood, as the family lived in a rural location distanced from other socially acceptable families. However, after one of the recording sessions, she described that prior to his marriage her father had had a close friendship with the beautiful Indian-born actress Merle Oberon. She explained that he had distanced himself when he suspected she had Indian ancestry, which turned out to be correct. What emerged from these comments, although not actively stated, was the ambiguity, double standards, and isolation that resulted in the social constructs of race and racial imagining. Verna Perry's father had ended the relationship with Oberon due to a fear of being socially shunned, although she "passed" as white. He, in turn, restricted his daughter from friendships that would have alleviated loneliness. Thus, the family had absorbed the overriding racial narratives present in the British community, despite the negative personal impact. Although we have no way of knowing the extent of Verna's father's feelings, the presence of photos of Oberon within the family archive suggests something other than mere nostalgia.

Wallace Burnet-Smith raised the subject of Anglo-Indians in the first session when describing that his mother had been encouraged to move to India to become a governess after the First World War, as it was socially unacceptable for British men to marry "native women."[51] Later in the same session, I asked about the clothing he wore as a boy, and he explained that sola topis (cork helmets) were worn to protect them from the sun but also to "keep their skin white." In a later session he mentioned that when he attended Brighton College in England, boys remarked on his sun tanned skin. Therefore, although Wallace never actively connected skin, racial acceptance, and the process of exclusion, throughout the interview, in separate comments, he suggested there was an active process of exclusion based on racial perception and prejudice. In India, he benefited from this process as he was seen as "white," although others were actively excluded. However, in Britain he was not quite "white" enough, as he was marked out as different by his Indian connections. This suggests that embedded within the psyche of the British in India was the importance of racial separation and of racial "purity." John Outram described the difference in these terms: "It was a barrier of such huge strength that even to call it a racial barrier or colour barrier would be to reduce it from what it was really was . . . it was simply built in to the culture."[52] However, there were many instances in which the concept and the actuality collided, resulting in disquiet and personal loss to those involved. Jill Gowdey was able to deconstruct the racial basis of this prejudice and the personal discomfort this caused on a domestic level, but secondary narratives present in the interviews reveal how this embedded prejudice not only caused personal loss but also created an atmosphere of discomfort, where guarding against the loss of one's "white" status was a permanent and constant feature. This challenged the dominant official narrative of the positive role of the British in India. The principle of trusteeship supported the view that the British presence aimed to elevate the country to a position of self-government and in so doing bequeath reforms in government and infrastructure—but these insights suggest a darker element of British rule.

Migratory Identity or Postcolonial Melancholia

In the first chapter I argued that the British in India were not truly "at home" and existed within an imperial framework rather being rooted in the physical space of India. This was in contrast to southern Irish Protestants, who actively sought to remain as part of an imperial family, but who often had strong and deep-rooted connections to home and the landscape in Ireland. On independence, the majority of the British in India returned to Britain, as did a large proportion of southern Irish Protestants. However, "although Britain might have been imagined as home at a distance, it was much harder to resettle in practice, particularly at a time of rationing and economic hardship."[53] Women traveling to India and other parts of the empire were provided with guidebooks to instruct them on household management, control of disease, and child care,[54] but those returning to Britain following independence had no such guides, and yet in many ways Britain was an unfamiliar place.[55] This section suggests that, for a substantial number of those from India and Ireland, "return" to Britain proved that they were situated primarily within a British imperial diaspora, rather than in the metropolitan center. As Alison Blunt noted with regard to the Anglo-Indian community, resettlement in the metropole complicated ideas of home and belonging.[56] For those interviewed, this often resulted in feelings of discomfort, which led to the decision to relocate again within the boundaries of the Empire-Commonwealth and reflected their ties to a wider British world that had been created by the empire and was still reflected in its people, laws, and customs. As noted with many immigrants arriving from the Commonwealth, there were active ways in which they were prevented from fully accessing jobs and housing. This was not the case for white returnees from Ireland and India, yet the expectation that they would be settling in a familiar and comfortable environment was often challenged in subtle rather than overt ways. The desire to return was confounded by reality and reflected "complex and contesting geographies of home, identity and diaspora."[57]

Homi Bhabha argues that from difference and translation emerges a third strand that creates a hybrid. This hybridity emerges from "the act of cultural translation." He suggests that forms of culture are continually in a process of hybridity.[58] "For me, the importance of hybridity is not to be able to trace two original moments from which the third emerges, rather hybridity to me is the 'third space,' which enables other positions to emerge.'" Bhabha argues that third space displaces the originating histories and sets up new structures, thus giving rise to new meaning and representation.[59] His theory of hybridity is a useful way in which to consider an imperial diasporic consciousness—neither colonial nor metropolitan, but influenced by both—not a facsimile of either but a merging of both strands. In the postcolonial world, a new migratory identity emerged from those who originally came from a colonial environment but were discomforted by the metropolitan center.

Anne Hodkinson arrived in Britain in the early 1950s from Dublin. Shortly after having met her English husband Brian, they planned to migrate to New Zealand. This was postponed due to a family illness, but in 1962 they availed themselves of the opportunity of assisted passage to move to Australia. Anne attributed this to a shared spirit of adventure, a desire to see and experience new places and climates. However, after approximately a decade they returned to live in Ireland and finally moved back to Britain in the 1990s.[60] When asked about the decision to migrate to Australia, and then to return to the British Isles, Anne was initially pragmatic on both accounts. She cited the desire for adventure as the initial reason for moving to Australia and a difficulty in coping with the heat as a reason for return. However, it is telling that the family relocated to Ireland after this period and stayed there for many years. Anne finally relocated to London after retirement, as she wanted to be near her children. While her decision making was rooted in practicalities and a desire for new opportunities, the fluidity of the family suggests they were in an in-between space; they chose to locate themselves within a transitional space.

Betty and Fred Gascoyne came from India in the late 1940s. They both found life in England difficult, and he decided to rejoin the army. They were posted to Germany and then served in Singapore. On returning to England in 1963, Betty and her children found adjustment difficult. Her son Brian described the cold and the "black and white" landscape around Peterborough, as well as the "horrible cave-like house" they initially lived in.[61] Adjusting to life in Britain was made more difficult by the lack of interest in their experiences from Peterborough locals who thought they were "showing off" when they described their life in Germany and Singapore. These combined factors caused Betty to feel dislocated and her children to feel alienated and isolated. These feelings were alleviated only by a chance encounter when she was volunteering at the local hospital. She heard a woman crying out in Urdu. Unable to speak English, the woman was terrified by the clinical environment. Betty's linguistic abilities meant she was able to explain the treatment in Urdu to the woman and reassure her that she would soon be well. This chance encounter proved to be the conduit through

TWILIGHT OF EMPIRE * 187

which Betty was able to find a place in Britain. She became a translator to the small number of Indian and Pakistani patients at the hospital. In so doing, she was able to both link elements of her life and find a useful role, whereas previously she had felt unable to connect to life in Peterborough. It was through direct personal connections that Betty was able to acclimatize to life in England, find an active role, and feel part of the local community. Interestingly, this was through a connection with the Indians and Pakistanis with whom she had grown up rather than the British people she thought were her "kith and kin."[62]

Paddy Reilly's family was originally from Ireland but had lived and worked in India since the mid-nineteenth century. When asked about his feelings about the empire as a young man in India, he responded, "I was proud of being part of the empire, because I thought we did do a lot of good things, . . . I was pleased to be a part of the empire and I don't mean that in a jingoistic way, being an Irishman I wasn't necessarily . . . I was interested in the history of the empire."[63] After independence, some of his family went to England, but Paddy decided to relocate to South Africa and then Rhodesia. In the process, he was able to consider the contrasting racial policies toward native people of color in each country. His perception was that discriminatory policies were much more marked in Africa than in India, which made him decide to join the Better World Movement, which aimed to increase contact between Africans and Europeans. Increasingly concerned after the Unilateral Declaration of Independence in 1965, Paddy considered moving to Australia but eventually relocated to Britain in the 1970s. When asked about his sense of belonging as an older man living in Britain, he replied,

> It's a good question, where do I belong? I feel that I loved India dearly; I felt most at home in Rhodesia until it began to go bad, which saddened me terribly, and I've grown to like England. I still think of Ireland and visit it, but I am a Rhodesian, although it doesn't exist any more. My world is a vanished world, in a sense, but I am relaxed about it, and if I get to heaven, I'll say thanks very much! And I've learnt to love people of every colour and creed, even the English![64]

Paddy's description contains multiple elements of imperial consciousness. He connected to his Irish antecedents, although they date to a different century and transnational geography. He proclaimed his love for his childhood home in India, which is part of his lived experience. His chosen national identity is Rhodesian: the site of his early adult life and where he met his wife and raised a young family. Yet Paddy acknowledged that every aspect of this world had irrevocably changed: "My world is a vanished world." Each of the countries was imprinted on his consciousness: Ireland, India, Rhodesia, and even England had been transformed by the end of empire. And yet Paddy was sanguine about this transformation.

Conclusion

John Outram asserted that relocating from a colonial environment to the metropole was an easy transition. However, this process was taking place as Britain was forced to reconsider its place in the world. Southern Irish Protestants and the British in India migrated to the place they considered "home." Imperial narratives in the postwar period presented the process of decolonization as the logical outcome of the process of trusteeship. However, when British rule was challenged in Kenya and Egypt in the 1950s, narratives in the media presented the protagonists as barbaric, unlawful, and irresponsible. Several returnees from Ireland and India played an active role in the decolonization process. While not overtly critical, their responses suggested disenchantment with the governing class in Britain, as they witnessed the consequences of rapid decolonization. Relocation to the metropole caused members of the British diaspora to consider their sense of connection and belonging. Using firsthand accounts of those who returned in this period, it posits that both southern Irish Protestants and the British in India did, in fact, reconsider this connection over the course of their lifetimes, although the way in which they did so was dependent on several factors: country of origin, journey through life, and their own individual sense of self. For some, the process of relocation was not the easy transition suggested by John Outram. There were those who despite returning to Britain remained imaginatively part of the British diaspora, feeling neither entirely rooted in their country of origin nor part of metropolitan Britain, but rather existing in a diasporic space.

Conclusion

Homeward Bound has explored how an imperial connection was formed and retained in two distinct imperial sites in the twentieth century and considered the impact of return migration on returnees' sense of Britishness. Through examining original oral history recordings with those who were previously overlooked by official histories of the period and contrasting these with existing recordings, personal documents, memoirs, and, importantly, official records such as parliamentary debates and legislation and contemporaneous newspaper accounts, this book discovered that imperial homes were not neutral spaces but rather the sites of imperial values that were transmitted from generation to generation. Implicit in this was the clear demarcation between the indigenous population and their imperial rulers. The belief in the superiority of the latter provided the justifying principle for governing the former. This was reinforced through the close, but sometimes contested, relationship between the colonized "other" in the home, on which the colonizer was dependent for fundamentals such as food preparation and child care. This close but unbalanced relationship brought the imperial dynamic into the home in both comfortable and challenging ways.

This work has discovered that it is not possible to speak of a unified imperial consciousness. One of the principal ways in which southern Irish Protestants and the British in India differed was in their relationship to the physical space of home and the connection to land and landscape. There were multiple understandings of home in each country: some rooted in a physical space, others in a sense of national consciousness or located within an imperial diasporic identity. A fundamental way in which imperial identity differed in Ireland and India was over conceptualizations of home. The British were located in India but imaginatively connected to Britain as "home." In Ireland, there were multilayered identities—British, Irish, and imperial—that sometimes existed simultaneously. This was partly linked to the relationship to climate and landscape, as those in Ireland felt a strong connection with both, often emerging from generations of occupancy. In contrast, the British in India often saw the climate and landscape as a threat, a site of danger, disease, and discomfort and potential racial degeneration. They rarely owned property and often moved frequently.

Education was used in a metropolitan and colonial setting in both countries to implicitly and explicitly encourage an imperial worldview. In both India and Ireland, the preferred means, among those who could afford to, was to return children to Britain for their education as this route gave access to the values of metropolitan Britain, which, in turn, guaranteed higher social status on their return to the colony. For the British in India, this ensured their racial status, as proximity to the metropole meant they were part of the "home-born" community and thus much less likely to have mixed ancestry. As well as ensuring increased social capital, a metropolitan education introduced pupils from both countries to a curriculum that emphasized British achievements in literature, history, and technical subjects. Pupils from both countries frequently attended boarding school where they were also exposed to imperial values through sport, debating societies, and the architecture and material culture of the school. Thus, attending school in Britain had definite social consequences. However, by contrasting personal recollections with official narratives, one can see that pupils from Ireland and India had different responses to the experience. Evidence suggests that those from Ireland developed a stronger sense of their connection to Ireland when at school in Britain, whereas pupils from India often did imbue the imperial ethos and returned to India to become part of the next generation of imperial administrators and military officers. Nevertheless, not all families could afford a metropolitan education. Those who educated their children in Ireland and India could still be assured of a curriculum that promoted British values and achievements.

Education also demarcated the ruling class from the majority of the population by ensuring separate education establishments for Irish Protestants and the British in India. The separation was strictly patrolled: through religion in Ireland, and through racial difference in India. Interestingly, in Ireland, the Roman Catholic hierarchy aided this separation by insisting on Catholic education for Catholic children. Education in India and Ireland gave hegemonic status to British language, culture, and history while diminishing that of the "native" population. This in turn allowed the imperial class to access advantageous positions in the administration and thus created a continuation of difference and separation. However, in Ireland, an unintended consequence of the education policy was to create a legitimate site of resistance to British rule, as the Catholic Church insisted on managing the education of Catholic children, thus subtly subverting control from the authorities. Class position was neither a mirror of the metropole nor unified in a colonial setting. In Ireland, class and economic differences were put aside as Protestants unified behind their religion and cultural and political similarities. In contrast, in India rigid differences existed in colonial society based on links to the metropolitan center and official position.

Both southern Irish Protestants and the British community in India left as a direct response to the formation of new states in Ireland and India. The decision to return was prompted by a range of factors: a reduction in their employment prospects after independence; the covert threat of violence, particularly for southern Irish Protestants; and a lack of cultural affinity on the part of both groups with the new states of Ireland and India. These former elites no longer had a clearly defined role in the new postcolonial era. However, the main factor was the desire to remain as part of an imagined community of imperial British subjects. Britain was chosen as the return destination because of the continuing connection with it as "home," as remigrants considered themselves as part of an imperial British diaspora. However, with the decision to return to the imagined homeland there was a collision of notions of "home" for both groups, as they considered different conceptualizations of home: physical, national, imagined, and imperial.

The British in India became aware of their changing imperial position on the return voyage as the cramped conditions and lack of servants visibly illustrated their changed circumstances. This was compounded by the shock of arrival, as many of them were confronted with the contrast between their imagined vision of Britain and the reality of postwar, war-torn Britain. This was less true for southern Irish Protestants as they had greater familiarity with the environment and also had a less privileged lifestyle in Ireland than the British in India. Both groups experienced great difficulties in finding work and accommodation, a common response for many arriving migrants, but both these groups were confronted with the reality that their social capital was not immediately transferrable from the colony to the center. Women, in particular, expressed their emotional response to this difficult transitional period. Yet very few were able to seek help; rather, they felt that stoicism was the required response. However, interviews reveal how the same events are perceived differently according to age, gender, class, and outlook. Therefore, for young women from both countries, this process opened up hitherto unexplored possibilities and opportunities. The Irish Grants Committee files, a rarely used contemporary resource, illustrate how official reactions to each group varied. In response to loyalist refugees from Ireland, the government set up the Irish Grants Committee in order to provide financial assistance. This was widely supported in Parliament and in the media, as the Protestant returnees were seen as "kith and kin." Conversely, those arriving from India in the period following independence in 1947 received less support, primarily only what was due to them under the terms of their contracts.

Homeward Bound has demonstrated that returnees adjusting to Britain in the postwar period—whether from Ireland or India—were quickly aware of the changing political and social climate, and visibly aware of the counterflows of empire. A variety of sources, visual, architectural, and textual, have been used to consider how those in power were interpreting Britishness in this period. These indicate that there were various, apparently contradictory, narratives occurring at this time. The Festival of Britain in 1951 presented Britain as a modern, progressive nation and used art and design to illustrate this, whereas the coronation of Elizabeth II promoted dynastic monarchy and a traditional, and Protestant, nation. The 1948 British Nationality Act appeared to anticipate the ethos of the festival with its universal, inclusive, definition of British nationality, both of which were sponsored under the radical Labour government of 1945, whereas the Commonwealth Immigrants Act of 1962 appeared to revert to a traditional view that gave greater status to those born in Britain over those born overseas. Among these debates, interviews with returnees showed their various and multiple interpretations of British nationality in the postwar period. Some accepted Commonwealth migrants as part of an imperial family; others chose to reclaim an English consciousness, which precluded those of color.

The relocation from Ireland and India prompted members of the British diaspora to reconsider their sense of belonging. Interviews revealed a fluid sense of connection that changed in relation to time and context. Many southern Irish Protestants revealed how, despite being brought up with British affiliations and loyalties, they reconnected with a sense of Irish identity later in their life. The British in India also reconsidered their position in the latter part of their lives and in so doing often moved away from national identity to connection with something more personally linked to family and faith. The process of relocation was not always an easy transition. Returnees imagined they were part of a community of Britishness, but when the image collided with the reality, they found they were situated within an imperial diaspora rather than a metropolitan elite.

ACKNOWLEDGMENTS

I wish to offer my heartfelt thanks to all those I interviewed: for sharing their sometimes difficult, often untold, stories with generosity and patience. And to my editor, Clara Platter, without whom their words would never have been printed.

APPENDIX

Interviews

Name	Place and Date of Birth	Biography
Ron Alcock	Dublin, Ireland, 1938	He was one of eleven children born to father who was a carpenter and a stay-at-home mother. They lived in Dublin in a predominantly Catholic neighborhood. The family lived in Dublin, but his grandfather was a shoemaker in Wicklow. He went to a Protestant National school and successfully passed his matriculation exam, at which point he left school. Ireland was in a period of economic stagnation, and his older brothers were working in London, so while still a young man, Ron joined them. He worked in retail, becoming the manager of a shoe store in London, and then as a director of a shoe retailer in Essex, which became his home. In the latter part of his life, he became a Conservative councilor.
Wallace Burnet-Smith	Calcutta (Kolkata), India, 1922	Both his parents were born in England and went to India for work: his father joined the Eleventh Hussars in Yorkshire after failing to qualify as an accountant, and his mother lost her mother as a girl and became a governess in India. WBS was brought up in the military compound of Fort William in Calcutta and was aware of the strength of the military presence and also the racial divide that existed between British and Indians. He was educated in India, then sent to boarding school in Brighton on the English south coast aged eight. His feelings about return were conflicted: extreme homesickness while feeling very "at home" in England. He had been encouraged to follow in his father's footsteps and joined the RAF at the outbreak of the Second World War. He met his wife Jean, from Newcastle, in 1945. He remained in the RAF for the duration of his career. At the time he felt Indian independence was handled very badly, but in hindsight he thinks it was inevitable.
Elizabeth Carver	Bombay (Mumbai), India, 1943	Her maternal family lived in India for many generations while her father came from Kent, trained as a pharmacist, and was the first in his family to go out to India. As a young child, she grew up in Bombay and remembers the many faiths present in the city. She also remembered the precautions taken to keep skin white, such as wearing layers of clothes. She returned to England after Indian independence and grew up in Kent near her father's family.
Sue Elmes	Dublin, Ireland, 1940	Her father's family had a farmed estate in New Ross, Wexford, where they had lived for many generations. Sue mentioned that although socially limited because of the farm, they did mix, predominantly with other local Protestant families. During the civil war, the family farm was not targeted. Her father initially went to marine school and joined the merchant marine service but then trained as a doctor in Dublin. Sue mentioned that medicine was segregated along religious lines. Her father served in the Second World War, during which time he met Sue's mother. Although born in Dublin, Sue grew up in England, where her father had a medical practice. The family continued to have strong links to New Ross, and her father intended to be buried there, although eventually he was buried in England. Sue has always had an Irish passport and is proud to have one.

Name	Place and Date of Birth	Biography
Betty Gascoyne	Jubbulpore, India, 1925	Her maternal family had been in India since 1796 and worked for the East India Company, there was German ancestry on her father's side. She lived with her two sisters in a house provided by the railway company where her father worked in the Central Provinces. As her mother was in England due to ill health, she had a very close relationship with her Indian nanny. The family was Catholic, and she was sent to boarding school, St. Joseph's, in Sorga, aged five. The school had a British curriculum that was taught in English, with Urdu and Hindi as additional subjects. After finishing school at 17 she joined the Fourteenth Army; her mother was already serving as a Quartermaster. Here she met her husband Fred, who was from London. They planned to stay in India, but her husband's regiment was recalled because of independence. Betty traveled to England with two young children; she found life in postwar London very difficult and eventually her husband rejoined the army, and they were posted to Germany. Their married life was spent in the army: Germany, Austria, and Singapore. On retirement, they settled in Peterborough, and Betty found adjustment very difficult until she did voluntary work in the local hospital translating for South Asian patients.
Charles Giles	Lake District, England, 1932	Although born in England, Charles relocated to India aged one. His family had been involved in India since the 1760s; his father had returned to England to study at Oxford University and subsequently became a managing agent for Killick Nixon and Co. As he was in business, the family did mix with Indians socially as well as professionally. They lived in an apartment in Bombay and spent the hot season in Mount Abu. Charles was initially educated at Government House with a tutor and then sent to Raj Kumar College, as one of five British boys and 150 Maharajas and their sons, before returning to England as his ancestors had regularly done, aged ten to attend Horris Hill boarding school followed by naval college at Dartmouth aged thirteen. He spent his working life in the Royal Navy. His wife, Jane, also had family connections to India, and she grew up in Bombay until the family relocated to England in the late 1940s.
Jill Gowdey	Lichfield, England, 1930	Both of Jill's parents were from the U.K. and had no real connection to India. Her father joined the South Staffordshire regiment in 1916 and was sent to India in 1934. The family moved according to her father's postings but settled in Bangalore in the south. Jill and her two brothers had home tutors, one of whom was Anglo-Indian. Through this connection, Jill became aware of the racial inequality present in India and British attitudes to race. She later went to a boarding school. The family returned to England at the end of the Second World War. Jill was delighted that the family was all resident in one place, but her mother found the adjustment very difficult. Jill studied home economics at Battersea Polytechnic and married her husband who was a Church of England vicar. They lived in Derbyshire and had three children, and she was very involved in the pastoral side of parish life.

Name	Place and Date of Birth	Biography
Anne Hodkinson	Dublin, Ireland, 1941	Her mother was a Catholic from Northern Ireland who came to Dublin to train as a chef. She met Anne's father, Willie Lang, when working at one of the most established gentlemen's clubs in Dublin. He was a Protestant from Dublin, and she converted in order to marry. Anne's paternal grandfather was in the Royal Irish Constabulary but left after the Troubles of the 1920s. Her father was a wine waiter and later became Head Steward at Church of Ireland House in central Dublin, where Anne grew up. She went to the Kildare Place Model school, which was Church of Ireland. She noted how religious segregation was widespread throughout her childhood and affected almost every part of life, although she had many Catholic friends in her neighborhood. On leaving school, she trained as a secretary and worked for a linen manufacturer in Dublin before coming to London aged 19 with friends. She met her husband Brian when ice skating, and after some years they emigrated to Australia with their young family. Anne found acclimatization difficult, and they eventually returned to Ireland, during which time she converted to become a Quaker. After her children were adults, she came to England with her husband for work and settled in London, although her children and grandchildren are mainly in Ireland and Australia.
Robert Maude	Dublin, Ireland, 1929	He grew up in large house in North County Dublin. One grandfather was a "gentlemen's gentleman" in the Viceregal Lodge in Dublin; the other was senior in the Royal Irish Constabulary. Both parents were Protestants; his mother was from a large family and at independence three of his maternal uncles moved to Belfast as they felt they had no future in the new state. His father trained as an optician and had his own practice in the Quays in Dublin. Robert was one of three children. He remembers his family disapproving of Irish neutrality during the Second World War. He attended the Erasmus Smith secondary school in Dublin, a private school that provided an education for Protestant and Jewish boys. He says that the family had pro-British views but also felt free to practice their religion and never felt threatened or intimidated. He studied natural sciences at Trinity College Dublin and later a master's degree in mycology at Nottingham University. He gave his reasons for coming to the U.K. as the pursuit of his career as a biologist rather than any feelings of discomfort living in Dublin. Working in a research institute, he never felt any discrimination as colleagues were more focused on their work. In later life, having learned Irish in school, he is currently a member of a conversational Irish study group. The rest of his family remained in Dublin.
John Outram	Taiping, Malaya (Malaysia), 1934	His father was born in India and served in the Burma Rifles as aide-de-camp to the governor, and the family moved to India at the beginning of the Second World War. His mother had grown up in Argentina. John would have been sent to boarding school in England but the outbreak of the war preventing this, and instead he went to one in Kashmir aged eight. He was aware from a very early age of the parallel lives of the British and Indians yet at the same time his closest relationships were with his Indian servants. He returned to England aged twelve and attended Wellington College. On finishing, he studied architecture in London before working for the London County Council and private practices before establishing his own practice in the late 1970s. His architecture uses a strong visual iconography and is considered as exemplary of postmodern architecture.

Name	Place and Date of Birth	Biography
Verna Perry	Kent, England, 1939	The family moved to India when she was a baby and lived in an apartment in Bombay. They had long-standing connections to India. Her father was a senior manager at asbestos cement company Turner and Newall. She remembers riots during independence; the family had guns in case of a violent attack. They felt independence was ushered in too quickly and were horrified by the violence that accompanied it. They were briefly sent to boarding school in England and then traveled back to Bombay. As with other families working in commerce, they mixed socially with Indians but only ones who had been educated in England. Unlike military families, they left in the 1950s and Verna and her sister went to boarding school in Kent. She wanted to become an artist but her family advised her to become a teacher. She married, her husband was a geologist/engineer, and they traveled the world with his job. Later in life, she returned to teaching and established a school in Abu Dhabi when her husband was based there. They later moved to London.
James "Paddy" Reilly	India, 1927	His ancestors were Irish on both sides and arrived in India in the 1830s to join the East India Company army. They fought in the Uprising of 1857. He noted how the links with Ireland were kept—they celebrated the 1916 Easter Rising—while also being firmly part of the British empire. His father worked on the railways which covered the costs of educating Paddy at St. Joseph's CBS in the Himalayas. They were part of the "country born" that made their lives in India and as such, had no plans to leave. Independence in 1947 precipitated this, and they family decided to relocate: initially to South Africa, and then to Rhodesia, where the Civil Service were actively recruiting. He wanted to train as a teacher but was recruited to the Income Tax division. He met his English born wife Val in Rhodesia and their children were born in a rural part of the countryside when Paddy worked as a cost clerk in the Roads Department, later becoming Deputy Director of the Government Audit department. They were part of a Better World movement to encourage integration but after the Unilateral Declaration of Independence the family were concerned about the direction in which the country was going and feared their sons would be drafted into the army. In the mid 1970s they moved to Tunbridge Wells—Paddy found it extremely difficult to adjust but finally did so through his strong family links and religious faith.
Sue Sloan	Quetta, India, 1934	Her father was originally from Kent. He fought in the First World War and wanted a different future so joined the Indian Army. Her mother was born into a British family in Singapore who migrated to India. The family was based in the north as her father was fighting on the North West Frontier. During the Second World War, her mother joined the Women's Auxiliary Corps and Sue was sent to boarding school which she disliked. On partition the family was living near the border in the Punjab so were relocated back to England. They settled in Essex, which was a huge cultural shock for Sue and her mother. Sue found it hard to fit it to school in Essex and remarked on how little people knew or cared about India. Her education in India had been limited so she was not able to apply to university, instead she went to secretarial college in London and got a job with British Transport Films. She found life in postwar London liberating, contrasting it with the limited opportunities open to women in India. Her husband was a Protestant from Dublin who was a GP. After their marriage, Sue assisted in the practice while raising their two sons.

Name	Place and Date of Birth	Biography
Olive Stevenson	Surrey, England, 1930	Both of her parents were Protestants who were born and raised in Dublin. In 1920, as they were both working in the civil service—her mother in the Bank of Ireland, her father in the Post Office, they decided their position in the new state was tenuous and moved to south London. Olive describes growing up in a place where neither she nor her family had any connection. She remembered her mother's extreme loneliness and difficulties in adjusting to life in England, and her regular visits to family in Dublin. Olive was studious and encouraged to be so, achieving a place at Oxford University. This was followed by a course in social work at the Tavistock Clinic leading to a professional career in practice, later in teaching. Her insights into the nature of family relationships and dynamics were particularly useful in thinking about diasporic identity.
Peter Walton	North Wales, 1939	His mother's family originated in Scotland and moved to the north of Ireland, migrating south to acquire land in Co. Carlow in the nineteenth century. They built a large home and had a farmed estate. His parents met when his father was a British soldier stationed at the house in the 1920s. Peter's early years were spent in Carlow, he was then sent to boarding school in Dublin, followed by a boarding school in England. There were long-standing family connections to the British Army and as a boy, Peter wanted to join an Indian regiment. He joined the British Army in a logistics role and spent his entire career in places that were in the throes of decolonization; Cyprus, Malaya, Aden, Borneo. He has a long-standing interest in family history and after retirement traced his family tree. He is also involved in a voluntary capacity in the Prince of Wales's Leinster Regiment, one of the Irish regiments disbanded in 1922. He lives in Kent.
Mollie Warner	Jhansi, India, 1913	Her father was originally from Yorkshire but joined the Royal Hussars, her maternal grandfather was also in the army. The family lived in a military cantonment and Mollie attended Wynberg Allen boarding school in Musoorie. There were several wealthy Indian girls in her class. She noted how protected girls were, always chaperoned and never allowed out alone. She met her husband in India, he was an engineer who often worked away from home while she was responsible for raising their children. On independence, she feared for her children's future and decided to travel to England, although she had limited family connections. She settled in north London, educated her five children, married again and moved to Leeds, her father's birthplace.

NOTES

PREFACE
1 Central Statistics Office, "Census 1926 Reports," www.cso.ie; Delaney, *Demography, State and Society*, 71.

INTRODUCTION
1 Lyons, *Ireland since the Famine*; Brown, *Ireland*; Buckland, *Irish Unionism*, 3–7.
2 Kenny, "Irish Emigrations in a Comparative Perspective," 407; Billings and Farrell, *Irish in Illinois*.
3 MacRaild, *Irish Diaspora in Britain*; Delaney, *Demography, State and Society*.
4 Trew, *Leaving the North*, 10.
5 Ida Milne and Ian d'Alton, "Content and Context," in d'Alton and Milne, *Protestant and Irish*, 8.
6 Foster, "Protestant Accent," xxii.
7 Robinson, *Big House*; Casey, *Silver Tassie*; Bowen, *Last September*.
8 Ferriter, *A Nation and Not a Rabble*; Foster, *Vivid Faces*.
9 Hart, *IRA and Its Enemies*, 288–91.
10 Wilson, "Ghost Provinces, Mislaid Minorities," 82; Borgonovo, *Spies, Informers*, 180.
11 Crawford, "Southern Irish Protestants and 'Irishness,'" 54; Bury, *Buried Lives*.
12 D'Alton and Milne, *Protestant and Irish*.
13 Brown, "India," 423.
14 Brown, "India," 424–26.
15 Satia, *Time's Monster*, 199.
16 Darwin, *Unfinished Empire*, 321.
17 Crosbie, "Ireland, Colonial Science, and the Geographical Construction of British Rule."
18 Claeys, "Survival of the Fittest."
19 Dalrymple, *White Mughals*, 115–24.
20 "Introduction," in MacRaild, Bueltmann, and Clark, *British and Irish Diasporas*.
21 Satia, *Time's Monster*, 246.
22 Manchester University Press, "Studies in Imperialism" (2022), www.manchesteruniversitypress.co.uk.
23 Hall and Rose, *At Home with the Empire*.
24 Lester, *Imperial Networks*, 7.
25 Lester, *Imperial Networks*, preface.

203

26 Lester, *Imperial Networks*, preface.
27 Crosbie, "Ireland, Colonial Science, and the Geographical Construction of British Rule," 973–75.
28 Cohn, *Colonialism and Its Forms of Knowledge*, 3.
29 Schwarz, *Memories of Empire*.
30 Paul, *Whitewashing Britain*, xv.
31 Curtis, *Apes and Angels*, xi–xiv; Foster, *Paddy and Mr Punch*; Hickman et al., "Limitations of Whiteness," 161.
32 Anderson, *Imagined Communities*, 6.
33 Cohen and Fischer, *Routledge Handbook of Diaspora Studies*.
34 Cohen, *Global Diasporas*, ix.
35 Seeley, *Expansion of England*; Colley, *Britons*; Hall, *Cultures of Empire*.
36 "The British Empire and Empire Migration, 1815 to the 1960s," in Harper and Constantine, *Migration and Empire*, 2–4.
37 Cohen, *Global Diasporas*, 67.
38 "Introduction," in MacRaild, Bueltmann, and Clark, *British and Irish Diasporas*.
39 Kenny, "Irish Emigrations in a Comparative Perspective."
40 Cohen and Fischer, *Routledge Handbook of Diaspora Studies*, 6
41 Chowdhury, "Between Dispersion and Belonging," 104–5.
42 Brah, *Cartographies of Diaspora*, 192.
43 Blunt and Dowling, *Home*, 142.
44 Potter, "Empire, Cultures and Identities," 55; George, "Homes in the Empire," 98.
45 Buettner, *Empire Families*; Collingham, *Imperial Bodies*.
46 Moulton, *Ireland and the Irish*, 217.
47 Lyons, *Ireland since the Famine*, 15–16.
48 Mitchel, *Last Conquest of Ireland*, 218.
49 Gleeson, "Emigrants and Exiles."
50 Satia, *Time's Monster*, 265.
51 Said, *Orientalism*.
52 Hickman et al., "Limitations of Whiteness"; Ryan and Webster, *Gendering Migration*; MacRaild, *Irish Diaspora in Britain*; Delaney, *Demography, State and Society*; Moulton, *Ireland and the Irish*; O'Sullivan, *Irish World Wide*; Chatterji and Washbrook, *Routledge Handbook of the South Asian Diaspora*; Chatterji and Alexander, *Bengal Diaspora*.
53 Finnegan, "Family Myths, Memories and Interviewing," 178.
54 Thompson with Bornat, *Voice of the Past*, 1–8.
55 Dillon, *National Life Stories*.
56 Perks, "'Corporations Are People Too!,'" 41.
57 Portelli, "What Makes Oral History Different?," 33–36.
58 Portelli, "What Makes Oral History Different?"
59 Portelli, "What Makes Oral History Different?"
60 Popular Memory Group, "Popular Memory, Theory, Politics, Method."
61 Trew, *Leaving the North*, 16–17, chap. 7.

62 Buettner, *Empire Families*, 2.

63 Kennedy, *Magic Mountains*, 3–4.

64 Brennan, "Political Minefield," 406.

65 Brennan, "Political Minefield"; Taylor, *Heroes or Traitors?*

66 Metcalf, *Ideologies of the Raj*, 34.

67 Akenson, *Irish Education Experiment*, 253–54.

68 CO 762/212: Report on the Irish Grants Committee.

69 Lunn, "Reconsidering 'Britishness,'" 83–84.

70 Lyons, *Ireland since the Famine*; Brown, *Ireland*; Buckland, *Irish Unionism*, 3–7.

1. HOMES IN THE EMPIRE

1 Blunt and Dowling, *Home*; George, "Homes in the Empire."

2 Blunt and Dowling, *Home*, 2.

3 Blunt and Dowling, *Home*, 159.

4 Kennedy, *Magic Mountains*, 8.

5 Blunt, *Domicile and Diaspora*, 4.

6 Blunt, *Domicile and Diaspora*, 4–5.

7 Sloan oral history, track 2.

8 Outram oral history, track 2.

9 Walton oral history, track 2.

10 Maude oral history, track 1.

11 Alcock oral history, track 3.

12 CO 762/212: Report on the Irish Grants Committee.

13 CO 762/15/161: Mrs. E. M. Troy.

14 CO 762/80/1312: George Tyner.

15 CO 762/86/1400: Samuel Byford.

16 CO 762/86/1400: Samuel Byford.

17 CO 762/180/3145: George Daunt.

18 CO 762/86/1416: Cecil Stoney.

19 Safran, "Diasporas in Modern Societies," 83–84.

20 Brown, *Ireland*, 18–22.

21 Alcock oral history, track 1.

22 Oral history, track 3.

23 Collingham, *Imperial Bodies*, 82–84.

24 MSS EUR T.7 Vere Birdwood.

25 Sloan oral history, track 5.

26 Pioneers in Charity and Social Welfare, track 1.

27 Hodkinson oral history, track 2.

28 Fleming, *Head or Harp*, 35.

29 Fleming, *Head or Harp*, 36.

30 Collingham, *Imperial Bodies*, 15.

31 Harrison, *Climate and Constitutions*.

32 MSS EUR T.4 Colonel Rivett Carnac, 3/8.

33 Collingham, *Imperial Bodies*, 165.

34 Collingham, *Imperial Bodies*, 171.

35 MSS EUR T.28 Lady Dring.

36 Perry oral history, track 2.

37 Outram oral history, track 2.

38 Bowen, *Bowen's Court*, 3.

39 Bowen, *Bowen's Court*, 367.

40 Fleming, *Head or Harp*, 15.

41 Fleming, *Head or Harp*, 39.

42 Bowen, *Bowen's Court*, 384–85.

43 Walton oral history, track 2.

44 CO 762/212: Report on the Irish Grants Committee.

45 Strong, *Visions of England*, 145–90.

46 Pooley, "From Londonderry to London," 192.

47 Said, *Orientalism*, 7.

48 Davidoff and Hall, *Family Fortunes*.

49 Collingham, *Imperial Bodies*, 99–101.

50 Collingham, *Imperial Bodies*, 106.

51 Burnet-Smith oral history, track 3.

52 Outram oral history, track 2.

53 MSS EUR T.7 Vere Birdwood, 2/1.

54 Walton oral history, track 2.

55 Elmes oral history, track 1.

56 The National Archives, Kew (TNA), Irish Grants Committee case files.

57 MSS EUR T.4 Colonel Rivett Carnac 4.

58 Walton oral history, track 2.

59 TNA, Irish Grants Committee case files.

60 MSS EUR T.28 Lady Dring, 5/9; Outram oral history.

61 MSS EUR T.20 Irene Edwards, 2/12.

62 Alcock oral history; Walton oral history.

63 Bowen, *Bowen's Court*, 193.

64 Dalrymple, *White Mughals*, 23–32.

65 Levine, "Sexuality, Gender and Empire," 136.

66 Levine, "Sexuality, Gender and Empire," 140.

67 Davin, "Imperialism and Motherhood," 13.

68 Steel and Gardiner, *Complete Indian Housekeeper and Cook*, 16.

69 MSS EUR T.7 Vere Birdwood, 5/9.

70 Procida, "Good Sports and Right Sorts," 460.

71 Procida, "Good Sports and Right Sorts," 454–88.

72 Kennedy, *Magic Mountains*, 118.

73 MSS EUR T.32 Lady Kathleen Griffiths, 9/5.

74 MSS EUR T.28 Lady Dring 6/6.

75 Levine, "Sexuality, Gender and Empire," 140.

76 Warner oral history, track 3.
77 Perry oral history, track 1.
78 Levine, "Sexuality, Gender and Empire," 154.
79 CO/762/161 Mrs. E. M. Troy.
80 CO/762/120/2073: Mrs. Appelby.
81 CO 762/100/1698: M. K. Madden.
82 CO 762/100/1691: Annabella Rainey.
83 Urquhart, "Unity of Unionism."
84 Kynaston, "Uncovering the Unspoken."
85 Harding and Pribram, *Emotions*; Plamper, *History of Emotions*.
86 Thomson, "Indexing and Interpreting Emotion."
87 Institute of Historical Research, "Oral History Spring School."
88 Thomson, "Indexing and Interpreting Emotion."
89 Bornat, "Remembering and Reworking Emotions," 49.
90 Bornat, "Remembering and Reworking Emotions," 49.
91 Bew, *Ideology and the Irish Question*, 68.
92 Ferriter, *Transformation of Modern Ireland*, 122.
93 Walton oral history, track 9.
94 Harding, "Talk about Care," 33.
95 Walton oral history, track 9.
96 Walton oral history, track 9.
97 Alcock oral history, track 1.
98 Alcock oral history, track 1.
99 Alcock oral history, track 1.
100 Alcock oral history, track 1.
101 Sloan oral history, track 5.
102 Gowdey oral history, track 2.
103 Gowdey oral history, track 2.
104 Gascoyne oral history, track 7.
105 Bornat, "Remembering and Reworking Emotions," 48.
106 Anderson and Jack, "Learning to Listen," 129.
107 Anderson and Jack, "Learning to Listen," 130.
108 Hoirns, "Crying in the Archive."
109 Hoirns, "Crying in the Archive."
110 Steel and Gardiner, *Complete Indian Housekeeper and Cook*, 18.

2. READING THE NATION

1 Bratton, *Impact of Victorian Children's Fiction*, 13–14.
2 Heathorn, *For Home, Country and Race*, 4–5.
3 Heathorn, *For Home, Country and Race*, 6.
4 Heathorn, *For Home, Country and Race*, 20.
5 Steel and Gardiner, *Complete Indian Housekeeper and Cook*, 160–69.
6 Fayrer, *European Child-Life in Bengal*, 29–30.

7 Kennedy, *Magic Mountains*, 132.
8 Buettner, *Empire Families*, 110.
9 MSS EUR T.32 Sir Percival Griffiths, 7/3.
10 Walton oral history, track 2.
11 MSS EUR T.7 Vere Birdwood, 2/4.
12 MSS EUR T.7 Vere Birdwood, 2/4.
13 Bratton, *Impact of Victorian Children's Fiction*, 14.
14 Heathorn, *For Home, Country and Race*, 12.
15 Heathorn, *For Home, Country and Race*, 6.
16 Walsh, "'Paltry Abridgements,'" 56.
17 MacKenzie, *Propaganda and Empire*, 175.
18 Castle, "Imperial Legacies, New Frontiers," 145.
19 Mangan, *Athleticism in the Victorian and Edwardian Public School*.
20 Jones oral history, track 2.
21 *Great Public Schools*, 303.
22 *Great Public Schools*, 303.
23 *Great Public Schools*, 303.
24 Jones oral history, track 2.
25 Jones oral history, track 2.
26 Godber, *Harpur Trust*, 109–10.
27 Godber, *Harpur Trust*, appendix.
28 Godber, *Harpur Trust*, 109–10.
29 Godber, *Harpur Trust*, 109.
30 Godber, *Harpur Trust*.
31 Jones oral history, track 2.
32 MacKenzie, *Propaganda and Empire*, 175.
33 MacKenzie, *Propaganda and Empire*.
34 MacKenzie, *Propaganda and Empire*, 176.
35 Buettner, *Empire Families*, 165.
36 Godber, *Harpur Trust*, 115.
37 Jones oral history, track 2.
38 Godber, *Harpur Trust*, 110.
39 Clarke, *History of the Cheltenham Ladies College*, 53.
40 Clarke, *History of the Cheltenham Ladies College*, 56.
41 Clarke, *History of the Cheltenham Ladies College*, 57.
42 Clarke, *History of the Cheltenham Ladies College*, 55.
43 Godber, *Harpur Trust*, 111.
44 MSS EUR T.55 Colonel Rivett-Carnac.
45 Giles oral history, track 4.
46 Burnet-Smith oral history, track 5.
47 Burnet-Smith oral history, track 5.
48 Burnet-Smith oral history, track 5.
49 Burnet-Smith oral history, track 5.

50 Burnet-Smith oral history, track 5.
51 MSS EUR T.7 Vere Birdwood, 3.
52 Bowen, *Bowen's Court*, 419–20.
53 Bowen, *Bowen's Court*, 420.
54 Day-Lewis, *Buried Day*, 96.
55 Fleming, *Head or Harp*, 72.
56 Fleming, *Head or Harp*, 72.
57 Fleming, *Head or Harp*, 73.
58 Fleming, *Head or Harp*, 76.
59 Fleming, *Head or Harp*, 73.
60 Fleming, *Head or Harp*, 78.
61 Fleming, *Head or Harp*, 77.
62 Buettner, *Empire Families*, 72–73.
63 Buettner, *Empire Families*, 74.
64 Buettner, *Empire Families*, 82.
65 "Report on the Progress of Education of European Children," 1.
66 "Report on the Progress of Education in European Schools," 2–3.
67 "Report on the Progress of Education in European Schools," 2.
68 "Report on the Progress of Education in European Schools," 35.
69 "Report on the Progress of Education in European Schools," 3.
70 Kennedy, *Magic Mountains*, 132–36.
71 Kennedy, *Magic Mountains*, 138.
72 Baly, *Employment of Europeans in India*, 20.
73 Baly, *Employment of Europeans in India*, 19.
74 Kennedy, *Magic Mountains*, 144.
75 "Report on the Progress of Education of European Children."
76 Kennedy, *Magic Mountains*, 8.
77 Farren, *Politics of Irish Education*, 13.
78 Akenson, *Irish Education Experiment*, 253–54.
79 Akenson, *Irish Education Experiment*, 25.
80 Akenson, *Irish Education Experiment*, 384.
81 Akenson, *Irish Education Experiment*, 385.
82 Said, *Orientalism*, 3–7.
83 "Report on the Progress of Education of European Children," ii.
84 "Report on the Progress of Education of European Children," iv.
85 "Report on the Progress of Education of European Children."
86 Akenson, *Irish Education Experiment*, 384.
87 Akenson, *Irish Education Experiment*, 238.
88 Lyons, *Ireland since the Famine*, 89.
89 Akenson, *Irish Education Experiment*, 382.
90 *Third Book of Lessons for the Use of Irish National Schools*, 145.
91 Warner oral history, track 1.
92 Outram oral history, track 6.

93 Gascoyne oral history, track 1.
94 Kennedy, *Magic Mountains*, 118.
95 Fleming, *Head or Harp*, 46.
96 Fleming, *Head or Harp*.
97 Fleming, *Head or Harp*.
98 Fleming, *Head or Harp*.
99 Fleming, *Head or Harp*, 48.
100 Fleming, *Head or Harp*.
101 Lyons, *Ireland since the Famine*, 89.
102 Farren, *Politics of Irish Education*, 50.
103 McDowell, *Crisis and Decline*, 179.
104 Walton oral history, track 4.
105 Maude oral history, track 1; Walton oral history; Hodkinson oral history; Alcock oral history.
106 Hodkinson oral history, track 3.
107 Hodkinson oral history, track 3.
108 Alcock oral history, track 2.
109 MN and MG oral history.
110 Cannadine, *Ornamentalism*, 5–9, 11.
111 Bowen, *Protestants in a Catholic State*, 80–94.
112 Select Committee on Colonization and Settlement, iii.
113 Mizutani, *Meaning of White*, 22.
114 Mizutani, "Rethinking Inclusion and Exclusion," 1.
115 Stoler, "Rethinking Colonial Categories," 139–43.
116 Baly, *Employment of Europeans in India*, 14.
117 Reilly oral history, track 4.
118 MSS EUR T.32 Sir Percival Griffiths 6.
119 Mizutani, "Rethinking Inclusion and Exclusion."
120 "Rethinking Inclusion and Exclusion," 12
121 MSS EUR T.32 Sir Percival Griffiths.
122 MSS EUR T.32 Lady Percival Griffiths.
123 Burnet-Smith oral history, track 6.
124 *Warrant of Precedence in India*, 1–13.
125 *Warrant of Precedence in India*, 14–17.
126 Cannadine, *Ornamentalism*, 43.
127 MSS EUR T.32 Sir Percival Griffiths.
128 Outram oral history, track 2.
129 White, *Minority Report*, 56.
130 Aughey, "What Is Living and What Is Dead in the Ulster Covenant of 1912?"
131 Aughey, "What Is Living and What Is Dead in the Ulster Covenant of 1912?"
132 Fitzpatrick, *Descendancy*, 10.
133 Alcock oral history, track 2.
134 Hodkinson oral history, track 1.

135 Fleming, *Head or Harp*, 63.
136 Fitzpatrick, *Descendancy*, 9–13.

3. ENDINGS AND NEW BEGINNINGS

1 Central Statistics Office, "Census 1926 Reports," www.cso.ie; Delaney, *Democracy, State and Society*, 71.
2 Brown, "India," 423.
3 Cohen, *Global Diasporas*, 67.
4 Kenny, "Diaspora and Comparison," 136.
5 Hickman, "Census Ethnic Categories and Second-Generation Identities."
6 MacRaild, *Irish Diaspora in Britain*, 90.
7 MacRaild, *Irish Diaspora in Britain*, 5.
8 Bielenberg, "Exodus," 202–26.
9 Bielenberg, "Exodus," 227.
10 Brennan, "Political Minefield," 406.
11 Bielenberg, "Exodus," 228–29.
12 Delaney, *Democracy, State and Society*, 95.
13 Moulton, *Ireland and the Irish*, 217.
14 Belchem, *Irish Catholic and Scouse*, xii.
15 Pooley, "Getting to Know the City."
16 Kenny, "Diaspora and Comparison," 136.
17 Miller, *Emigrants and Exiles*.
18 Hart, *IRA and Its Enemies*, 288–91.
19 McDowell, *Crisis and Decline*, 95, 135–36.
20 Fitzpatrick, *Descendancy*, 188.
21 Brennan, "Political Minefield," 407.
22 CO 762/1: Letter from Leo Amery on appointments to Irish Grants Committee.
23 CO 762/212: Report on Irish Grants Committee, 13.
24 CO 762/212: Report on Irish Grants Committee, 13.
25 CO 762/50/776: William Bateman.
26 CO 762/120/2080: Richard Wordsworth Cooper.
27 CO 762/15:170 Lord Ashtown.
28 CO 762/15: Lord Ashtown.
29 CO 762/170/2908: H. L. Stopford.
30 Brown, *Ireland*, 279.
31 Transfer of Power Collection, Mountbatten Papers, 267.
32 Warner oral history; Burnet-Smith oral history.
33 MSS EUR T.17 Lady Sylvia Corfield, 9.
34 MSS EUR T.17 Lady Sylvia Corfield, 9–10.
35 Metcalf, *Ideologies of the Raj*, 28–33.
36 Warner oral history, track 1.
37 Sloan oral history, track 2.
38 Sloan oral history; Perry oral history.

39 Borgonovo, *Spies, Informers*, 180.

40 Passaris, "Immigration and the Evolution of Economic Theory."

41 *Warrant of Precedence in India*, 1–13.

42 Satia, *Time's Monster*, 72–73.

43 James, *Rise and Fall of the British Empire*, 219–22.

44 Metcalf, *Ideologies of the Raj*, 39–41.

45 Brown, "India," 423.

46 Transfer of Power Collection, Indian Independence Act.

47 India Compensation for the Services.

48 "Debates in the Dail," *Weekly Irish Times*, 7 January 1922, 2.

49 Brown, *Ireland*, 119.

50 Bielenberg, "Exodus," 231.

51 Brown, *Ireland*, 37–41.

52 White, *Minority Report*, 97–99.

53 Bowen, *Protestants in a Catholic State*, 16

54 Bowen, *Protestants in a Catholic State*, 92.

55 Moulton, *Ireland and the Irish*, 215.

56 Ferriter, *Transformation of Modern Ireland*, 66.

57 Delaney, *Democracy, State and Society*, 37–38.

58 CO 762/1: Royal Irish Constabulary, Terms of Disbandment

59 Delaney, *Democracy, State and Society*, 37–38.

60 Transfer of Power Collection, Mountbatten Papers, Viceroy's Interview, 165.

61 Transfer of Power Collection, Viceroy's Personal Report No. 13.

62 Transfer of Power Collection, Indian Independence Act, 242.

63 India Compensation for the Services.

64 Gascoyne oral history, track 4.

65 Perry oral history, track 1.

66 MSS EUR T.7 Vere Birdwood, 6/12.

67 Moulton, *Ireland and the Irish*, 217.

68 Moulton, *Ireland and the Irish*, 218.

69 CO 762/212: Report on the Irish Grants Committee 1930.

70 Moulton, *Ireland and the Irish*, 220.

71 Gascoyne oral history, track 7.

72 Gowdey oral history, track 3.

73 Gowdey oral history, track 3.

74 Gascoyne oral history, track 7.

75 Warner oral history, track 3.

76 Gascoyne oral history, track 7.

77 Sloan oral history, track 1.

78 Collis, *Irishman's England*, 15.

79 Pooley, "Getting to Know the City," 220.

80 Fleming, *Head or Harp*, 72.

81 Fleming, *Head or Harp*, 74.

82 Alcock oral history, track 3.

83 Hobsbawm, *Age of Extremes*, 90.

84 Hobsbawm, *Age of Extremes*, 92–93.

85 Orwell, *Road to Wigan Pier*.

86 CO 762/196/ 2168: Francis Henry Pakenham.

87 CO 762/120/2078: Agnes Clarke.

88 CO 762/120/2071: Mrs. B. Meade.

89 CO 762/4/18: Ernest Ince Allen.

90 Paul, *Whitewashing Britain*, 4–5.

91 Kynaston, *Austerity Britain*, 22.

92 Sloan oral history, track 5.

93 Gascoyne oral history, track 8.

94 Outram oral history, track 2.

95 Gowdey oral history, track 4.

96 Sloan oral history, track 5.

97 CO 762/86/1418: James Glynn.

98 CO 762/120/2071: Mrs. B. Meade.

99 Kynaston, *Austerity Britain*, 20.

100 National Archives, "The Cabinet Papers" (n.d.), www.nationalarchives.gov.uk.

101 Powers, *Britain*, 89–95.

102 Warner oral history, track 1.

103 Letter to Niamh Dillon, 23 July 2013.

104 Gascoyne oral history, track 1.

105 Reilly oral history, track 9.

106 Pioneers in Charity and Social Welfare, track 1.

107 Pioneers in Charity and Social Welfare, track 1.

108 Pioneers in Charity and Social Welfare, track 1.

109 Sloan oral history, track 5.

110 Gowdey oral history, track 4.

111 Outram oral history, track 6.

112 Burnet-Smith oral history, track 4.

113 Pooley, "From Londonderry to London," 197.

114 Hodkinson oral history, track 3.

115 Alcock oral history, track 3.

116 Pooley, "From Londonderry to London," 190–91.

117 Brennan, "Political Minefield," 406.

118 Brennan, "Political Minefield," 407.

119 CO 762/212: Report on the Irish Grants Committee, 4.

120 DO 35/343/10159/10: Lunn Memo.

121 Hansard 5 (Commons), vol. 166.

122 CO 762/212: Report on the Irish Grants Committee.

123 CO 905/17: Minutes of First Meeting of Dunedin Committee.

124 Hansard 5 (Commons), 20 February 1928.

125 CO 762/212: Report on the Irish Grants Committee, 38.
126 CO 762/212: Report on the Irish Grants Committee, 13.
127 CO 762/212: Report on the Irish Grants Committee.
128 India Compensation for the Services.
129 India Compensation for the Services.
130 India Compensation for the Services, table 1.
131 Hansard 5 (Commons), vol. 445.
132 Hansard 5 (Commons), vol. 445.
133 Hansard 5 (Commons), vol. 445.
134 Hansard 5 (Commons), vol. 445.
135 Evens, *Public Opinion on Colonial Affairs*, ii.
136 Evens, *Public Opinion on Colonial Affairs*, iii.
137 Evens, *Public Opinion on Colonial Affairs*, iii.
138 Evens, *Public Opinion on Colonial Affairs*, 5.
139 Evens, *Public Opinion on Colonial Affairs*, 10.
140 Evens, *Public Opinion on Colonial Affairs*, 13.
141 Evens, *Public Opinion on Colonial Affairs*, 16.
142 MacKenzie, *Propaganda and Empire*, 1.

4. BRAVE NEW WORLD?

 1 Immigration from the Commonwealth 1965, Cmnd. 2739.
 2 Harper and Constantine, "Immigration and the Heart of Empire," 197.
 3 British Nationality Act 1948, 1.
 4 British Nationality Act 1948, 4.
 5 British Nationality Act 1948, 3.
 6 Parliamentary Session 1947–48.
 7 Parliamentary Session 1947–48.
 8 Parliamentary Session 1947–48.
 9 Paul, *Whitewashing Britain*, 22.
10 Parliamentary Session 1947–48; Hansard 5 (Commons), vol. 454.
11 Hansard 5 (Commons), vol. 454.
12 Hansard 5 (Commons), vol. 454.
13 Hansard 5 (Commons), vol. 454.
14 British Nationality Bill, 13 July 1948.
15 British Nationality Bill, 7 July 1948.
16 British Nationality Bill, 19 July 1948.
17 Paul, *Whitewashing Britain*, 6–9.
18 Paul, *Whitewashing Britain*, 76–82.
19 Paul, *Whitewashing Britain*, 123.
20 Webster, *Imagining Home*, 25.
21 Harper and Constantine, "Immigration and the Heart of Empire," 202.
22 Gilroy, *Black Teacher*.

23 Harper and Constantine, "Immigration and the Heart of Empire," 203; Hodkinson oral history; Elmes oral history.
24 Curtis, *Apes and Angels*; De Nie, *Eternal Paddy*.
25 Beddoe, *Races of Britain*, 149.
26 Moulton, *Ireland and the Irish*, 292.
27 Moulton, *Ireland and the Irish*, 294.
28 Mohanram, *Imperial White*, 152.
29 Conekin, *Autobiography of a Nation*, 2.
30 Turner, *Beacon for Change*, 11.
31 Bowyer oral history, track 6.
32 Rennie, *Festival of Britain*, 19.
33 Powers, *Britain*, 13.
34 Johnston, "Ernö Goldfinger at Open House 2019."
35 Grindrod, *Concretopia*, 80–86.
36 Rennie, *Festival of Britain*, 32.
37 Cox, *South Bank Exhibition*.
38 Conekin, *Autobiography of a Nation*, 12.
39 Rennie, *Festival of Britain*, 41.
40 Rennie, *Festival of Britain*, 41.
41 Morrison oral history, track 11.
42 Games, Moriarty, and Rose, *Abram Games Graphic Designer*, 75–77.
43 Pugh, *We Danced All Night*, 400–402.
44 Conekin, *Autobiography of a Nation*, 3.
45 Conekin, *Autobiography of a Nation*, 3.
46 Leaders of National Life.
47 Conekin, *Autobiography of a Nation*, 4–6.
48 Conekin, *Autobiography of a Nation*, 8.
49 Conekin, *Autobiography of a Nation*, 8–10.
50 Turner, *Beacon for Change*, 56.
51 Turner, *Beacon for Change*, 56.
52 Rennie, *Festival of Britain*, 35.
53 Turner, *Beacon for Change*, 226.
54 Knight, *A Queen Is Crowned*.
55 Knight, *A Queen Is Crowned*.
56 Rutherford, *After Identity*, 43.
57 Rutherford, *After Identity*.
58 Knight, *A Queen Is Crowned*.
59 Knight, *A Queen Is Crowned*.
60 Webster, *Imagining Home*, 93.
61 Webster, *Imagining Home*, 93.
62 Webster, *Imagining Home*, 102.
63 Festival of Britain Office, *Festival of Britain*, 15.

64 Festival of Britain Office, *Festival of Britain*, 17.
65 Sloan oral history, track 5.
66 Webster, *Imagining Home*, 6.
67 Sloan oral history, track 5.
68 Leaders of National Life.
69 Sloan oral history, track 5.
70 Gowdey oral history, track 5.
71 Sloan oral history, track 5.
72 Burnet-Smith oral history, track 2.
73 Warner oral history, track 3.
74 Burnet-Smith oral history, track 7.
75 Burnet-Smith oral history, track 2.
76 Interviewees' views of Mountbatten ranged from disappointment to despair: Sloan, Gowdey, Reilly, Perry, Burnet-Smith oral histories.
77 British Nationality Bill, 19 July 1948.
78 Cannadine, *Ornamentalism*, 45.
79 Perry oral history, track 2.
80 Gowdey oral history, track 5.
81 Carver, oral history, track 2.
82 Warner oral history.
83 Warner oral history.
84 Sloan oral history, track 3.
85 Burnet-Smith oral history, track 7.
86 Sloan oral history, track 5.
87 Walton oral history, track 8.
88 Paul, *Whitewashing Britain*, 132.
89 Delaney, *Demography, State and Society*, 165.
90 Harper and Constantine, "Immigration and the Heart of Empire," 186.
91 Harper and Constantine, "Immigration and the Heart of Empire," 180.
92 Harper and Constantine, "Immigration and the Heart of Empire," 181.
93 Paul, *Whitewashing Britain*, 66.
94 Commonwealth Immigrants Act, 1–2.
95 Commonwealth Immigrants Act, 3.
96 Commonwealth Immigrants Act, 3–4.
97 Commonwealth Immigrants Act, 3.
98 Commonwealth Immigrants Act, 6–10.
99 Commonwealth Immigrants Act, 12.
100 Paul, *Whitewashing Britain*, 106.
101 Hickman, *Religion, Class and Identity*; Moulton, *Ireland and the Irish*, 274–76.
102 Moulton, *Ireland and the Irish*, 274–75.
103 Hansard 5 (Commons), vol. 653.
104 Hansard 5 (Commons), vol. 653.
105 Hansard 5 (Commons), vol. 653.

106 Hansard 5 (Commons), vol. 653.

107 Hansard 5 (Commons), vol. 653.

108 Hall, *Cultures of Empire*, 2.

109 Hodkinson oral history, track 3.

110 Gowdey oral history, track 6.

111 Burnet-Smith oral history, track 3.

112 Burnet-Smith oral history, track 3.

113 Peter Walton oral history, track 8.

114 Oral history.

115 Oral history.

116 British Nationality Act 1948, 4.

117 Oral history.

118 Oral history.

119 Burnet-Smith oral history, track 2.

5. TWILIGHT OF EMPIRE

1 Lunn, "Reconsidering 'Britishness,'" 83–84.

2 Thompson, "Introduction," 18.

3 Paul, *Whitewashing Britain*, 1.

4 Heinlein, *British Government Policy and Decolonization*,. 20.

5 Whiting, "Empire and British Politics," 181.

6 Whiting, "Empire and British Politics," 162.

7 Alcock oral history, track 3.

8 Alcock oral history, track 3.

9 Alcock oral history, track 3.

10 Burnet-Smith oral history, track 7.

11 Walton oral history, track 7.

12 Reilly oral history, Track 3.

13 "A Student of Politics," "Return to Eden," *Sunday Times*, 9 December 1956, 9.

14 "Heavy Costs of Crisis," *Daily Mail*, 11 October 1956, 8.

15 "British Role in Europe Vital," *The Times*, 26 September 1956.

16 "Parliament Meeting Today; Critical Survey of Policy," *The Times*, 12 September 1956, 8.

17 "Life amid the Mau Mau," *Sunday Times*, 14 December 1952, 6.

18 "Mau Mau—'The Terror by Night,'" *Sunday Times*, 27 September 1953, 4.

19 Graham Greene, "Mau Mau, the Black God," *Sunday Times*, 4 October 1953, 4.

20 Greene, "Mau Mau," 4.

21 Burnet-Smith oral history, track 6.

22 Warner oral history, track 3.

23 Chaudhuri, "Memsahibs and Their Servants in Nineteenth-Century India," 555.

24 Hall, "Cultural Identity and Diaspora," 222.

25 Hall, "Cultural Identity and Diaspora," 225.

26 Hall, "Cultural Identity and Diaspora," 225.

27 Maude oral history, track 1.
28 Walton oral history, track 7.
29 Walton oral history, track 7.
30 Hodkinson oral history, track 3.
31 Hodkinson oral history, track 3.
32 Hodkinson oral history, track 3.
33 Pooley, "From Londonderry to London," 207.
34 Alcock oral history, track 2.
35 Alcock oral history, track 2.
36 Alcock oral history, track 3.
37 Outram oral history, track 2.
38 Outram oral history, track 2.
39 Gascoyne oral history, track 8.
40 Reilly oral history, track 9.
41 Reilly oral history, track 9.
42 Gowdey oral history, track 6.
43 Portelli, "What Makes Oral History Different?," 33–36.
44 Maude oral history, track 1.
45 Maude oral history, track 1.
46 Maude oral history, track 1.
47 Perry oral history, track 2.
48 Burnet-Smith oral history, track 2.
49 Gowdey oral history, track 1.
50 Gowdey oral history, track 1.
51 Burnet-Smith oral history, track 2.
52 Outram, oral history, track 3.
53 Blunt, *Domicile and Diaspora*, 108.
54 Fayrer, *European Child-Life in Bengal*; Steel and Gardiner, *Complete Indian House-keeper and Cook*.
55 Blunt, *Domicile and Diaspora*.
56 Blunt, *Domicile and Diaspora*, 105.
57 Blunt, *Domicile and Diaspora*, 137.
58 Rutherford, "Third Space," 211.
59 Rutherford, "Third Space."
60 Hodkinson oral history, tracks 1–5.
61 Gascoyne oral history, track 8.
62 Gascoyne oral history, track 8.
63 Reilly oral history, track 3.
64 Reilly oral history, track 9.

BIBLIOGRAPHY

Akenson, Donald H. *The Irish Education Experiment: The National System of Education in the Nineteenth Century*. London: Routledge & Kegan Paul, 1970.

Anderson, Benedict. *Imagined Communities*. 2nd ed. London: Verso, 1983.

Anderson, Kathryn, and Dana C. Jack. "Learning to Listen: Interview Techniques and Analyses." In *The Oral History Reader*, edited by Robert Perks and Alistair Thomson, 129–43. London: Routledge, 2006.

Ashcroft, Richard T., and Mark Bevir. "British Multiculturalism after Empire: Immigration, Nationality, and Citizenship." In *Multiculturalism in the British Commonwealth: Comparative Perspectives on Theory and Practice*, edited by Richard T. Ashcroft and Mark Bevir, 25–45. Oakland: University of California Press, 2019.

Aughey, Arthur. "What Is Living and What Is Dead in the Ulster Covenant of 1912?" Paper presented at the Conference on the Ulster Covenant 1912–2012, Kings College London, 6–7 September 2012.

Baly, J. *The Employment of Europeans in India*. Calcutta: Bengal Science Association, 1879.

Beddoe, John. *The Races of Britain: A Contribution to the Anthropology of Western Europe*. London: Hutchinson, 1885. Reprint, 1971.

Belchem, John. *Irish Catholic and Scouse: The History of the Liverpool Irish 1800–1940*. Liverpool: Liverpool University Press, 2007.

Bew, Paul. *Ideology and the Irish Question: Ulster Unionism and Irish Nationalism 1912–1916*. Oxford: Clarendon, 1994.

Bielenberg, Andy. "Exodus: The Emigration of Southern Irish Protestants during the Irish War of Independence and the Civil War." *Past and Present*, no. 218 (February 2013): 202–26.

Billings, Mathieu W., and Sean Farrell. *The Irish in Illinois*. Carbondale: Southern Illinois University Press, 2020.

Blunt, Alison. *Domicile and Diaspora: Anglo Indian Women and the Spatial Politics of Home*. Malden, MA: Blackwell, 2005.

Blunt, Alison, and Robyn Dowling. *Home*. London: Routledge, 2006.

Borgonovo, John. *Spies, Informers and the "Anti–Sinn Fein Society": The Intelligence War in Cork City 1920–1921*. Dublin: Irish Academic Press, 2007.

Bornat, Joanna. "Remembering and Reworking Emotions: The Reanalysis of Emotion in an Interview." *Oral History* 38, no. 2 (2010): 43–52.

Bowen, Elizabeth. *Bowen's Court and Seven Winters*. London: Vintage, 1999.

———. *The Last September*. London: Vintage, 1998.

Bowen, Kurt. *Protestants in a Catholic State: Ireland's Privileged Minority*. Montreal: McGill-Queen's University Press, 1983.

Brah, Avtah. *Cartographies of Diaspora*. London: Routledge, 1996.

Bratton, J. S. *The Impact of Victorian Children's Fiction*. London: Routledge, 1981. Reprint, 2016.

Brennan, Niamh. "A Political Minefield: Southern Loyalists, the Irish Grants Committee and the British Government, 1922–21." *Irish Historical Studies* 119 (May 1997): 406–19.

Brown, Judith M. "India." In *The Oxford History of the British Empire:* Vol. 4: *The Twentieth Century*, edited by Wm. Roger Louis and Judith M. Brown, 421–46. Oxford: Oxford University Press, 1999.

Brown, Terence. *Ireland: A Social and Cultural History 1922–2002*. London: Harper, 2004.

Buckland, Patrick. *Irish Unionism*. London: Historical Association, 1973.

Buettner, Elizabeth. *Empire Families: Britons and Late Imperial India*. Oxford: Oxford University Press, 2004.

Bury, Robin. *Buried Lives: The Protestants of Southern Ireland*. Stroud: History Press, 2017.

Cannadine, David. *Ornamentalism: How the British Saw Their Empire*. London: Allen Lane, 2001.

Casey, Sean O. *The Silver Tassie*. London: Macmillan, 1928.

Castle, Kathryn. "Imperial Legacies, New Frontiers: Children's Popular Literature and the Demise of Empire." In *British Culture and the End of Empire*, edited by Stuart Ward, 145–62. Manchester: Manchester University Press, 2001.

Chatterji, Joya, and Claire Alexander. *The Bengal Diaspora*. London: Routledge, 2015.

Chatterji, Joya, and David Washbrook. *Routledge Handbook of the South Asian Diaspora*. London: Routledge, 2013.

Chaudhuri, Nurpur. "Memsahibs and Their Servants in Nineteenth-Century India." *Women's History Review* 3, no. 4 (1994): 549–62.

Chowdhury, Amitava. "Between Dispersion and Belonging: At Home in the Diaspora." In *Between Dispersion and Belonging: Global Approaches to Diaspora in Practice*, edited by Amitava Chowdhury and Donald H. Akenson. Montreal: McGill-Queen's University Press, 2016.

Claeys, Gregory. "The 'Survival of the Fittest' and the Origins of Social Darwinism." *Journal of the History of Ideas* 61, no. 2 (2000): 223–40.

Clarke, A. K. *A History of the Cheltenham Ladies College: 1853–1979*. Suffolk: John Catt Limited, 1979.

Cohen, Robin. *Global Diasporas: An Introduction*. London: University College Press, 1997.

Cohen, Robin, and Carolin Fischer, eds. *The Routledge Handbook of Diaspora Studies*. London: Routledge, 2019.

Cohn, Bernard S. *Colonialism and Its Forms of Knowledge*. Princeton, NJ: Princeton University Press, 1996.

Colley, Linda. *Britons: Forging the Nation 1707–1837*. New Haven, CT: Yale University Press, 2005.

Collingham, E. M. *Imperial Bodies: The Physical Experience of the Raj c1800–1947*. Cambridge: Polity, 2001.

Collis, John Stewart. *An Irishman's England.* London: Cassell & Company, 1937.

Conekin, Becky E. *The Autobiography of a Nation: The 1951 Festival of Britain.* London: Festival Publications, 1951.

Cornell, Stephen, and Douglas Hartman. *Ethnicity and Race: Making Identities in a Changing World.* Thousand Oaks, CA: Pine Forge Press, 2007.

Cox, Ian. *The South Bank Exhibition: A Guide to the Story It Tells.* London: HMSO, 1951.

Crawford, Heather. "Southern Irish Protestants and 'Irishness.'" *Oral History* 39 (2011): 53–64.

Crosbie, Barry. "Ireland, Colonial Science, and the Geographical Construction of British Rule in India, c. 1820–1870." *Historical Journal* 52, no. 4 (2009): 963–87.

Curtis, L. P. *Apes and Angels: The Irishman in Victorian Caricature.* Washington, DC: Smithsonian Institution Press, 1997.

Dalrymple, William. *White Mughals: Love and Betrayal in Eighteenth-Century India.* London: HarperCollins, 2002.

d'Alton, Ian, and Ida Milne, eds. *Protestant and Irish: The Minority's Search for Place in Independent Ireland.* Cork: Cork University Press, 2019.

Darwin, John. *Unfinished Empire: The Global Expansion of Britain.* New York: Bloomsbury, 2012.

Davidoff, Leonore, and Catherine Hall. *Family Fortunes: Men and Women of the English Middle Class 1780–1850.* London: Routledge, 1994.

Davin, Anna. "Imperialism and Motherhood." *History Workshop*, no. 5 (Spring 1978): 9–65.

Day-Lewis, Cecil. *The Buried Day.* London: Chatto and Windus, 1960.

Delaney, Enda. *Demography, State and Society: Irish Migration to Britain, 1921–1971.* Liverpool: Liverpool University Press, 2000.

De Nie, Michael. *The Eternal Paddy: Irish Identity and the British Press 1798–1882.* Madison: University of Wisconsin Press, 2004.

Dillon, Niamh. "Ernö Goldfinger at Open House 2019." *Sound and Vision Blog*, 18 September 2019. https://blogs.bl.uk/sound-and-vision.

Evens, G. K. *Public Opinion on Colonial Affairs.* London: NS. 119, June 1948.

Farren, Sean. *The Politics of Irish Education 1920–65.* Belfast: University of Belfast Institute of Irish Studies, 1995.

Fayrer, Sir Joseph. *European Child-Life in Bengal.* London, 1873.

Ferriter, Diarmaid. *A Nation and Not a Rabble: The Irish Revolution 1913–23.* London: Profile Books, 2015.

———. *The Transformation of Modern Ireland 1900–2000.* London: Profile Books, 2005.

Festival of Britain Office. *The Festival of Britain 1951.* London: Festival of Britain Office, 1951.

Finnegan, Ruth. "Family Myths, Memories and Interviewing." In *The Oral History Reader*, edited by Robert Perks and Alistair Thomson, 177–84. London: Routledge, 2006.

Fitzpatrick, David. *Descendancy: Irish Protestant Histories since 1795.* Cambridge: Cambridge University Press, 2014.

Fleming, Lionel. *Head or Harp*. London: Barrie and Rockliffe, 1965.

Foster, R. F. *Paddy and Mr Punch: Connections in Irish and English History*. London: Allen Lane, 1993.

———. "The Protestant Accent." In *Protestant and Irish: The Minority's Search for Place in Independent Ireland*, edited by Ian d'Alton and Ida Milne, xxi–xxiv. Cork: Cork University Press, 2019.

———. *Vivid Faces: The Revolutionary Generation in Ireland 1890–1923*. London: Penguin, 2015.

Fussell, Elizabeth. "Space, Time and Volition: Dimensions of Migration Theory." In *The Oxford Handbook of the Politics of International Migration*, edited by Marc R. Rosenblum and Daniel J. Tichenor, 25–52. Oxford: Oxford University Press, 2012.

Games, Naomi, Catherine Moriarty, and June Rose. *Abram Games Graphic Designer: Maximum Meaning, Minimum Means*. Aldershot: Lund Humphries, 2003.

George, Rosemary Marangoly. "Homes in the Empire, Empires in the Home." *Cultural Critique* 26 (1993–94): 95–127.

Gilroy, Beryl. *Black Teacher*. London: Bogle-L'Ouverture, 1994.

Gleeson, David T. "Emigrants and Exiles: The Political Nationalism of the Irish Diaspora since the 1790s." In MacRaild, Bueltmann, and Clark, *British and Irish Diasporas*.

Godber, Joyce. *The Harpur Trust 1552–1973*. Bedford: Harpur Trust, 1973.

Great Public Schools. London: Edward Arnold, 1892.

Grindrod, John. *Concretopia: A Journey Around the Rebuilding of Postwar Britain*. London: Old Street Publishing, 2013.

Hall, Catherine, ed. *Cultures of Empire: Colonizers in Britain and the Empire in the Nineteenth and Twentieth Centuries. A Reader*. Manchester: Manchester University Press, 2000.

Hall, Catherine, and Sonya O. Rose. *At Home with the Empire: Metropolitan Culture and the Imperial World*. Cambridge: Cambridge University Press, 2006.

Hall, Stuart. "Cultural Identity and Diaspora." In *Identity, Community, Culture, Difference*, edited by Jonathan Rutherford, 222–38. London: Lawrence and Wishart, 1990.

Harding, Jenny. "Talk about Care: Emotions, Culture and Oral History." *Oral History* 38, no. 2 (2010): 33–42.

Harding, Jenny, and Deidre Pribram. *Emotions: A Cultural Studies Reader*. London: Routledge, 2009.

Harper, Marjorie, and Stephen Constantine. "Immigration and the Heart of Empire." In *Migration and Empire*, 180–211. Oxford: Oxford University Press, 2014.

Harrison, Mark. *Climate and Constitutions: Health, Race, Environment, and British Imperialism in India 1600–1850*. Oxford: Oxford University Press, 2002.

Hart, Peter. *The IRA and Its Enemies: Violence and Community in Cork, 1916–1923*. Oxford: Oxford University Press, 1998.

Heathorn, Stephen J. *For Home, Country and Race: Constructing Gender, Class and Englishness in the Elementary School, 1880–1914*. Toronto: University of Toronto Press, 2000.

Heinlein, Frank. *British Government Policy and Decolonization 1945–1963*. London: Frank Cass, 2002.

Hickman, Mary J. "Census Ethnic Categories and Second-Generation Identities: A Study of the Irish in England and Wales." *Journal of Ethnic and Migration Studies* 37, no. 1 (2011): 79–97.

———. *Religion, Class and Identity: The State, the Catholic Church and the Education of the Irish in Britain*. Aldershot: Avebury, 1995.

Hickman, Mary, et al. "The Limitations of Whiteness and the Boundaries of Englishness: Second-Generation Irish Identifications and Positionings in Multi-ethnic Britain." *Ethnicities* 5 (2005): 160–82.

Hobsbawm, Eric. *Age of Extremes: The Short Twentieth Century 1914–1991*. London: Michael Joseph, 1994.

Hoirns, Sara. "Crying in the Archive: The Story of Diana Bromley." *History of Emotions Blog*, 21 December 2015. https://emotionsblog.history.qmul.ac.uk/2015/12/crying-in-the-archive-the-story-of-diana-bromley/.

Howe, Stephen. *The New Imperial Histories Reader*. London: Routledge, 2010.

Institute of Historical Research. "Oral History Spring School." 25–27 April 2013.

James, Lawrence. *The Rise and Fall of the British Empire*. London: Abacus, 2008.

Jeffrey, Keith. *"An Irish Empire?" Aspects of Ireland and the British Empire*. Manchester: Manchester University Press, 1996.

Kennedy, Dane. *The Magic Mountains: Hill Stations and the British Raj*. Berkeley: University of California Press, 1996.

Kenny, Kevin. "Diaspora and Comparison: The Global Irish as a Test Case." *Journal of American History* 90, no. 1 (June 2003): 134–62.

———. "Irish Emigrations in a Comparative Perspective." In *The Cambridge Social History of Modern Ireland*, edited by Eugenio F. Biagini and Mary E. Daly, 405–22. Cambridge: Cambridge University Press, 2017.

Knight, Castleton. *A Queen Is Crowned*. Rank Organisation, 1953. DVD.

Kynaston, David. *Austerity Britain: 1945–51*. London: Bloomsbury, 2007.

———. "Uncovering the Unspoken: Memory and Post-war Britain." National Life Stories Annual Lecture, British Library, February 2017.

Lester, Alan. *Imperial Networks: Creating Identities in Nineteenth-Century South Africa and Britain*. London: Routledge, 2001.

Levine, Philippa. "Sexuality, Gender and Empire." In *Gender and Empire*, edited by Philippa Levine, 134–55. Oxford: Oxford University Press, 2004.

Lunn, Kenneth. "Reconsidering 'Britishness': The Construction and Significance of National Identity in Twentieth-Century Britain." In *Nation and Identity in Contemporary Europe*, edited by Brian Jenkins and Spyros A. Sofos, 83–101. London: Routledge, 2007.

Lyons, F. S. L. *Ireland since the Famine*. London: Weidenfeld & Nicolson, 1971.

MacKenzie, John M. *Propaganda and Empire: The Manipulation of British Public Opinion, 1880–1960*. Manchester: Manchester University Press, 1984.

MacRaild, Donald M. *The Irish Diaspora in Britain 1750–1939.* Basingstoke: Palgrave Macmillan, 2011.

MacRaild, Donald, Tanja Bueltmann, and J. C. D. Clark, eds. *British and Irish Diasporas: Societies, Cultures and Ideologies.* Manchester: Manchester University Press, 2019.

Mangan, J. A. *Athleticism in the Victorian and Edwardian Public School: The Emergence and Consolidation of an Educational Ideology.* Cambridge: Cambridge University Press, 1981.

McDowell, R. B. *Crisis and Decline: The Fate of the Southern Unionists.* Dublin: Lilliput Press, 1997.

Metcalf, Thomas R. *Ideologies of the Raj.* Cambridge: Cambridge University Press, 1995.

Miller, Kerby A. *Emigrants and Exiles: Ireland and the Irish Exodus to North America.* Oxford: Oxford University Press, 1985.

Mitchel, John. *The Last Conquest of Ireland (Perhaps).* Dublin: University College Dublin Press, 2005.

Mizutani, Satoshi. *The Meaning of White: Race, Class and the Domiciled Community in British India 1858–1930.* Oxford: Oxford University Press, 2011.

———. "Rethinking Inclusion and Exclusion: The Question of Mixed-Race Presence in Late Colonial India." *University of Sussex Journal of Contemporary History*, no. 5 (2002): 1–22.

Mohanram, Radhika. *Imperial White: Race, Diaspora and the British Empire.* Minneapolis: University of Minnesota Press, 2007.

Moulton, Mo. *Ireland and the Irish in Interwar Britain.* Cambridge: Cambridge University Press, 2014.

Orwell, George. *The Road to Wigan Pier.* 1936. Reprint, London: Penguin, 2001.

O'Sullivan, Patrick. *The Irish World Wide.* Leicester: Leicester University Press, 1996.

Passaris, C. "Immigration and the Evolution of Economic Theory." *International Migration* 27, no. 4 (1989): 525–42.

Paul, Kathleen. *Whitewashing Britain: Race and Citizenship in the Postwar Era.* Ithaca, NY: Cornell University Press, 1997.

Perks, Rob Perks. "'Corporations Are People Too!' Business and Corporate Oral History in Britain." *Oral History* 38 (Spring 2010): 36–54.

Plamper, Jan. *A History of Emotions.* Oxford: Oxford University Press, 2017.

Pooley, Colin G. "From Londonderry to London: Identity and a Sense of Place for a Protestant Northern Irish Woman in the 1930s." In *The Great Famine and Beyond: Irish Migrants in Britain in the Nineteenth and Twentieth Centuries*, edited by Donald M. MacRaild, 189–213. Dublin: Irish Academic Press, 2000.

———. "Getting to Know the City: The Construction of Spatial Knowledge in London in the 1930s." *Urban History* 31 (2004): 210–27.

Popular Memory Group. "Popular Memory, Theory, Politics, Method." In *The Oral History Reader*, edited by Robert Perks and Alistair Thomson, 43–53. London: Routledge, 2006.

Portelli, Alessandro. "What Makes Oral History Different?" In *The Oral History Reader*, edited by Robert Perks and Alistair Thomson, 32–43. London: Routledge, 2006.

Potter, Simon J. "Empire, Cultures and Identities in Nineteenth and Twentieth-Century Britain." *History Compass* 5, no. 1 (2007): 51–71.

Powers, Alan. *Britain: Modern Architectures in History*. London: Reaktion Books, 2007.

Procida, Mary A. "Good Sports and Right Sorts: Guns, Gender and Imperialism in British India." *Journal of British Studies* 40, no. 4 (2001): 454–88.

Pugh, Martin. *We Danced All Night: A Social History of Britain between the Wars*. London: Vintage, 2009.

Rennie, Paul. *Festival of Britain: Design 1951*. Woodbridge: Antique Collectors Club, 2007.

Robinson, Lennox. *The Big House*. London: Macmillan, 1928.

Rutherford, Jonathan. *After Identity*. London: Lawrence and Wishart, 2007.

———. "The Third Space: Interview with Homi Bhahba." In *Identity, Community, Culture, Difference*, edited by Jonathan Rutherford, 207–21. London: Lawrence and Wishart, 2007.

Ryan, Louise, and Wendy Webster. *Gendering Migration: Masculinity, Femininity and Ethnicity in Postwar Migration to Britain*. Aldershot: Ashgate, 2008.

Safran, William. "Diasporas in Modern Societies: Myths of Homeland and Return." *Diaspora: A Journal of Transnational Studies* 1, no. 1 (Spring 1991): 83–99.

Said, Edward W. *Orientalism*. London: Penguin, 2003.

Satia, Priya. *Time's Monster: History, Conscience and Britain's Empire*. London: Penguin, 2020.

Schwarz, Bill. *Memories of Empire: The White Man's World*. Oxford: Oxford University Press, 2011.

Seeley, J. R. *Expansion of England*. London: Macmillan, 1888.

Steel, Flora Annie, and Grace Gardiner. *The Complete Indian Housekeeper and Cook*. 1904. Reprint, Oxford: Oxford University Press, 2011.

Stoler, Ann. "Rethinking Colonial Categories: European Communities and the Boundaries of Rule." *Comparative Studies in Society and History* 31, no. (1 January 1989): 134–61.

Strong, Roy. *Visions of England*. London: Bodley Head, 2011.

Taylor, Paul. *Heroes or Traitors? Experiences of Southern Irish Soldiers Returning from the Great War 1919–1939*. Liverpool: Liverpool University Press, 2015.

Third Book of Lessons for the Use of Irish National Schools. Glasgow: William Collins, 1870.

Thompson, Andrew. "Introduction." In *Britain's Experience of Empire in the Twentieth Century*, edited by Andrew Thompson, 1–32. Oxford: Oxford University Press, 2016.

Thompson, Paul, with Joanna Bornat. *The Voice of the Past*. Oxford: Oxford University Press, 2000.

Thomson, Alistair. "Indexing and Interpreting Emotion: Joy and Shame in Oral History." *Oral History Australia Journal*, no. 41 (2019): 1–12.

Trew, Johanne Devlin. *Leaving the North: Migration and Memory, Northern Ireland 1921–2011*. Liverpool: Liverpool University Press, 2013.

Turner, Barry. *Beacon for Change: How the Festival of Britain Shaped the Modern Age*. London: Aurum Press, 2011.

Urquhart, Diane. "Unity of Unionism: Women and the Third Home Rule Crisis." Paper presented at the Ulster Covenant 1912–2012 Conference, 7 September 2012.

Walsh, Patrick. "'Paltry Abridgements': School Texts and Teaching History in Nineteenth-Century India and Ireland." In *Irish Classrooms and British Empire: Imperial Contexts in the Origin of Modern Education*, edited by David Dickson, Justyna Pyz, and Christopher Shepard, 53–61. Dublin: Four Courts Press, 2012.

Warrant of Precedence in India. Allahabad: Government Press, United Provinces, 1921.

Webster, Wendy. *Englishness and Empire: 1939–65*. Oxford: Oxford University Press, 2005.

———. *Imagining Home: Gender, "Race" and National Identity, 1945–64*. London: UCL Press, 1998.

White, Jack. *Minority Report: The Anatomy of the Southern Irish Protestant*. Dublin: Gill and Macmillan, 1975.

Whiting, Richard. "The Empire and British Politics." In *Britain's Experience of Empire in the Twentieth Century*, edited by Andrew Thompson, 161–210. Oxford: Oxford University Press, 2016.

Wilson, Tim. "Ghost Provinces, Mislaid Minorities: The Experience of Southern Ireland and Prussian Poland Compared, 1918–23." *Irish Studies in International Affairs* 13 (2002): 61–86.

ORAL HISTORY INTERVIEWS
The British Library, London, The British Diaspora, Recorded by Niamh Dillon

Alcock, Ron. C1508/2. Born in Dublin in 1938. Tracks 1–3. Recorded 5 July, 16 July, 14 September 2012.

Burnet-Smith, Wallace. C1508/4. Born in Calcutta in 1922. Tracks 1–7. Recorded 20 October 2012, 1–2 February 2013.

Carver, Elizabeth. C1508/11. Born in Bombay in 1943. Tracks 1–2. Recorded 1 August 2013.

Elmes, Sue. C1508/6. Born Dublin in 1940. Tracks 1–2. Recorded 17 October 2012.

Gascoyne, Betty. C1508/10. Born in Jubbulpore, India in 1925. Tracks 1–8. Recorded 25 June, 16 July, 10 December 2013.

Giles, Charles. C1508/12. Born in the Lake District, England in 1932. Tracks 1–4. Recorded 10 September, 16 October 2013.

Gowdey, Jill. C1508/7. Born in Lichfield, England in 1930. Tracks 1–6. Recorded 11–12 March 2013.

Hodkinson, Anne. C1508/14. Born in Dublin in 1941. Tracks 1–5. Recorded on 21 November 2014, 10 February 2015.

Maude, Robert. C1508/3. Born in Dublin in 1929. Track 1. Recorded 12 July 2012.

Perry, Verna. C1508/13. Born in Dartford in Kent in 1939. Tracks 1–3. Recorded on 4 February, 14 March 2014.

Reilly, Paddy. C1508/9. Born in India in 1927. Tracks 1–9. Recorded 18 June, 11 October, 16 November 2013.

Sloan, Sue. C1508/8. Born in Quetta in 1934. Tracks 1–5. Recorded 16 April, 9 May, 24 May 2013.

Walton, Peter. C1508/5. Born in 1939 in north Wales. Tracks 1–12. Recorded 13 November, 27 November 2012, 21 February 2013.

Warner, Mollie. C1508/1. Born in 1913 in Jhansi, India. Tracks 1–3. Recorded 15–16 June 2012.

The British Library, London, Architects' Lives, Recorded by Niamh Dillon
Bowyer, Gordon. C467/109. Born in Twickenham in 1923. Tracks 1–10. Recorded 2013.
Epstein, Gabriel. C467. Born in Duisberg, Germany in 1918. Tracks 1–7. Recorded 24–26 September 2009.
Hunt, Tony. C467/135. Born in London in 1932. Tracks 1–35. Recorded 2016–17.
Jones, Edward. C467/98. Born in Hertfordshire in 1939. Tracks 1–11. Recorded 2011–12.
Morrison, Graham. C467/139. Born in Kilmarnock in Scotland in 1951. Tracks 1–17. Recorded 2017–19.
Outram, John. C467/86. Born in Malaya in 1934. Tracks 1–27. Recorded 2007–8.

The British Library, London
Leaders of National Life. Reference C408/016/F1089-Transcript. Interview with Hugh Casson. Recorded by Cathy Courtney.
Pioneers in Charity and Social Welfare. Reference C1155/01. Interview with Olive Stevenson. Recorded by Niamh Dillon. Tracks 1–29. 2004–5.
Pioneers in Qualitative Research. Ruth Finnegan. Recorded by Paul Thompson.

MANUSCRIPTS AND PAPERS IN ARCHIVE COLLECTIONS
The British Library, London
PLAIN TALES FROM THE RAJ
MSS EUR R 7. T.7. Vere Birdwood.
MSS EUR R 55. T.4. Colonel Rivett Carnac.
MSS EUR R 11. T.11. 105. T. George Carroll.
MSS EUR R 17. T.17. Lady Sylvia Corfield.
MSS EUR R 28. T.28. Lady Deborah Dring.
MSS EUR R 29. T.20. Irene Edwards.
MSS EUR R 32 T.32. Lady Kathleen Griffiths.
MSS EUR R 31 T.31. Sir Percival Griffiths.
British Nationality Act 1948. Northern Rhodesia: Government Printer, Lusaka, 1949.
British Nationality Bill, 13 July 1948.
British Nationality Bill, 19 July 1948.
Commonwealth Immigrants Act 1962. HMSO.
Immigration from the Commonwealth 1965. Cmnd. 2739. HMSO.
Conekin, Becky E. *The Autobiography of a Nation: The 1951 Festival of Britain*. London: Festival Publications, 1951.
Evens, G. K. *Public Opinion on Colonial Affairs*. London: NS. 119.
Festival of Britain Office. *The Festival of Britain 1951*. London: Festival of Britain Office, 1951.
Hansard 5 (Commons), 20 February 1928.
Hansard 5 (Commons), vol. 166. 16 July 1923.

Hansard 5 (Commons), vol. 445. India and Pakistan, 11 December 1947.

Hansard 5 (Commons), vol. 454. British Nationality Bill, 19 July 1948.

Hansard 5 (Commons), vol. 653. Commonwealth Immigrants Bill, 6 February 1962.

India Compensation for the Services, CMD 7116, April 1947, table 2. June 1948.

Parliamentary Session 1947–48, 7 July 1948, British Nationality Bill, Second Reading.

"Report on the Progress of Education in European Schools in Bengal: During the Quinquennium 1917–19—1921–1922." Calcutta: Bengal Secretariat Book Depot, 1923.

"Report on the Progress of Education of European Children during the Quinquennium 1912–13—1916–17." Calcutta: Bengal Secretariat Book Depot, 1923.

Select Committee on Colonization and Settlement (India). London: House of Commons, 23 July 1858.

Transfer of Power Collection. Indian Independence Act. 1947. L/P & J/10/124: ff 2–12.

Transfer of Power Collection. Mountbatten Papers. 267. 29 July 1947.

Transfer of Power Collection. Mountbatten Papers. Viceroy's Interview No. 116 (Doc 1130).

Transfer of Power Collection. Viceroy's Personal Report No. 13. L/Po/6/123: ff 182–89. 18 July 1947.

Warrant of Precedence in India. Allahabad: Government Press, United Provinces, 1921.

NEWSPAPER ARCHIVE

Church of Ireland Gazette
Daily Mail
The Economist
Irish Independent
Irish Times
Sunday Times
The Times
Weekly Irish Times

The National Archives, Kew
IRISH GRANTS COMMITTEE

CO 762/1: Royal Irish Constabulary, Terms of Disbandment.

CO 762/1: Letter from Leo Amery appointing members to the Irish Grants Committee.

CO 762/212: Report on the Irish Grants Committee 1930.

CO 762/4/18: Ernest Ince Allen.

CO 762/15/170: Lord Ashtown.

CO 762/50/776: William Bateman.

CO 762/80/1312: George Tyner.

CO 762/86/1400: Samuel Byford.

CO 762/86/1416: Cecil Stoney.

CO 762/86/1418: James and Mrs. B. M. Glynn.

CO 762/100/1691: Annabella Rainey.

CO 762/100/1698: M. K. Madden.

CO 762/120/2071: Mrs. B. Meade.

CO 762/120/2073: Mrs. Appelby.

CO 762/120/2078: Agnes Clarke.

CO 762/120/2080: Richard Wordsworth Cooper.

CO 762/15/161: Mrs. E. M. Troy.

CO 762/170/2908: Henrietta L. Stopford.

CO 762/180/3145: George Daunt.

CO 762/196/2168: Francis Henry Pakenham

CO 905/17: Minutes of First Meeting of Dunedin Committee 20 January 1926.

DO 35/479/3: Irish Grants Committee.

DO 35/343/10159/10: Lunn Memo 1928.

INDEX

academic rigor, at Cheltenham Ladies College, 62

Academy Awards, 144

accent: acceptance and, 63–64; British, 37–39, 56; Irish brogue, 38–39, 56

accommodations, living, 102, 117, 137; in postwar Britain, 91, 113–14, 115, 116, 131, 168, 191–92; for returnees from India, 108–9, 116, 129; for returnees from Ireland, 115–16, 129

Act of Union (1801), Britain, 4

Adenauer, Konrad, 171

Africa: British imperialism in, 171–72; discrimination in, 187

Akenson, Donald H., 73

Alcock, Ron (interviewee), 22, 25, 47–48, 78, 111, 197; on employment and religion, 87–88; fluid sense of Britishness for, 177; on freedom of London, 121–22; on National Service, 168

Algeria, French war with, 167

Aliens Act (1905), 151

ambivalent notions, of home: of British in India, 51, 184; of Irish Protestants, 21, 22

America. See United States

Amery, Leo, 124

Anderson, Benedict, 141

Anderson, Kathryn, 49–50

Anglicization, of Ireland and India, 5, 137

Anglo-Indian community, 19, 28, 37–38, 53, 61, 70; discrimination against, 181–82, 183; passing as white by, 68; relocation to Britain of, 106

Anglo-Irish community, 11, 38–39, 88, 101; Catholic abuse of, 47–48; Irish Protestants and Britain linked as, 25–26, 51, 106

Anglo-Irish Treaty, 124

Anglo-Irish war, 76

Appelby, E., Irish Grants Committee case files, 42

architecture, modern, 138–39

Army: British, 17, 21, 23, 42, 94, 102, 112, 116, 186; Fourteenth, 21; Indian, 4, 19, 62, 100, 102–3; Women's Auxiliary Corps, 19. *See also* Irish Republican Army

Arnold, Thomas, 54

Ascendancy class, in Ireland, 88, 89, 92, 96–97; Gwynn as, 106; in Parliament, 100

Ashtown (Lord), Irish Grants Committee case files, 96, 97

Attlee, Clement, 113, 131, 166

Auchinleck, Claude, 102

Aughey, Arthur, 86–87

Baldwin, Stanley, 125

Ballyhoura country, County Cork, 32

Balniel (Lord), 153–54

Baly, J, 70

Bateman, William, from Irish Grants Committee case files, 95

Beale, Dorothea, 62

Beddoe, John, 137

Bedford Girls, marriage and employment and, 62–63

belonging, sense of, 16, 166; as fluid, 174–79, 193

Bhabha, Homi, 185–86

Bielenberg, Andy, 92

Birdwood, Vere, Plain Tales from the Raj archive, 17, 18, 27, 34–35, 56–57; on public school ethos, 65; on return to Britain, 104–5; on women in British India, 40

Black presence, in Britain, 151

Blunt, Alison, 19, 185

cultural nationalism, of Irish Free State, 77–78, 80

culture, British: education supporting, 57–58, 190–91; imperial elite, 174; as separate from Indian, 28; superiority of, 7, 42

curriculum, educational: British values from, 67, 72–73, 75, 76, 99, 190–91; Education Code widening, 58; games in, 58

Dáil, of Irish Free State, 100–101

d'Alton, Ian, 4

Daunt family (from Irish Grants Committee case files), 24

Davin, Anna, 39

Day-Lewis, Cecil, 65

day school, for middle class, 58

Decline and Fall of the Roman Empire (Gibbon), 59

decolonialization, failure of trusteeship from rapid, 15, 170, 173, 188

decolonialization, of British Empire, 9, 15, 103; Irish Protestants and, 106, 109; as outcome of trusteeship principle, 15, 170, 173, 188; returnee resignation to, 167–68; sadness of, 169

Delaney, Enda, 92–93

demise, of British Empire, 142, 166

demobilization, of colonial military, 102

Demography, State and Society (Delaney), 92–93

deportation, of immigrants, 152, 154

depression, from relocation strains, 118

diaspora, Imperial British, 2, 7, 90, 185, 188; axes of, 8; education reinforcing British values of, 53, 55, 59, 75–76, 190–91; employment opportunities and, 99, 129; idea of home to, 18–19, 91, 189; metropolitan elite contrasted with, x, 193; "spatial imaginary" of, 8–9

differentiation, 61, 67, 122, 190–91; in India by race, 53; between India domiciled and home-born British, 74–75, 82–83, 84–85, 155, 189, 190; in Ireland by religion, 10, 53, 79–80

discrimination, 138; in Africa, 187; against Anglo-Indian community, 181–82, 183; against Caribbean immigrants, 136–37; against Irish, 137; against Irish Protestants, 3, 22; outlawing color-based, 135

Disraeli, Benjamin, 148

domestic sense of home, 18, 103, 105; British and Indian separate, 27

Dominions, of Britain: citizenship of, 133–34; survey on interest in, 127–28; white dominions and, 133

Dowling, Robyn, 19

Dring (lady), Plain Tales from the Raj archive, 30, 41

duality: India home and not home, 19–20, 21, 104–5, 189; of Irish and imperial identity, 25, 106

Dublin, Ireland, 1

Dunedin (Lord), 124

dyarchy government, in India, 126

Easter Rising (1916), Ireland, 22, 45, 77, 180–81

East India Company, 4, 5, 39, 40, 69, 80–81

economic activity, of women in Ireland, 42, 52

Ede, James Chuter, 131, 133

Eden, Anthony, 171

education, 58–59, 61, 65, 154; Anglicization from boarding school, 17, 20, 21, 28, 34, 50, 55–56, 190–91; British hegemony through, 68, 69, 80, 190–91; class and gender emphasized in, 61, 62–63; as compulsory and state run in Britain, 54; consequences of colonial, 67; cultural nationalism of Irish Free State and, 77–78, 80; Education Code for improving, 61; imperial identities supported by, x, 5 14, 53, 55, 75–76; of Indianized English, 70; for Irish identity and pride, 77, 79; Irish loyalty through, 73, 76; Irish nationalists rejecting British, 73; for leadership skills, 60; migration and, 26; national identity through, 57–58; nationalism changing, 77; as nondenominational in Ireland, 71–72, 79, 80; politicization of, 79; reforming system of, 131; return to metropolitan center of British Empire for, 55, 56–57, 63–64, 79; through Lawrence Military Asylum, 69; young women benefit from tertiary, 120–21, 130

Perry, Verna (interviewee), 30, 41, 103–4, 148, 149, 200; on Anglo-Indian discrimination, 182, 183; British education of, 120–21; on India independence violence, 98
personal link, between monarch and subject, 146–47
personal memories, social context of, 10–11
physical space, of home, 19, 33–35, 103
politicians: as appealing to emotions, 44–45; decolonization deaths caused by, 170
politics: British schools instruments of, 54; of domiciled community in India, 82–83, 84; Elizabeth II as neutral in, 147; women in Ireland and, 43, 52
Pooley, Colin, 33
Portelli, Alessandro, 179
postimperial/postcolonial world, Britain in, 7, 10, 15, 90–91, 131, 185–86, 191–92
postwar Britain: acclimatizing to, 109, 191–92; Elizabeth II unifying force in, 147, 192; employment and accommodations in, 91, 113–14, 115, 116, 120–22; Festival of Britain and coronation in, 141, 144, 192; racial differences and, x, 7; as second-tier power, 128, 130
Procida, Mary, 40
Propaganda and Empire (MacKenzie), 61, 167
property loss, in Irish Grants Committee case files, 94–95
Protestants, Irish. *See* Irish Protestants

Quakers, Society of Friends, 163–64
A Queen Is Crowned (film), 141–144

race, 8, 19, 92, 132, 161; British education and white, 55; British fear degradation of, 33, 42, 68–69, 81; British Nationality Act and, 135, 136–37, 151; Commonwealth Immigrants Act on, 151–55; differentiation in India by, 34, 53; immigration and, 151–55; interracial marriage and, 39, 41, 173, 181–82; proximity to metropole and, 16, 83–84, 156, 190; "purity" of, 184; "social Darwinism" and, 5; "whiteness" construction of, 7, 184
Race, Ernest, 139

The Races of Britain (Beddoe), 137
Rainey, Annabella (Irish Grants Committee case files), 42
Raymont, Thomas, 57
Reilly, Paddy (interviewee), 1–2, 83, 118, 166, 171, 200; fluid sense of Britishness for, 178, 179; imperial consciousness of, 187–88
relationships, with servants, 18, 20; of British children, 34–35, 36–37
religious segregation, 10; in India, 4–5, 73, 79; in Ireland, 53, 71–72, 79–80; social divisions and, 163–64; through English language, 38
religious similarities, working classes and, 86–88
religious tolerance, in Ireland, 29, 44
"Remembering and Reworking Emotions" (Bornat), 49
Republic of Ireland, 152–53, 154
retrenchment: of British Empire, 169–72, 192; in British living spaces in India, 27
returnees, 10, 91, 104–5, 114, 115, 173; accommodations for, 108–9, 116–17; connection with monarchy of, 149; coronation of Elizabeth II and, 144–46; debates on nationality of, 156–57, 161, 193; emotional responses of, 122, 185; as imperial elite no longer, 174; imperial process role of, 162, 167, 171; as part of British community, 132; social position lost by, 112–13, 190, 192, 193
revival, of Irish literature and music, 67
R.I.C. *See* Royal Irish Constabulary
Ride to Khiva (Burnaby), 60
riots, Notting Hill and Nottingham, 151, 162
Rivett-Carnac (colonel), Plain Tales from the Raj archive, 29, 36, 63
The Road to Wigan Pier (Orwell), 111
Roman Catholic Church, 53, 71, 79
Roman empire, British empire aligned with, 59
Royal Colonial Institute, 57–58
Royal Irish Constabulary (R.I.C.): Irish Grants Committee and, 102; targeting of, 23, 112; withdrawal of, 101–2
Ruskin, John
Rutherford, Jonathan, 142

Said, Edward, 33, 72
Sālote (Queen), of Tonga, 142–43, 145
SCCS. *See* Select Committee on Colonization and Settlement
second-tier power, postwar Britain as, 128, 130, 131
Second World War: aftermath of, 109, 113, 128, 140, 141; British destruction from, 109, 110, 116; post colonial era of, 91, 131
Seeley, J. R., 6
Select Committee on Colonization and Settlement (SCCS), 80–81
self-determination, U.S. supporting, 173
sense of belonging, 16, 166; as fluid, 174–79
separation, of British from Indians, 54, 67, 184; cultural, 28; in hill station schools, 71; in separate towns, 27
servant and master relationships, 18, 20, 33–36, 51; as non-existent for returnees, 107–8, 114
Shawcross, Hartley, 134
Simla hill station, 76
Sinn Fein, 24, 95
skills, immigration and, 154, 155
skin color: colonial differentiation by, 155–56; racial status and, 63–64, 137–38, 151–55
Sloan, Sue (interviewee), 19–20, 27, 48, 49, 150, 200; on coronation of Elizabeth II, 144–45; on employment in Britain, 113–14, 120, 121; on Festival of Britain, 144; on India independence violence, 98; on lack of servants, 115; on small scale of Britain, 109
"social Darwinism," 5
society, classes of: Parliament debates on, 133–35, 158. *See also* class, social
sola topi (cork hat/helmet), 30, 183–84
Southern Irish Loyalist Relief Association, 124
Soviet funding, of Kenya and Suez uprisings, 172
"spatial imaginary," of diaspora, 188; of colony and metropole hybrid, 185–86; from colony to metropole, 8–9, 44
spiritual life, in India, 31
spiritual salvation, contrasted with national identity, 57
sports: British women and, 40; English contrasted with Gaelic, 78–79; leadership learned through, 60–61

Sports Pavilion, Festival of Britain, 131, 138–40
status, British: for Dominion and Commonwealth born, 132; English accent and, 37–39, 56; fear of losing, 33, 129; hegemonic, 33, 68, 80, 190–91; metropolitan and colonial students differences in, 65; partition changing, 107
Steel, Flora Annie, 39–40, 51, 55
Stepney boys' clubs, 62
Stevenson, Olive (interviewee), 28, 90, 119–20, 201
stigma, of mental illness, 118, 129
Stoler, Ann, 82
Stoney, Cecil (from Irish Grants Committee case files), 24
Stopford, Henrietta (from Irish Grants Committee case files), 96
strategies, for coping, from boarding school, 50
Strong, Roy, 33
Suez Canal crisis, 167, 168, 171
Sumner Scale, for compensation, 125
superiority: British cultural, 7, 42; of Gaelic cultural ethos, 26

"Talk about Care" (Harding), 45
Taunton Commission (1873), 62
Tavistock Square, 127
technical education system, in India, 69–70
technical progress, Festival of Britain and, 138–39, 140, 165
Thames, compared to Ganges, 109–10
Third Book of Lessons (William Collins), 73–74
Thomson, Alistair, 43
Thornville, Carlow, Ireland, 32, 45–46
Tilbury Docks, 117
Today through Yesterday (textbook), 61
Town and Country Planning Act (1944), 116–17
Trades Union Congress, Britain, 113
transition: from Britain to England, 162; of British to Indian rule, 97; colonial to postcolonial, 10, 131, 185–86; from home in India to Britain, 108, 115, 120
transnational networks and forces, British Empire linked by, 6, 7, 8, 9, 92

ABOUT THE AUTHOR

NIAMH DILLON is Project Director at National Life Stories at the British Library and is also currently leading a corporate history of civil engineers, J Murphy & Sons. Prior to this, she worked on the Academy Award–winning *Into the Arms of Strangers* at Warner Bros. She has taught postgraduate seminars, presented at international conferences, and published in the *Oral History Journal*. She recently published a chapter in *Protestant and Irish: The Minority's Search for Place in Independent Ireland*.

Lightning Source UK Ltd.
Milton Keynes UK
UKHW010636161222
413998UK00004B/101/J